The New American Interventionism

POWER, CONFLICT, AND DEMOCRACY:
AMERICAN POLITICS
INTO THE TWENTY-FIRST CENTURY
ROBERT Y. SHAPIRO, EDITOR

Power, Conflict, and Democracy:
American Politics Into the Twenty-first Century

Robert Y. Shapiro, *Editor*

This series focuses on how the will of the people and the public interest are promoted, encouraged, or thwarted. It aims to question not only the direction American politics will take as it enters the twenty-first century but also the direction American politics has already taken.

The series addresses the role of interest groups and social and political movements; openness in American politics; important developments in institutions such as the executive, legislative, and judicial branches at all levels of government as well as the bureaucracies thus created; the changing behavior of politicians and political parties; the role of public opinion; and the functioning of mass media. Because problems drive politics, the series also examines important policy issues in both domestic and foreign affairs.

The series welcomes all theoretical perspectives, methodologies, and types of evidence that answer important questions about trends in American politics.

John G. Geer, *From Tea Leaves to Opinion Polls: A Theory of Democratic Leadership*

Kim Fridkin Kahn, *The Political Consequences of Being a Woman: How Stereotypes Influence the Conduct and Consequences of Political Campaigns*

Kelly D. Patterson, *Political Parties and the Maintenance of Liberal Democracy*

Dona Cooper Hamilton and Charles V. Hamilton, *The Dual Agenda: Race and Social Welfare Policies of Civil Rights Organizations*

Hanes Walton Jr., *African-American Power and Politics: The Political Context Variable*

Amy Fried, *Muffled Echoes: Oliver North and the Politics of Public Opinion*

Russell D. Riley, *The Presidency and the Politics of Racial Inequality: Nation-Keeping from 1831 to 1965*

Robert W. Bailey, *Gay Politics, Urban Politics: Identity and Economics in the Urban Setting*

Ronald T. Libby, *ECO-WARS: Political Campaigns and Social Movements*

Donald Grier Stephenson Jr., *Campaigns and the Court: The U.S. Supreme Court in Presidential Elections*

Kenneth Dautrich and Thomas H. Hartley, *How the New Media Fail American Voters: Causes, Consequences, and Remedies*

Douglas C. Foyle, *Counting the Public In: Presidents, Public Opinion, and Foreign Policy*

Ronald G. Shaiko, *Voices and Echoes for the Environment: Public Interest Representation in the 1990s and Beyond*

The New American Interventionism:

Lessons from Successes and Failures

Essays from

Political Science Quarterly

Edited by

DEMETRIOS JAMES CARALEY

COLUMBIA UNIVERSITY PRESS

New York

Columbia University Press
Publishers Since 1893
New York   Chichester, West Sussex

The articles in this volume are reprinted with permission from the following issues of *Political Science Quarterly*:

Barry Blechman and Tamara Cofman Wittes, "Defining Moment: The Threat and Use of Force in American Foreign Policy" 114 (Spring 1999): 1–30.

William C. Banks and Jeffrey D. Straussman, "A New Imperial Presidency? Lessons from U.S. Involvement in Bosnia" 114 (Summer 1999): 195–217.

James Burk, "Public Support for Peacekeeping in Lebanon and Somalia: Assessing the Casualties Hypothesis" 114 (Spring 1999): 53–78.

Eytan Gilboa, "The Panama Invasion Revisited: Lessons for the Use of Force in the Post Cold-War Era" 110 (Winter 1995–96): 539–562.

Morris Morley and Chris McGillion, "'Disobedient' Generals and the Politics of Redemocratization: The Clinton Administration and Haiti" 112 (Fall 1997): 363–384.

James Fowler, "The United States and South Korean Democratization" 114 (Summer 1999): 265–288.

Alan J. Kuperman, "The Stinger Missile and U.S. Intervention in Afghanistan" 114 (Summer 1999): 219–263.

LIBRARY OF CONGRESS CATALOGING-IN-PUBLICATION DATA

The new American interventionism: lessons from success and failures: essays from Political science quarterly / edited by Demetrios James Caraley.
    p. cm.
Includes bibliographical references.
ISBN 0-231-11849-X (alk. paper)
1. United States—Armed Forces—Foreign countries. 2. International police. 3. Intervention (international law) I. Caraley, Demetrios.
JZ6377.U6N49 1999   99-14696
327.1′17′0973—dc21

∞

Printed in the United States of America

p 10 9 8 7 6 5 3 2
□

For my wife, Vilma

T.A.S.P.

Contents

Foreword

DEMETRIOS JAMES CARALEY

The purpose of *The New American Interventionism* is to bring within one volume articles that talk to the general question of American military invervention since the end of the cold war. This collection does not purport to be a comprehensive overview of all the interventions that have taken place. Rather, the articles were written by individual authors who, on their own initiative or in response to my editorial suggestion, were moved to write about specific topics. I find it gratifying that the book as a whole has turned out to provide powerful lessons about the success or failure of the most important interventions and the general strategies and political processes that underlay them.

The scores of lessons in the book for policy makers and interested members of the public cannot be summarized in a foreword. But in rereading all the articles together in preparation for this book, I was struck by four patterns. First is the great complexity of the American government in reaching and implementing decisions to use military force, because proposals to use force generate conflict. The State Department, parts of the Defense Department, the CIA, and the national security adviser all have different perspectives and responsibilities and different relationships to the regime or the person to be influenced. In addition, foreign allies must be consulted to obtain their support or at least their acquiescence, as must organizations like the UN and NATO, under whose authority the military action may be taking place. The conflict and delay are simply in keeping with the United States's pluralistic political system. But in military matters, the internal conflict sends contradictory signals to those whom the United States is trying to target. As a result, the targets it wants to influence choose the signal they prefer to believe, which often leads them to disbelieve U.S. resolve and makes them refuse to comply until the United States actually uses force.

DEMETRIOS JAMES CARALEY is the Janet Robb Professor of the Social Sciences at Barnard College and professor of political science in the graduate faculties of Columbia University. He has published numerous books and articles on national security policy, congressional policy making, and urban politics and is the editor of *Political Science Quarterly*.

Second, *The New American Interventionism* shows that influence against a determined foe cannot be exerted, even by the world's sole remaining superpower, "on the cheap," that is, with verbal threats or limited air attacks or cruise missiles that carry the risk of only minimal casualties. The success in removing Raul Cedras as the head of Haiti's government and Manuel Noriega as the leader of Panama's government and in imposing and implementing a cease-fire in Bosnia with the agreement of Slobodan Milosevic all required use of ground troops. In the case of Haiti, Cedras capitulated when he was persuaded that American airborne troops had already taken off to invade his country; as a result, the troops did not have to go in fighting. In the Gulf War, however, more than five weeks of the heaviest air attacks with nonnuclear bombs and missiles in the history of warfare did not coerce Saddam Hussein and the Iraqi government to take troops out of Kuwait. Only a massive campaign by ground troops with the risk of substantial casualties—which in actuality did not occur—forced the Iraqis out.

Neither this foreword nor this book is a brief in favor of incurring large American casualties. But to be seen as unwilling to absorb *any* casualties severely limits the ability of the United States's overwhelmingly superior weaponry and trained military personnel to coerce compliance even from a Slobodan Milosevic or Saddam Hussein, who are heads of third-rate powers. They have learned that because the United States is so reluctant to use military power, and especially ground troops, they can safely and repeatedly ignore deadlines and ultimatums and score tactical gains while receiving no or only acceptable damage in retaliation.

Third, the book shows how predominantly ad hoc the American use of military power has been against regimes it has been trying to influence since the end of the Soviet communist containment policy. Sometimes America intervenes to roll back an invasion, sometimes to try to stop massacres of civilians, sometimes to guarantee cease-fires in civil wars (while almost always tilting in favor of the underdog of the moment), sometimes to bring about democratization, sometimes to retaliate against terrorist attacks, and sometimes to displace foreign leaders it doesn't like. But often America does not intervene in similar situations at all. Having a consistent grand strategy for all contingencies of intervention may be impossible in the complexities of the post-cold war era. But couldn't the president and congressional leadership agree to articulate some general principles for classes of interventions, such as civil wars involving civilian ethnic cleansing and other atrocities? Such principles could speed up decisions on new interventions and deter massacres by convincing would-be aggressors that American military force will be used to stop and possibly capture, try, and punish them.

Fourth, the book strikingly reminds us that in military interventions, Congress has largely been bypassed concerning the use of military force and has allowed the presidency—however much weakened domestically—again to become an "imperial" one. Once the president decided to act, he normally did not ask Congress for authority or for specific appropriations. The president simply declared that his Article II designation as commander in chief gave him his own constitutional authority to use force and to finance it with money already granted to the military in lump-sum appropriations. The one exception was President George Bush, who asked for congressional authority to use American force in the Gulf War. But even that request came some five months after huge American military forces had already been deployed at positions from which they could strike immediately. And Bush's request came after strong off-the-record statements that even if the resolution failed in Congress, he would go ahead and risk impeachment. President Bush explicitly admitted this in a January 1999 lecture to the Senate. Not only was Congress not asked for authority in most military attacks, but many were already in progress or finished before the president—Reagan, Bush, or Clinton—even made a case to Congress as a whole or to the public justifying the action.

This is not to say that Congress has clamored to get formally involved in deciding to use military force. For the most part, members have preferred to avoid such involvement because of the inherent complexities of intervention decisions and because if the venture fails, they can second-guess the president. Leaks to the media created stories about most of the actions being planned; but, except in the Gulf War, Congress showed little interest in doing anything about them. Indeed, the Senate showed only the slightest interest in the Clinton administration's proposed treaty change to expand NATO to include former Soviet satellites, although this change will probably have much longer-term military policy consequences than any of the recent military interventions have had.

By bypassing Congress when initiating military attacks, the president implicitly asserts as irrelevant Congress's Article I constitutional power to "declare war," an untenable constitutional position.[1] But he also puts himself at an intellectual disadvantage. By not having to persuade independently elected majorities in Congress of the case's merits, the president loses the opportunity of engaging in a give-and-take with equals through which he can gain fresh perspectives to balance those generated and debated in secrecy by his subordinates in the executive branch. It was this failure of the president to consult more broadly and to rely instead on executive branch groupthink that played a large part in the 1961 Bay of Pigs fiasco and in the disastrous decisions starting in 1964 to expand the war in Vietnam.

As of this writing at the end of the NATO air war against Serbia, U.S. post–cold war military interventions have not caused any major disasters—though the outcome of the war in Serbia is unclear and other interventions have produced some notable successes. But the seeds of disasters have already been planted in the Balkans, Middle East, the Korean peninsula, and the Taiwan

---

[1] The claims of Congress for the control of warmaking rest on its Article I powers to "provide for the common defense," to "declare war," to "raise and support armies," and "to provide and maintain a navy."

Acknowledgments

I wish to thank the authors of the articles in this collection for having them published in the *Political Science Quarterly* and for now granting permission to reprint them in this volume. I am especially grateful to Robert Jervis for providing a special introduction and concluding essay for the book. Bob Jervis has been on *PSQ*'s editorial advisory board ever since I became its editor and has given me thousands of hours of wise counsel affecting every aspect of the journal's operation. I thank Bonnie Hartman for assuming most of the burden of transforming the articles into a published book and in general for doing an excellent job as *PSQ*'s managing editor. I thank Vilma Caraley, Jean Highland, Richard Pious, and Robert Shapiro for editorial advice, and I also thank the small staff at the Academy of Political Science—Philip Biondo, Loren Morales, Allison Pretto, and Grace Wainer—for keeping the Academy running smoothly and efficiently. Finally, I am grateful to John Michel and Alex Thorp for facilitating the publication at Columbia University Press.

D.J.C.

Introduction

ROBERT JERVIS

Wherever the standard of freedom and independence has been or shall be unfurled, there will [America's] heart, her benedictions and her prayers be. But she goes not abroad in search of monsters to destroy. She is the well-wisher to the freedom and independence of all. She is the champion and vindicator only of her own.

—John Quincy Adams

When America talks of the defense of interests, and not just territories, it leads to continued suspicions that the United States is seeking a globalized NATO.

—An anonymous NATO official[1]

American intervention abroad, especially that utilizing force, is the subject of increased attention in the post-cold war era. Of course, the United States intervened extensively during the cold war itself. Indeed, John Quincy Adams notwithstanding, intervention is as American as apple pie, although it usually has been for the purpose of defending narrow national interests as well as for spreading American values. The first two American administrations sent considerable sums to the Barbary pirates to protect American shipping, and Thomas Jefferson resorted to force when their demands became exorbitant and the United States had built a navy that could do the job. Covert action was also not unknown to early American statesmen.[2] Bribery, the support of foreign friends, conspiracies to overthrow unfriendly regimes, propaganda—both "white" (open) and "black" (disguised)—as well as the use of force were not newly discovered in 1945.

[1] Quoted in Roger Cohen, "A Policy Struggle Starts Within NATO," *New York Times*, 27 November 1998.

[2] Stephen Knott, *Secret and Sanctioned: Covert Operations and the American Presidency* (New York: Oxford University Press, 1996).

ROBERT JERVIS is the Adlai E. Stevenson Professor of International Politics and a member of the Institute of War and Peace Studies at Columbia University. He has written numerous articles and books on foreign policy and international relations, including *Perception and Misperception in International Politics* and *System Effects: Complexity in Political and Social Life*.

During the cold war, the United States intervened in the domestic affairs of almost every country in the world, usually by covert means. It sought to subvert communist regimes, albeit with little success,[3] while in the rest of the world, covert action more frequently took the form of supporting chosen individuals and factions, notwithstanding the fact that the dramatic attempts to overthrow governments received the most attention. This is not to imply either that the United States was unique or that its behavior was immoral. International politics is built on the concept of sovereignty yet has always involved serious efforts by states to interfere in the domestic affairs of others. Americans may be outraged at the thought that China sought to influence the 1996 presidential election and gain Bill Clinton's favor by contributing to his campaign. While we may wonder at Chinese sophistication if they believed that the sum of $100,000 would go far or that influence could be obtained by a contribution whose source had to be kept hidden, the more important point is that this kind of behavior is hardly unusual.

Despite its long history, the concept of intervention has no precise definition. In common parlance, intervention predominantly means either of two quite different things. First, it can refer to interference in another state's domestic affairs with a view either to influence or to replace the government. Support for a leader or regime that might otherwise fall or be overthrown can also be considered a form of intervention. Such activities are usually covert or at least subject to "plausible deniability," for the related reasons that they violate the norm of sovereignty and that a leader or faction whose overthrow is believed to be sought by the outside power may gain domestic support for that very reason. A second meaning of intervention is military, which can be undertaken to replace a government, support a regime against rebellion, repel (and, if our definition were to be truly evenhanded, assist) aggression against a third party, or end civil strife.[4] In the post-cold war era, a third kind of intervention has become important as well: open efforts to establish and maintain democratic processes, irrespective of the identities of the individuals and factions that may gain power, subject only to the proviso that they will continue democratic practices.

States can also engage in what might be called "permissive intervention": permitting others, including their own private citizens, to act where the state itself does not. Thus, during the war in Bosnia, the United States allowed arms to flow to that country and Croatia and also sanctioned the use of American

---

[3] The best study is that by Gregory Mitrovich, *Compellence and Coexistence: The Transformation of America's Cold War Objectives, 1947–1956* (Ithaca, NY: Cornell University Press, forthcoming); also see Walter Hixson, *Parting the Curtain: Propaganda, Culture, and the Cold War* (New York: St. Martin's Press, 1996).

[4] For good treatments of intervention for the latter purpose, see Ariel Levite, Bruce Jentleson, and Larry Berman, eds, *Foreign Military Intervention* (New York: Columbia University Press, 1992); and Barbara Walter and Jack Snyder, eds., *Civil Wars, Insecurity, and Intervention* (New York: Columbia University Press, forthcoming).

military consultants to retrain the Croatian army as an effective force that could expel the native Serbs from eastern Croatia, thereby fundamentally changing the course of the war.

Because of its great size and power, the United States cannot help strongly influencing the fates of other countries, including their domestic arrangements. Most obviously, the state of the American economy has a major influence over the economic fortunes of all countries. An America that absorbs imports helps others grow and thereby contributes to the political success of the parties and regimes that happen to be in power. Conversely, when the Unites States raised interest rates in the 1970s, the effects were not only to increase the economic burden on debtor nations but also to weaken their governments.

American power means not only that its intervention can be inadvertent but also that it can occur by anticipation. Thus American opposition to Salvador Allende in Chile was sufficiently well known so that Augusto Pinochet and his colleagues did not have to be told that they would receive American support if they took control. Similarly, today, those who would make their countries more democratic know that some American support is likely, at least if they do not strongly oppose American policies.

The objectives of intervention are often broader than those sought by "normal" diplomacy. Normal diplomacy is usually aimed at securing specific policies such as deterring attacks on neighbors, opening markets, or gaining diplomatic support. Intervention often has the much more general objective of changing the orientation of another government, if not changing the government itself. During the cold war, the United States intervened with four objectives in mind: to secure regimes that would support or at least not oppose overall U.S. foreign policy; conversely, to prevent the establishment of communist regimes or, if this was not possible, to remove them; to ensure local and regional stability; and to support democracy. Sometimes these goals were linked: the desire for stability can often work in tandem with support for democracy. This was most notably the case with the American intervention in Western Europe in the late 1940s. Although some American rhetoric implied a fear of Soviet invasion, the real concern was that Western Europe would disintegrate from within, that economic collapse and the loss of faith would lead to political collapse and a communist takeover. Most obviously, this motivated the Truman Doctrine and Marshall Plan. But it also led to American covert action in support of democracy in Western Europe, especially in France and Italy. These fears also provided the main impetus for the American endorsement of a military alliance. The primary purpose of NATO in American eyes was not to deter a Soviet military attack, which was seen as extremely unlikely, but to give Western Europeans the sense that their futures were secure from external threat and that it was therefore worthwhile for them to devote their energies to internal recovery. The security guarantee was a security blanket; the target was less the USSR than the Europeans' psyche.[5]

---

[5] For further discussion, see Robert Jervis, *The Meaning of the Nuclear Revolution* (Ithaca, NY: Cornell University Press, 1989), 206–212.

In other cases, however, one objective was gained only by sacrificing another. Thus the United States intervened to unseat the governments of Iran in 1953, Guatemala a year later, and Chile in 1973, even though the last one was a democracy and the first two were more democratic than the regimes that replaced them. The dilemma was most famously summarized by President John Kennedy when he discussed what the United States should do in the Dominican Republic after the dictator Rafael Trujillo was assassinated, an outcome that owed more than a little to American encouragement of the opposition. "There are three possibilities in descending order of preference: a decent democratic regime, a continuation of the Trujillo regime or a Castro regime. We ought to aim at the first, but we really can't renounce the second until we are sure that we can avoid the third."[6] Although the fear of communism vanished with the Soviet Union, the perceived tension between stability and order, on the one hand, and radicalism and instability, on the other, continue, as Morris Morley and Chris McGillion show in their study of the Clinton administration's policy toward Haiti. Similar conflicts cloud U.S. policy in the Congo and Eastern Africa and are likely to prove central in the more important arena of policy toward China, although in these cases even more than in Haiti, it is difficult to identify the democrats and the paths to democracy.

The cold war witnessed disagreement over whether American interventions were motivated primarily by security or economic concerns, over whether what the United States feared was the growth of Soviet power or indigenous left-wing regimes that would threaten American economic penetration.[7] But it is likely that intervention was most likely when both interests were involved. Because relatively minor covert actions, and certainly anything more, entailed significant costs and risks and therefore would not be undertaken lightly, action was likely when the decision makers believed that what was at risk was not security *or* economic stakes *or* democratic values, but instead two—if not all three—of these values.

With the end of the cold war, interventions are even more likely to require multiple objectives, which now also include humanitarian concerns. At least where military intervention is concerned, it is likely to take several impulses to move the United States. Such intervention is not likely to come quickly. I do not think that it is an accident that American involvement in Somalia, Haiti, and Kosovo came only after slow deliberation, false starts, and procrastination. Whereas a shock like the Iraqi invasion of Kuwait can produce a fairly prompt

---

[6] Quoted in Arthur Schlesinger Jr., *A Thousand Days* (Boston: Houghton Mifflin, 1965), 769.

[7] A good general discussion of the causes of the American military intervention in this period is that by Herbert Tillema, *Appeal to Force* (New York: Crowell, 1973); also see Herbert Tillema, *International Conflict Since 1945: A Bibliographic Handbook of Wars and Military Intervention* (Boulder, CO: Westview Press, 1991); Benjamin Fordham, "The Politics of Threat Perception and the Use of Force," *International Studies Quarterly* 42 (September 1998): 567–590; Mi Yung Yoon, "Explaining U.S. Intervention in Third World Internal Wars, 1945–1989," *Journal of Conflict Resolution* 41 (August 1997): 580–602.

response, even there several months were required to turn an embargo and defensive deployment into a military offensive.

Military intervention is, of course, different from other kinds not only because it is often inconsistent with the rule of law but also because it is likely to entail the expenditure of significant blood and treasure. Even relatively small operations like those in Grenada, Panama, and Haiti kill some American soldiers and innocent civilians and run risks whose upward bounds are hard to estimate. James Burk critically scrutinizes the popular view that American public opinion is particularly sensitive to casualties and argues, I believe correctly, that the public looks at the objectives for which the United States is intervening as well as at the costs and that it was splits within the elite rather than between it and the general public that produced the pressure to withdraw from Lebanon and Somalia.[8] But it would be strange indeed if decisions to intervene were not to be influenced by estimates of costs. Symmetrically, the credibility of American threats to use force is influenced by the adversary's estimate of what the United States thinks is at stake and the casualties it believes the United States foresees. So even if Burk is correct that the U.S. public is not as sensitive to casualties as many people believe, if other countries accept the conventional wisdom, they will develop strategies to threaten and inflict casualties and may discount American threats to act in the face of such costs.

Three major themes emerge from the essays that comprise this book. First, the effects of American intervention do not flow from American actions alone. Instead, what is crucial is the interaction between what the United States and other outside actors do and the politics on the scene. This point is perhaps only common sense, but it is often missed by those whose desire to criticize or defend American policy leads them to focus exclusively on American motives and actions. Alan Kuperman shows that many of the arguments about the effects of the American introduction of Stinger missiles into the Afghan conflict—and especially the claims that this escalation forced out the Soviets or, to the contrary, delayed Mikhail Gorbachev's withdrawal—ignore the internally driven Soviet changes and the ways in which the groups doing the fighting reacted to the new technology. More generally, the "success" or "failure" of American policy cannot be explained without taking full account of the degree of overlapping interests between the United States and the targets of the intervention. As Barry Blechman and Tamara Wittes show, the different outcomes of American attempts are often attributable less to differences in American behavior than to differences in the objectives sought and, therefore, in the amount of local resistance.[9] Similar considerations affect the credibility of American threats to intervene, which are more likely to be believed when what is at stake is very

---

[8] For a general discussion of current public attitudes toward intervention, see Bruce Jentleson and Rebecca Britton, "Still Pretty Prudent: Post–Cold War American Public Opinion on the Use of Military Force," *Journal of Conflict Resolution* 42 (August 1998): 395–417.

[9] For a general appreciation of this point, see David Baldwin, *Economic Statecraft* (Princeton: Princeton University Press, 1985).

important to the United States but not as vital to the local actors who must comply in order to avoid intervention. Stating the problem in this way illustrates why threats to intervene are often insufficient and why it is so hard for the United States to bend local actors to its will, notwithstanding superior American material resources: especially in the post-cold war world, the stakes tend to be of only peripheral concern to the United States though are crucial to the local actors. Who rules in Iraq and what form of government prevails in the former Yugoslavia obviously matter to the United States, or its forces would not be there. But the outcomes matter much more to the actors in the region, who will therefore go to greater lengths to get their way.

Turning to the causes of American intervention, two factors stand out. First, intervention, like all foreign policy, remains deeply domestic. Whether and how the United States intervenes is shaped by domestic political processes, the values and interests of the participating groups in the United States, and the actors' domestic political stakes. The structure of American government plays a crucial role here. As William Banks and Jeffrey Straussman explain, the Constitution gives Congress crucial powers through the appropriations process. But the cold war saw an erosion: a possible nuclear attack precluded congressional debate; presidents acted on their own in situations short of this; and Congress saw delegating power as expeditious and safe. These habits have maintained their hold, but whether they will continue to do so into the future remains unclear.[10] Whether or not they do, the multiple domestic pressures on the president can neither be ignored nor encapsulated in a parsimonious theory of foreign policy. This was one reason that the American threats to oust the Panamanian dictator Manual Noriega were ineffective. As Eytan Gilboa shows, the administration was incapable of speaking with one voice, and even someone who listened carefully and had no bias would have had trouble guessing what the United States would do.

The second factor is the role of the past. Political scientists often overlook the guiding principle of historians: what happens at one time is strongly influenced by what has come before and strongly influences what comes later. No intervention is discrete and separate; instead, each instance changes the political landscape in which the actors operate. Forces and beliefs are generated, validated, nourished, and diminished by each case of intervention. Starting with the familiar point that Vietnam reduced both the American willingness to intervene and the credibility of American threats, Blechman and Wittes show that the course of subsequent interventions also affected both the United States's willingness to use force and others' perception of this likelihood. Sometimes rather striking lessons are drawn, ones that may not be detected by all the actors involved. Thus, behind the attack on Belgian peacekeepers at the start of the

---

[10] For other discussions, see Randall Ripley and James Lindsay, eds., *Congress Resurgent: Foreign and Defense Policy on Capitol Hill* (Ann Arbor: University of Michigan Press, 1993); and Eugene Wittkopf and James McCormick, "Congress, the President, and the End of the Cold War: Has Anything Changed?" *Journal of Conflict Resolution* 42 (August 1998): 440–466.

genocide in Rwanda were the lessons that the Hutu extremists learned from the American behavior in Somalia and the concomitant prediction that the Western powers would remove their forces once it was clear that they would suffer casualties if they stayed.[11] Blechman and Wittes similarly find a Somali leader telling an American envoy, "We have studied Vietnam and Lebanon and know how to get rid of Americans, by killing them so that public opinion will put an end to things."

James Fowler's article finds that the prevailing lessons from other cases provide a parallel explanation of the paradox of the American acquiescence, if not support, for repression in Korea in 1979 under a liberal and human rights-oriented president and its support for liberalization in 1987 under a conservative administration. In 1979, American leaders were most impresssed (and depressed) by the fact that the liberalization of the shah of Iran and their refusal to support domestic repression led to a disastrous revolution and the seizure of American hostages; in 1987 what was salient was the success of the Philippine nonviolent revolution, which received at least a modicum of American support. Although states do not blindly repeat policies that were followed by success and shun those that seemed to produce failure, each important event does influence future behavior. The outcome of the NATO intervention in Kosovo is likely to prove to be a real turning point for the alliance and American foreign policy. Later behavior will be different because of it. By altering beliefs and domestic incentives, Kosovo will deeply affect how American national interest is defined, what policies are seen as effective and appropriate, and the priority given to humanitarian objectives if not to foreign policy in general.

Robert Jervis argues that the strong role of domestic politics and the impact of each episode on later beliefs and preferences mean that the United States will not be able to develop a coherent grand strategy for intervention and that other states will have difficulty predicting American behavior. The results will not be satisfying to scholars, citizens, or statesmen at home or abroad, but all will have to live with an inconsistent, if not contradictory, set of American policies.

At the end of this volume, we do not have a complete and parsimonious theory of intervention, and given the complexities and contingencies involved, we may never have one. But these essays bring to bear converging perspectives on these vital questions and make clear many of the multiple causes and effects that are at work. As we move into a world in which there is good reason to believe that covert action will continue and military intervention will increase, these arguments and analyses should help us to understand where we are going as well as where we have been.

---

[11] Bruce Jones, "Keeping the Peace, Losing the War: Military Intervention in Rwanda's 'Two Wars'" in Walter and Snyder, eds., *Civil Wars, Insecurity, and Intervention.*

Defining Moment:
The Threat and Use of Force in American
Foreign Policy

BARRY M. BLECHMAN
TAMARA COFMAN WITTES

The use of military force has been a difficult subject for American leaders for three decades. Ever since the failure of American policy and military power in Vietnam, it has been hard for U.S. policy makers to gain domestic support for the use of force as an instrument of statecraft. U.S. military power has been exercised throughout this thirty-year period, but both threats of its use and the actual conduct of military operations have usually been controversial, turned to reluctantly, and marked by significant failures as well as successes. The American armed forces are large, superbly trained, fully prepared, and technologically advanced. Since the demise of the Soviet Union, U.S. forces are without question the most powerful by far on the face of the earth. Their competence, lethality, and global reach have been demonstrated time and again. Yet with rare exceptions, U.S. policy makers have found it difficult to achieve their objectives by threats alone. Often they have had to use force—even if only in limited ways—to add strength to the words of diplomats. And at more times than is desirable, the failures of threats and limited demonstrative uses of military power have confronted U.S. presidents with difficult choices between retreat and all-out military actions intended to achieve objectives by the force of arms alone.

In the 1980s, most U.S. military leaders and many politicians and policy makers drew a strong conclusion from the failure of U.S. policy in Vietnam.

BARRY M. BLECHMAN is the founder and president of DFI International and the cofounder and chairman of the Henry L. Stimson Center. This article was prepared initially for the National Academy of Sciences. TAMARA COFMAN WITTES is a university fellow and doctoral candidate in the Department of Government, Georgetown University. Her dissertation concerns techniques for ethnic conflict resolution. She also writes on coercive diplomacy and U.S. counterterrorism policy.

This viewpoint was spelled out most clearly by then Secretary of Defense Caspar Weinberger in 1984: force should only be used as a last resort, he stated, to protect vital American interests and with a commitment to win. Threats of force should not be used as part of diplomacy. They should be used only when diplomacy fails and, even then, only when the objective is clear and attracts the support of the American public and the Congress.[1]

General Colin Powell, former chairman of the Joint Chiefs of Staff, was and remains a proponent of what was called the Weinberger doctrine. "Threats of military force will work," he says, "only when U.S. leaders actually have decided that they are prepared to use force." In the absence of such resolution, U.S. threats lack credibility because of the transparency of the American policy-making process. For this reason, "the threat and use of force must be a last resort and must be used decisively."[2] Powell has argued that any use of force by the United States should accomplish U.S. objectives quickly while minimizing the risks to U.S. soldiers.[3]

Other U.S. policy makers have taken a more traditional geopolitical view, believing that the U.S. failure in Vietnam needs to be understood on its own terms. Regardless of what was or was not achieved in Southeast Asia in the late 1960s and early 1970s, the United States, they believe, can and should continue to threaten and to use limited military force in support of diplomacy to achieve limited ends without resorting to all-out contests of arms. In the words of then Secretary of State George Shultz in December 1984, "Diplomacy not backed by strength will always be ineffectual at best, dangerous at worst."[4] Moreover, Shultz insisted, a use of force need not enjoy public support when first announced; it will acquire that support if the action is consonant with America's interests and moral values. In 1992, Les Aspin, then chairman of the House Armed Services Committee and later secretary of defense, branded the Weinberger doctrine an "all-or-nothing" approach. He asserted that the United States should be willing to use limited force for limited objectives and that it could pull back from such limited engagements without risk.[5] From this perspective, force should be used earlier in a crisis, rather than later, and need not be displayed in decisive quantities. The limited-objectives school describes the threat of force as an important and relatively inexpensive adjunct to American diplomatic suasion.

As the Soviet Union disintegrated and the cold war came to an end, this debate began to wane. U.S. policy makers began to wrestle with an array of

[1] Remarks by Secretary of Defense Caspar W. Weinberger to the National Press Club, 28 November 1984, published as Department of Defense News Release No. 609–84.

[2] Interview by Barry Blechman with General Colin Powell, 21 February 1997.

[3] Colin L. Powell, "Why Generals Get Nervous," *New York Times*, 8 October 1992; and Colin L. Powell, "U.S. Force: Challenges Ahead," *Foreign Affairs* 72 (Winter 1992–1993): 32–45.

[4] George Shultz, "The Ethics of Power" (address given at the convocation of Yeshiva University, New York City, 9 December 1985), *Department of State Bulletin*, 1–3 February 1985.

[5] Les Aspin, chairman of the House Armed Services Committee (address to the Jewish Institute for National Security Affairs, Washington, DC, 21 September 1992).

problems that were individually less severe than the threat posed by the USSR but collectively no less vexing. The military situation changed drastically as well. U.S. military power reigned supreme, and the risk that a limited military intervention in a third nation could escalate into a global confrontation quickly faded. During both the Bush and first Clinton administrations, it became increasingly evident not only that there were many situations in which limited applications of force seemed helpful but that in the complicated post-cold war world, opportunities for the pure application of Secretary Weinberger's maxims were rare. During this eight-year period, numerous challenges to American interests emerged that were too intractable for diplomatic solutions, that resisted cooperative multilateral approaches, and that were immune not only to sweet reason but to positive blandishments of any sort. Unencumbered by cold war fears of sparking a confrontation with the powerful Soviet Union, American policy makers turned frequently to threats and the use of military power to deal with these situations, sometimes in ways that conformed to the Weinberger guidelines but more often suggesting that—rightly or wrongly—the press of world events drives policy makers inevitably toward Secretary Shultz's prescriptions for limited uses of force in support of diplomacy.

The United States sometimes succeeded in these ventures and sometimes failed. Success rarely came easily, however; more often, the United States had to go to great lengths to persuade adversaries to yield to its will. Even leaders of seemingly hapless nations or of factions within devastated countries proved surprisingly resistant to American threats. Often U.S. leaders had to make good on threats by exercising U.S. military power. These further steps usually worked; but even when the United States conducted military operations in support of its post-cold war policies, the results were not always as clean and easy, or their consequences as far reaching, as decision makers had hoped. Given the overwhelming superiority of U.S. military power during this period, these results are hard to understand.

Indeed, even the greatest military success of the U.S. armed forces in the post-cold war period—the expulsion of the Iraqi occupation army from Kuwait in 1991—became necessary because U.S. diplomacy, including powerful threats of force, failed. Despite the most amazing demonstration of U.S. military capabilities and willingness to utilize force if necessary to expel the Iraqi military from Kuwait, despite the movement of one-half million U.S. soldiers, sailors, and air men and women to the region, the call-up of U.S. reserve forces, the forging of a global military alliance, even the conduct of a devastating air campaign against the Iraqi occupation army and against strategic targets throughout Iraq itself, Saddam Hussein refused to comply with U.S. demands and his troops had to be expelled by force of arms. The United States was not able to accomplish its goals through threats alone. The Iraqi leader either disbelieved the U.S. threats, discounted U.S. military capabilities, or was willing to withstand defeat in Kuwait in pursuit of grander designs.

Why was this the case? Why has it been so difficult for the United States to realize its objectives through threats of using military force alone? Why have U.S. military threats not had greater impact in the post-cold war period, and why have limited uses of force in support of diplomacy and in pursuit of political aims not been able to accomplish U.S. goals more often? Is this situation changing as it becomes indisputably clear that the United States is the only remaining military superpower? Or have history and circumstance made U.S. military superiority an asset of only narrow utility in advancing the nation's interests through diplomacy?

To answer these questions, we examined all the cases during the Bush and first Clinton administrations in which the United States utilized its armed forces demonstratively in support of political objectives in specific situations. There are eight such cases, several of which include multiple uses of force. In two of the cases, Iraq and Bosnia, threats or uses of force became enduring elements in defining the limits of the relationship between the United States and its adversary.

Actually, the U.S. armed forces have been used demonstratively in support of diplomatic objectives in literally more than a thousand incidents during this period, ranging from major humanitarian operations to joint exercises with the armed forces of friendly nations to minor logistical operations in support of the United Nations or other multinational or national organizations. Moreover, the deployment and operations of U.S. forces in Europe and in Southwest and East Asia on a continuing basis throughout the period are intended to support U.S. foreign policy by deterring foreign leaders from pursuing hostile aims and by reassuring friends and allies. In some cases, the presence of these forces, combined with the words of American leaders, may have been sufficient to deter unwanted initiatives. The presence of U.S. troops in South Korea, for example, is believed to deter a North Korean attack. We did not look at such cases of continuing military support of diplomacy in which "dogs may not have barked."[6] Instead, we looked only at the handful of specific incidents in which U.S. armed forces were used deliberately and actively to threaten or to conduct limited military operations in support of American policy objectives in specific situations.[7]

---

[6] A database listing all uses of the American armed forces since the end of the cold war was prepared by Defense Forecasts International (DFI) for the U.S. Air Force. It is based largely on official unpublished documents prepared by the major U.S. Air Force commands and other official data. For additional information, please contact Oliver Fritz, DFI International, 11 Dupont Circle, NW, Washington, DC 20036.

[7] In principle, there may also have been cases in which the United States achieved it ends through verbal threats alone, threats not backed by deliberate military activity. Some have suggested, for example, that President Bush was successful in preventing greater Serbian oppression in Kosovo through verbal warnings alone. In that specific case, however, Bush's warnings were given weight both by U.S. military activity in support of the UN Protection Force (UNPROFOR) in Bosnia and in enforcing the embargo on arms shipments to the region and by the deployment of U.S. troops to Macedonia. Overall, the authors could not identify any cases of verbal threats unaccompanied by military activity during this period, successful or unsuccessful, and would be grateful for any suggestion of such incidents.

We did not examine such military threats prior to the Bush administration, because, as noted above, the cold war placed significant constraints on U.S. uses of force. We believe that the demise of the USSR altered the global political and military environments so fundamentally as to make prior incidents irrelevant to understanding the effectiveness of contemporary military threats. The puzzle we seek to explain is the frequent inability of the United States to achieve its objectives through threats and limited uses of military power despite the political and military dominance it has enjoyed since 1989.

We supplemented published information about the cases with interviews with key U.S. policy makers during this period, including individuals who served in high positions in the Pentagon and at the State Department. At times these individuals are quoted directly. More often, their perspectives provide background and detail in the accounts of the incidents.[8]

We have concluded that the U.S. experience in Vietnam and subsequent incidents during both the Carter and first Reagan administrations left a heavy burden on future American policy makers. There is a generation of political leaders throughout the world whose basic perception of U.S. military power and political will is one of weakness, who enter any situation with a fundamental belief that the United States can be defeated or driven away. This point of view was expressed explicitly and concisely by Mohamed Farah Aideed, leader of a key Somali faction, to Ambassador Robert Oakley, U.S. special envoy to Somalia, during the disastrous U.S. involvement there in 1993–1995: "We have studied Vietnam and Lebanon and know how to get rid of Americans, by killing them so that public opinion will put an end to things."[9]

Aideed, of course, was proved to be correct. And the withdrawal from Mogadishu not only was a humiliating defeat for the United States but it also reinforced perceptions of America's lack of resolve and further complicated U.S. efforts to achieve its goals through threats of force alone.

This initial judgment, this basic "default setting" conditioning foreign leaders to believe that U.S. military power can be withstood, has made it extremely difficult for the United States to achieve its objectives without actually conducting military operations, despite its overwhelming military superiority. With the targets of U.S. diplomacy predisposed to disbelieve American threats and to believe they can ride out any American military initiative and drive away American forces, it has been necessary for the United States in many incidents to go to great lengths to change these individuals' minds. Reaching this defining moment—the point at which a foreign decision maker comes to the realization that, despite what may have happened in the past, in the current situation U.S.

---

[8] The individuals interviewed include Richard Cheney (secretary of Defense, 1989–1993); William Perry (secretary of Defense, 1994–1997); Walter Slocombe (undersecretary of Defense for policy, 1994–present); Colin Powell (chairman of the Joint Chiefs of Staff, 1989–1993); Strobe Talbott (deputy secretary of State, 1994–present); James Steinberg (director of policy planning, Department of State, 1994–1996).

[9] Letter from Robert Oakley to Barry Blechman, 7 August 1997.

leaders are committed and, if necessary, will persevere in carrying out violent military actions—has become a difficult challenge in U.S. diplomacy. It also creates a large obstacle to resolving conflicts and protecting U.S. interests while avoiding military confrontation.

How Threats are Evaluated

There is a rich literature on the use of force in world affairs and a considerable body of writing on the particular problems of the use of American military power in the post-cold war period.[10] There is also a large body of memoirs and contemporary histories testifying to the perceptions of American decision makers in particular incidents.[11]

The authors of this literature have made any number of observations as to the conditions that facilitate the effective use of military threats. Typically, these conditions are not proposed as prerequisites for effective threats but merely as elements that make it more likely that threats will succeed. We therefore term these variables "enabling conditions." The large number suggested in the literature, many of which differ from one another only in nuance, can be grouped into two broad categories. Most enabling conditions shape the credibility of the U.S. threat in the mind of the targeted foreign leaders; these include both conditions pertaining to the context in which the U.S. threat is made and to the character of the threat itself. Quite apart from the credibility of the U.S. threat, however, some demands are more difficult for foreign leaders to comply with than others, and some of the enabling conditions directly affect this perception of how costly it would be to comply with the demands. Together, the credibility of the threat and the degree of difficulty of the demands shape the targeted leader's evaluation of the likely cost of complying or of not complying

---

[10] Some voices in this debate include Christopher M. Gacek, *The Logic of Force: The Dilemma of Limited War in American Foreign Policy* (New York: Columbia University Press, 1995); Alexander L. George, "The Role of Force in Diplomacy: A Continuing Dilemma for U.S. Foreign Policy" in Gordon A. Craig and Alexander L. George, eds., *Force and Statecraft*, 3rd ed. (New York: Oxford University Press, 1995); Alexander L. George and William E. Simons, eds., *The Limits of Coercive Diplomacy* (Boulder, CO: Westview Press, 1994); Bruce W. Jentleson, "Who, Why, What and How: Debates Over Post-Cold War Military Intervention" in Robert J. Lieber, ed., *Eagle Adrift: American Policy at the End of the Century* (New York: Longman's, 1997); Lori Fisler Damrosch, ed., *Enforcing Restraint: Collective Intervention in Internal Conflicts* (New York: Council on Foreign Relations Press, 1993); Aspen Strategy Group, *The United States and the Use of Force in the Post-Cold War Era* (Queenstown, MD: Aspen Institute, 1995); and Joshua Murachik, *The Imperative of American Leadership: A Challenge to Neo-Isolationism* (Washington, DC: American Enterprise Institute, 1996).

[11] Some examples are James A. Baker and Thomas M. Defrank, *The Politics of Diplomacy: Revolution, War and Peace, 1989–1992* (New York: Putnam, 1995); Colin Powell with Joseph E. Persico, *My American Journey* (New York: Random House, 1995); Dan Quayle, *Standing Firm: A Vice-Presidential Memoir* (New York: HarperCollins, 1994); H. Norman Schwarzkopf with Peter Petre, *It Doesn't Take a Hero: General H. Norman Schwarzkopf, the Autobiography* (New York: Bantam Books, 1992); Bob Woodward, *The Commanders* (New York: Simon & Schuster, 1991); and George Bush and Brent Scowcroft, *A World Transformed* (New York: Alfred A. Knopf, 1998).

FIGURE 1
Evaluations of Threats

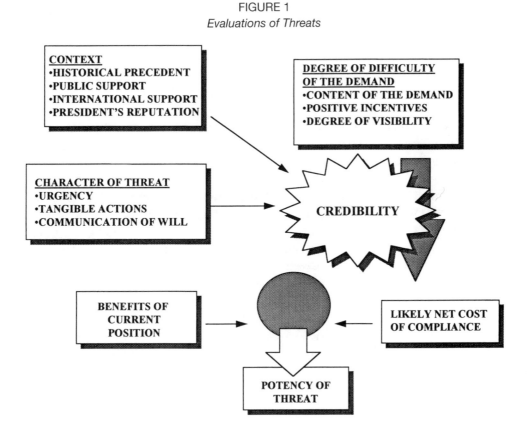

with U.S. demands. The balance between the cost of compliance and the cost of defiance represents the potency of the U.S. threat.[12] These relationships are expressed in Figure 1 and are discussed further below.

Enabling Conditions

The context in which a threat is made and the character of the threat itself together shape the credibility of the threat. The degree of difficulty of a demand is evaluated through this credibility screen to determine the likely costs of compliance and noncompliance.

Context of the threat. In previous work on this subject, Stephen Kaplan and Barry Blechman determined that coercive uses of military power by the United States were most likely to be successful when the United States acted in an appropriate historical context, when there was precedent for its demands and ac-

---

[12] This term was first suggested by Alexander George. See his discussion of credibility and of the magnitude of demands in George and Simons, *The Limits of Coercive Diplomacy.*

tions. This stands to reason. We know from experience that reaffirmations of long-standing positions are more likely to be taken seriously than declarations of new demands, particularly when the credibility of the traditional claim has already been tested through force of arms and found to be genuine. Targets of new claims of U.S. vital interests may quite naturally want to test the claimant's seriousness. Such a challenge, when it occurs, means that the threat is ineffective, and the goals of the U.S. demands must be asserted through direct military action. Precedents may also have negative effects; as we shall see, the fact that U.S. military power was resisted successfully in Vietnam and elsewhere by weaker military powers seems to have adversely affected the credibility of U.S. military threats in recent years.[13]

A second contextual factor believed to shape the credibility of U.S. military threats is the presence or absence of broad public support for military action and, particularly, whether or not there is wide support among members of Congress. Obviously, as in the case of Vietnam, domestic dissent raises the possibility either that the United States will not act on its threats if challenged or that even if it does act, the force of public opinion will sooner or later, probably sooner, compel a retreat. This does not necessarily mean that any dissent negates a president's threats; the effect of dissent presumably depends on the importance attributed to it by the intended target. Since Vietnam there only rarely has been broad public support for U.S. initiatives involving the threat or use of military force—at least prior to the actual and successful conduct of the operation—there is usually evidence that foreign leaders can cite in persuading themselves and their people that the Americans can be made to back down.[14]

The presence or absence of third-nation support for the U.S. position is a third contextual factor that seems to influence perceptions of the credibility of a U.S. threat. Allies' protests can curtail the willingness of the United States to act on its threats or to persevere in any military action needed to respond to a challenge for fear of incurring high costs in more important relationships. This factor has become increasingly important in assessments of threats or uses of force in recent years, as the United States has become increasingly reluctant to act without allies in the new types of situations that have emerged following the cold war. As with all the enabling conditions, what matters is not the reality of allied support but the targeted leader's perception of this factor. In explaining Saddam Hussein's disbelief of American threats during the Persian

---

[13] See Barry M. Blechman and Stephen S. Kaplan, *Force Without War* (Washington: DC, Brookings Institution, 1978); Robert Jervis, Richard Ned Lebow, and Janice G. Stein, *Psychology and Deterrence* (Baltimore: Johns Hopkins University Press, 1985); Thomas C. Schelling, *Arms and Influence* (New Haven: Yale University Press, 1966). Some scholars argue that forceful precedents are useful only when they reflect core U.S. interests; for example, see Alexander L. George and Richard Smoke, *Deterrence in American Foreign Policy: Theory and Practice* (New York: Columbia University Press, 1974).

[14] For discussion of the role that public opinion plays in America's ability to take effective military action abroad, see Jentleson, "Who, Why, What and How"; and J. Holl, "We the People Here Don't Want No War" in Aspen Strategy Group, *The United States and the Use of Force*.

Gulf conflict, for example, former Secretary of Defense Richard Cheney cited Hussein's belief that the United States could never carry out military operations in Iraq itself because—in Hussein's view—the Arab nations allied with the United States would make clear that in such circumstances they would have to leave the coalition.[15]

A final contextual factor often said to influence the credibility of U.S. threats is the reputation of the president and other high-level U.S. officials. The scholarly literature is mixed in its assessments of the importance of this factor, however, and the case studies examined for this project shed no light on the subject; no discernible difference could be seen in responses to threats by Presidents Bush or Clinton that would seem to pertain to the incumbent's reputation. More basic attributes of U.S. credibility and of the situation itself seem to have been more important.

Character of the threat. Other factors contributing importantly to the credibility of threats reflect the manner in which they are conveyed. A sense of urgency must be part of the threat or the targeted leader can believe that a strategy of delay and inaction will be effective in avoiding compliance. The establishment of deadlines appears to be particularly important.[16] In 1989 Panamanian strongman Manuel Noriega understood well that the United States would prefer to see him removed from power and democracy restored. But because the United States endorsed negotiations by the Organization of American States (OAS) with Noriega and never articulated an "either-or" threat of Noriega's forcible removal, he apparently interpreted U.S. rhetoric as bluster and dismissed stepped-up American military exercises in the Panama Canal zone as "mere posturing."[17]

Verbal threats are also more effective when accompanied by tangible military actions—steps that indicate the seriousness of the U.S. undertaking. Not only can movements or other actions by military units demonstrate actual capabilities, thus lending verisimilitude to threats, but by demonstrating the U.S. president's willingness to pay a price for the situation, they add credibility to his verbal demands. In this respect the greater the commitment demonstrated by the action, the more likely the threat is to be successful. Thus, Blechman and Kaplan[18] found the deployment of forces on the ground in the potential theater of operations to be a more effective means of making threats credible

---

[15] Interview by Barry Blechman with Richard Cheney, 15 January 1997. See also Janice G. Stein, "Deterrence and Compellence in the Gulf, 1990–1991: A Failed or Impossible Task?" *International Security* 17 (Fall 1992): 2; and George and Simons, *The Limits of Coercive Diplomacy.*

[16] George and Simons, *The Limits of Coercive Diplomacy.*

[17] See R. L. Grant, *Operation Just Cause and the U.S. Policy Process*, RAND Note N-3265-AF (Santa Monica, CA: RAND Corporation, 1991); Frederick Kempe, *Divorcing the Dictator: America's Bungled Affair with Noriega* (New York: Putnam, 1990); and J. B. Treaster, "Noriega Military Command Belittles General," *New York Times*, 27 December 1989.

[18] Blechman and Kaplan, *Force Without War.*

than the movement of naval forces, as ground deployments demonstrate a willingness to pay the political price by putting U.S. soldiers, or air men and women, at risk. Similarly, the mobilization of military reserves has been an effective means of adding credibility to threats. Disrupting the lives of U.S. citizens by placing them on active duty, separating them from their families and workplaces, indicates indisputably the president's willingness to pay a high political price to get his way.

Difficulty of the demand. The context and character of a threat determine its credibility in the mind of the target. But whether a foreign leader chooses to comply with a U.S. demand is also conditioned by the degree of difficulty of the demand itself. To be effective, a demand must obviously be specific, clearly articulated, and put in terms that the target understands. There is no shortage of cases in which the targets of military threats simply did not understand what was being asked of them and therefore could not have acted to satisfy U.S. demands even if they had wanted to.[19]

In addition, a demand can be more or less onerous for the targeted leaders to contemplate. In part, this evaluation will depend on the demand's specific content: What is, in fact, being demanded? At the extreme, some demands may not be satisfiable by the target. In some cases the United States (and other nations) have misread situations, demanding actions that the target of a threat was not capable of delivering. This may have been the case in U.S. relations with the Soviet Union over the Middle East in the 1960s and 1970s, for example, where the United States threatened repeatedly but seems to have misjudged the Soviet Union's ability to influence certain Arab nations and factions.[20]

The inclusion of positive incentives in the overall U.S. diplomatic strategy is an important way of improving the targeted leader's perception of a U.S. demand. Not only do positive incentives change perceptions of the content of a demand itself, they also provide a political excuse for the target to do what it might have wanted to do anyway: back down and accept the U.S. demand.

A targeted leader's perception of the difficulty of a demand also will be affected by the degree of visibility of the retreat required. Regardless of substance, an act of compliance that can be taken invisibly is far easier to accept, as it may not convey additional political costs. A retreat that is visible and humiliating may often be perceived as something to be resisted at any cost.[21]

---

[19] Paul G. Lauren, "Coercive Diplomacy and Ultimata: Theory and Practice in History" in Alexander L. George and William E. Simons, eds., *Limits of Coercive Diplomacy*, suggests that ultimatums are the most explicit and precise method of communicating demands and that they may lessen the chances of misperception or miscalculation by the opponent.

[20] Lawrence L. Whetten, *The Canal War: Four Power Conflict in the Middle East* (Cambridge, MA: MIT Press, 1974).

[21] On the effect that degree of difficulty and losing face have on the effectiveness of threats, see George and Simons, *The Limits of Coercive Diplomacy*.

It has been demonstrated in many studies that threats or limited uses of force are more likely to be effective when the behavior demanded of a target requires only that the target not carry out some threatened or promised action. This is a subset of the visibility factor: deterrent threats are more likely to succeed than compellent threats; the latter require the target to carry out a positive and, therefore, usually visible action. In the case of deterrent threats, on the other hand, it is usually unknown, and unknowable, whether or not in the absence of U.S. threats the target would have carried out the action being deterred. Would the Soviet Union have attempted to seize West Berlin in the late 1950s or early 1960s if the United States had not threatened to contest such an initiative with military force? No one can say with certainty. Thus, deterrent threats may appear to be more successful, because they are sometimes used to deter actions that would not be carried out in any event. Moreover, in those deterrent cases in which the initial threatened action would otherwise have been carried out, it is easier politically for the target to back down, as it need not be done in public; the target can always claim that, regardless of the U.S. threat, it would not have acted in any event. When the U.S. threat requires a positive act on the part of the target (for example, withdrawal from Kuwait), the retreat is publicly evident and could have dire consequences in national or regional politics.

Potency of the Threat

All of these enabling conditions—context of the threat, character of the threat, and degree of difficulty of a demand—contribute to a targeted leader's understanding of the cost of complying or of not complying with U.S. demands. In Alexander George's phrase, an effective threat must be potent relative to the demand. This means that the target must perceive that the threat, if carried out, would result in a situation in which the target would be worse off than if it complied with the U.S. demand. If, for example, the demand is that a ruler give up the throne, the only potent threat is likely to be that otherwise the ruler will be killed or that a situation would be created in which the ruler might be killed. Any threat less potent would likely be seen—even if it was carried out—as resulting in a situation no worse, and possibly better, than that which would have resulted from satisfying the demand. This evaluation, of course, will be filtered through the target's perception of the credibility of the threat: How likely it is that the anticipated punishment will be carried out? If the threat is perceived to be wholly incredible, the anticipated cost of noncompliance will be low. If the context and character of the threat add verisimilitude, however, the difficulty of the demand will be weighed carefully relative to the cost of noncompliance, and a sufficiently potent threat should produce compliance in a rational opponent.

CASE STUDIES

All these enabling conditions were examined for each of the eight major cases in which military force was threatened or used in limited ways in support of diplomacy during the Bush and first Clinton administrations. Although the authors examined each case extensively, only a brief summary of each can be presented in this article; the summaries highlight the key findings.

Panama, 1989–1990[22]

The Panamanian dictator Manuel Noriega was an agent of U.S. policy in Central America for many years. In the late 1980s, however, his value declined with settlement of the Nicaraguan insurgency, and he became increasingly and more openly involved with the Colombian drug cartels. After he was indicted in the United States in February 1988 for drug trafficking and money laundering, first the Reagan administration and then the Bush administration decided to seek his removal from office. As tensions grew between the two countries in 1988 and 1989, the Panamanian Defense Forces, one key source of Noriega's power, began to harass U.S. military personnel in the country and in the Canal Zone, as well as to step up repression of the democratic opposition in Panama.

Because of the upcoming presidential election, the U.S. government did not initiate serious pressures against Noriega until 1989. Beginning in April of that year, however, the United States tried to make clear that it considered Noriega an illegitimate ruler and that it wanted him to step down. It renewed economic sanctions against Panama, gave Panamanian opposition parties $10 million in covert assistance toward their effort in the scheduled May presidential elections, and provided election observers. After Noriega manipulated the elections, the United States initiated a variety of diplomatic actions, including recalling its ambassador. The Bush administration worked through the Organization of American States (OAS) to negotiate Noriega's resignation and also carried out a series of military exercises and other actions in the Canal Zone intended to make the U.S. military presence there more visible. Noriega continued to refuse to comply with U.S. demands, however, and survived a coup in which the United States played a minor role. When a U.S. naval officer was murdered in December 1989, President Bush quickly authorized the U.S. armed forces to invade Panama, capture Noriega, and bring him to the United States for trial.

In this case, therefore, both diplomacy and military threats failed, necessitating the direct use of military force in war to accomplish the U.S. objective. Why was this the case? The main reasons appear to be related to the context and character of the threat itself. Despite any number of statements by U.S.

---

[22] Sources used for this case study include contemporaneous news reports; Powell with Persico, *My American Journey*; Baker and DeFrank, *The Politics of Diplomacy*; Grant, *Operation Just Cause and the U.S. Policy Process*; Woodward, *The Commanders*; and Kempe, *Divorcing the Dictator*.

leaders indicating that they believed Noriega should step down and that they considered him an illegitimate ruler, it was never stated clearly and definitively that the United States would be willing to invade the country and throw Noriega out if he did not comply with the demand to relinquish office.[23] In short, no cost was ever specified for noncompliance with U.S. demands; hence, a potent threat was never made. The United States demanded that Noriega leave office, and although a threat to expel him by force might have been inferred from U.S. statements, it was never stated explicitly. Nor was any deadline set for his compliance with the demand to relinquish office; Noriega was permitted to defer action for months without any obvious penalty. Likewise, U.S. verbal demands were not directly supported by tangible military actions. Although reinforcements were sent to the Canal Zone and some exercises were held there, they were all downplayed by U.S. officials and explained by a general concern for the security of the Canal Zone in light of deteriorating U.S.–Panamanian relations.[24] Colin Powell has stated that the limited military actions taken by the United States in 1988 and 1989 probably reinforced Noriega's preexisting perception that the United Sates was irresolute and that he could persevere.[25] When the invasion force was assembled, it was done in secrecy and never displayed publicly or brandished in support of an ultimatum that Noriega surrender or face forceful expulsion. This approach, of course, was dictated by the Weinberger maxims of how to use military power effectively.

It was harder for U.S. officials to threaten effectively in this case, because the demand was extremely difficult for the target to contemplate. Noriega was being told to relinquish office; this was not a deterrent, but rather a compellent situation. Only a clear and potent threat might have had a chance of success, and in this case the target really did not understand that he faced a serious threat of U.S. action.

In the Panama case, in short, there was no defining moment because of the U.S. failure to make clear its compellent threat. The United States did not explicitly state the action it was prepared to take if its demand was not satisfied. Nor did it demonstrate a credible willingness to enforce the demand. No deadline for action by Noriega was established. The U.S. target, Noriega, never had to contemplate the seriousness of the U.S. resolve until it was too late for him to yield. U.S. leaders failed to press him into a defining moment.

U.S. Relations with Iraq, 1990–1996[26]

Eight months after the successful military operation in Panama, the Bush administration faced a far greater challenge in the Persian Gulf. In this case the

---

[23] President Bush even stated in a news conference on 13 October 1989 that using force in Panama was "a stupid argument that some very erudite people make." (Transcript printed in *New York Times*, 14 October 1989).

[24] Kevin Buckley, *Panama: The Whole Story* (New York: Simon & Schuster, 1991).

[25] Interview by Barry Blechman with General Colin Powell, 21 February 1997.

[26] Sources used in this case study included for the Persian Gulf crisis, Lawrence Freedman and Efraim Karsh, *The Gulf Conflict, 1990–1991* (Princeton: Princeton University Press, 1993); BBC World

threat of force was a central element of the U.S. strategy from nearly the outset of the crisis. President Bush and all other senior officials stated repeatedly and unequivocally that if Saddam Hussein did not withdraw Iraqi forces from Kuwait, the United States was prepared, with the help of its allies, to expel them by force of arms. The threat was made increasingly credible throughout the remainder of 1990 by the mobilization and deployment of an enormous U.S. and allied military force in the region, an operation that could have left no question in Hussein's mind about the president's willingness to run huge political risks to implement the threat. Furthermore, the president's credibility was strengthened by the forging of a broad coalition that backed the American action, including Arab nations as well as traditional U.S. allies, by authorization of the allied military action by the UN and of U.S. military action by Congress, and by the establishment of a clear deadline for compliance that imparted a definite sense of urgency. Finally, the United States initiated an air campaign prior to launching its ground offensive, providing even more evidence of its military prowess and will and offering a final opportunity for Iraq to withdraw from Kuwait rather than be thrown out.

The context and character of the U.S. threat would have predicted success. Yet all these measures failed; in the end, U.S. and allied armies had to invade Kuwait and compel the Iraqi retreat by force of arms. Why? Because of the opacity of the Iraqi regime, the answer may never be clear, although several possibilities come to mind.

Despite their visible display in the theater of operations, Hussein may still have underestimated U.S. military capabilities relative to Iraq's. He may have believed that the war would be far less one sided, causing sufficient U.S. casualties for Bush to end (or to be forced by U.S. and allied opinion to end) the hostilities short of the full expulsion of Iraqi forces from Kuwait. If so, he would have been counting heavily on the considerable opposition in the United States to the use of force prior to the authorizing legislation, as well as the obvious fragility of the coalition that had been brought together for the war.[27] He also simply may not have understood the extent of U.S. and allied power. Then Secretary of Defense Richard Cheney believes, for example, that Hussein's subordinates were afraid to bring him bad news or negative evaluations, as he was known to treat such messengers as traitors.[28]

Alternatively, the U.S. threat might simply not have been potent enough relative to the demand being made. The United States never threatened to un-

---

Service, *Gulf Crisis Chronology* (Essex, UK: Longman Current Affairs, 1991); Ofra Bengio, ed., *Saddam Speaks on the Gulf Crisis: A Collection of Documents* (Tel Aviv, Israel: Moshe Dayan Center, 1992); Baker and Defrank, *The Politics of Diplomacy*; Woodward, *The Commanders*; and Powell with Persico, *My American Journey*. For the post-1991 incidents, sources included Foreign Broadcast Information Service (FBIS) transcripts of statements by Iraqi officials, statements by U.S. officials, and contemporaneous Western news reports.

[27] Bengio, *Saddam Speaks on the Gulf Crisis*.

[28] Interview by Barry Blechman with Richard Cheney, 15 January 1997.

seat Hussein or to destroy his regime if Iraqi occupation forces were not with-drawn from Kuwait.[29] The threat was deliberately restricted to the destruction or expulsion of Iraqi forces in Kuwait, in part because Arab coalition members would not or could not support a more ambitious threat to destroy the Iraqi regime. From Hussein's perspective, in the context of his strategic vision, a mili-tary defeat while retaining power might have seemed preferable to an ignoble retreat. He might first have miscalculated and believed that the United States would not act to expel him from Kuwait; but subsequently, when he realized the error, he might have figured that in terms of his overall goals in the region and in terms of the likelihood of his being able to hold on to power in Baghdad, it would be better to be defeated militarily by the overwhelming forces that had been arrayed against him than to knuckle down to U.S. demands.[30] If this was the case, only a credible threat to destroy Hussein and his regime would have been potent enough to have achieved the objective—liberating Kuwait—without the direct use of military forces in war. In the absence of such a potent threat, Hussein never had to face a defining moment.

Because of this ambiguous outcome—military triumph for the United States but political survival for Saddam Hussein—threats and uses of force have remained a central element in U.S. relations with Iraq since the Gulf War ended. Immediately following the war, the United States and its allies, acting through the UN, intervened on the ground to protect the Kurds in Iraq's north and established no-fly zones in both the north and the south to protect the Kurds and the Shi'a minority from Iraq's air force. Both actions were accompa-nied by covert support for rebellious elements in the two regions intended to destabilize the Hussein regime. The no-fly zones have been enforced through combat air patrols and occasionally by air and missile strikes against radars, surface-to-air missiles, and command facilities.

Such an incident during the first Clinton administration took place in Sep-tember 1996, when the United States once again struck at air defense sites in the south of Iraq, this time in response to an Iraqi intervention in a conflict between two Kurdish factions in the north. The United States maintained that the Iraqi military action was unacceptable and responded both by reinforcing its forces in the Gulf region and by launching cruise missile attacks on newly rebuilt Iraqi air defense sites in the south. The United States took no action directly in the Kurdish region. When Hussein seemed to defy U.S. injunctions regarding the need for Iraq to respect the no-fly zone in the south, the United States threatened more devastating air strikes against Iraq and moved aircraft into the region that would be capable of carrying them out. Hussein seemed to comply with the U.S. demand.

---

[29] There have been some suggestions, however, that the United States made such a threat to deter the Iraqis from using chemical weapons. See James Baker's comments on his Geneva meeting with Tariq Aziz in January 1991, in *The Gulf War*, a BBC/WGBH Frontline coproduction, written and pro-duced by Eamonn Matthews (Seattle: PBS Video, 1996).

[30] Stein, "Deterrence and Compellence in the Gulf," 2.

In an odd incident earlier in the Clinton administration, the United States launched cruise missile attacks against Iraq in retaliation for a plot by Iraqi intelligence agents to assassinate former President Bush during a visit to Kuwait. The plot was uncovered before the assassination attempt could be made, but the United States retaliated anyway to punish Iraq and deter future incidents. The cruise missile attacks, which included a strike on an Iraqi military intelligence headquarters said to be implicated in the plot, were intended to indicate to Hussein that such acts of terror and similar covert operations would not be tolerated.

An even more dramatic threat of American military force in the Persian Gulf took place in August 1994, when in response to the movement of Iraqi armored forces toward Kuwait, the United States deployed substantial quantities of naval and land-based air and ground forces to the Persian Gulf and stated that it would resist any new invasion with force. The United States had been building up its capabilities and facilities in the Gulf ever since the 1991 war and used the occasion of the Iraqi armored movements to reinforce its presence there to deter any new invasion of Kuwait. The Iraqi units withdrew soon after the U.S. reinforcements arrived, and the Clinton administration claimed that its threats had succeeded. This claim is uncertain, however, as many observers maintained that the Iraqi leader could not possibly have contemplated an invasion given the experience in 1991, the much weaker state of the Iraqi armed forces, and the much greater preparedness of the United States and its allies three years later.

This sequence of incidents presents interesting evidence about the difficulty of utilizing military threats. In each episode the United States was apparently successful: the no-fly zones have generally been respected; there have been no publicly known Iraqi terrorist plots directed against American targets since U.S. retaliation for the planned assassination of Bush; and there have been no further overt threats against Kuwait since 1994. Yet in the larger strategic sense, the United States has failed. U.S. interests would be served most effectively either by the fall of the Hussein regime or by a radical change in Hussein's behavior such that he complies willingly with U.S. wishes. But the Hussein regime continues to skirt UN resolutions and the terms of the agreement that ended the war, continues to terrorize its minority populations, continues to behave belligerently towards Kuwait and other states in the region, and periodically continues to challenge the United States politically. In short, the United States has had to settle for a lesser objective: containment. In the words of one U.S. official, U.S. diplomacy and military activity have served at best "to put Hussein back in the box."

This failure has occurred despite the fact that most of the enabling conditions surrounding U.S. policy are positive. There is now precedent for the actions, the U.S. public is very supportive, and the allies have generally cooperated; when they have not, the United States has been willing to act unilaterally. All the enabling conditions that determine the context and character of the threats are positive. While the demands made have varied in their degree of difficulty, none has been onerous. The failure, then, appears to be the result of the potency of the threat relative to the demand. As in the Gulf War, the United States and its allies have not been willing to make and, if necessary, carry out the one threat that might accomplish their long-term strategic interest. It is evident that the United States is not willing to topple the Hussein regime through force of arms or even to enforce its more far-reaching demands.

The weakness of the U.S. and allied position became evident in the 1996 incident. In response to Iraq's military action against a Kurdish faction in the north, which U.S. leaders termed unacceptable, the United States was only willing to stage symbolic attacks against Iraqi air defense facilities in the south—far from the scene of the Kurdish conflict. This time, most of the allies were unwilling to go along with the action, and open dissent weakened the coalition. The crisis worsened for a time as Hussein seemed to defy U.S. demands about the southern no-fly zone. While he ultimately gave in, the broader U.S. strategic objective of containment was threatened. Hussein reasserted control over significant territory in the north and dismantled the Kurdish opposition. Once again, U.S. demands were not sufficiently potent to bring Hussein to a defining moment.

In late 1997, Hussein barred U.S. citizens from the UN teams inspecting Iraq for weapons of mass destruction in compliance with the agreements ending the war. He also refused to permit inspections of certain types of sites, such as presidential palaces. Although Hussein seemed to relent on the first issue, in January 1998 Iraqi officials refused to allow a particular inspection team, led by an American who Iraq claimed was a spy, to carry out its work. The United States and some of its allies threatened once again to carry out air strikes, and eventually UN Secretary Kofi Annan was able to negotiate an agreement to resume inspections that once more averted major confrontation but failed to resolve the underlying issues.[31]

Somalia, 1992–1995[32]

The disastrous U.S. intervention in Somalia probably did more to undermine worldwide perceptions of the efficacy of U.S. military power than any event in recent memory. Among other things, American actions in Somalia influenced the calculations of leaders in Haiti and Bosnia as they confronted U.S. threats simultaneously.

[31] See postscript for information on later developments.

[32] Primary sources for this case study include FBIS transcripts of Radio Mogadishu broadcasts; contemporaneous news reports; Baker and DeFrank, *The Politics of Diplomacy*; Powell with Persico, *My American Journey*; and Barry M. Blechman and J. M. Vaccaro, *Towards an Operational Strategy of Peace Enforcement: Lessons from Interventions and Peace Operations* (Washington, DC: Defense Forecasts International, 1995).

In Somalia, largely as a result of inattention at political levels, the United States allowed its military forces to transform their original humanitarian mission into a coercive activity intended to enforce a peaceful settlement of the underlying political conflict by disarming factions in a particular section of the country. When one faction resisted and killed twenty-four members of the Pakistani component of the United Nations peacekeeping force, the United States launched a low-level military offensive directed specifically against that faction. When U.S. forces suffered a tactical defeat in October 1993, Washington suddenly curtailed its objectives and announced that it would withdraw virtually all U.S. forces from the country.[33]

Once U.S. forces assumed the larger political role, the mission became extremely difficult. Most of the enabling conditions with respect to the context of the threat were negative. There was no significant precedent for U.S. involvement in Somali politics, and the American public did not support the mission beyond its initial humanitarian boundaries. Other countries with troops participating in the UN mission were extremely reluctant to undertake any actions implying a threat of conflict. The degree of difficulty of the demand escalated sharply once the U.S. offensive against Mohamed Farah Aideed began. Finally, because of the shifts in objectives, the U.S. demands were unclear—to U.S. officials and the U.S. public as well as to the Somali targets. Also, the Somali leaders were constrained by their mutual competition, as well as by internal conflicts within their respective factions, making it unclear whether compliance with U.S. demands was ever feasible.

Nonetheless, the character of the threat suggested potency. A clear sense of urgency was implied, and positive inducements for compliance were supplied. Yet the threat and use of force both failed. The clearest reason was noted previously and stated by the faction leader, Aideed, to the U.S. negotiator. Based on his understanding of recent U.S. history, he believed that the United States could not sustain a campaign against him in the face of casualties. The lack of precedent for the U.S. action in Somalia and the dissension already evident in the United States and among its allies served to confirm his preexisting view that the United States could not sustain its threats against even nominal opposition. The U.S. threat was not credible because contextual factors reinforced the target's preexisting judgment about U.S. credibility.

Macedonia, 1992–Present[34]

The deployment of U.S. and other nations' ground forces to Macedonia to deter any extension of the Bosnian war to that nation, or any other ethnic confla-

---

[33] U.S. forces initially entered Somalia in December 1992 as part of a multilateral mission, UNITAF, intended to secure the delivery of food and other relief supplies that would end the famine and prepare the way for a broader UN force. Having accomplished this limited mission, in May 1993 UNITAF gave way to UNOSOM II, which included only 4,500 U.S. troops. UNOSOM II's mission included disarming the various clan factions that were making the reestablishment of a central government impossible. U.S. forces and the entire UN peacekeeping mission had withdrawn from Somalia by March 1995.

[34] This and the following case study on Bosnian policy are based on public statements by President Clinton and then Secretary of State Warren Christopher, news reports, and extensive FBIS transcripts

gration, represents an apparent success for U.S. military threats. Despite their reluctance to become involved in Bosnia itself, first the Europeans and then the United States were willing to deploy troops to Macedonia as a means of guaranteeing their involvement should the conflict spread. The deployment also was intended to strengthen warnings to Serb leaders not to tighten oppression of the Albanian population in Kosovo. In a way, the unwillingness of U.S. leaders to take decisive action in Bosnia at the time made Macedonia seem more important in the eyes of Washington decision makers. It was a means of demonstrating some on-the-ground involvement and a willingness to prevent a widening conflict, thereby, it was hoped, earning some credits with the Europeans.

In this case, virtually all the enabling conditions were positive. There was support in the Congress, unanimity among the allies, the demand was stated clearly and reinforced by military actions, and the threat (automatic involvement in any extension of the Bosnian conflict) was potent relative to the demand. Its self-implementing nature intrinsically conveyed a sense of commitment and urgency.[35]

Of course, the U.S. threat with respect to Macedonia had another great advantage. It was intended to deter hostile actions whose likelihood was not clear. Whether or not the Serbs or anyone else might have tried to extend the Bosnian conflict to Macedonia absent the allied deployment of ground forces there is anyone's guess. The threat might have worked, because the degree of difficulty of the demand was low. Compliance with the demand required no visible action; in fact, it might have required no action at all.

Bosnia, 1992–Present

The Bosnian war and its accompanying humanitarian tragedies bedeviled both the Bush and the Clinton administrations. Throughout the conflict, threats and limited applications of force have been used for tactical purposes with mixed results. Early in the conflict, the United States and its allies established a no-fly zone to protect their humanitarian shipments and forces, and the threat of selective air strikes was employed to remind the Serbs of these rules, generally with some tactical success. On the other hand, the United States and its allies, working through the UN, threatened and used limited amounts of force repeatedly in efforts to protect the so-called safe areas from Serb encroachments and subsequent mass murders. These efforts failed miserably, climaxing with the occupation of Zepa and Srebrenica in 1995 and the murder of thousands of their residents.

---

of Croatian, Bosnian Serb, Serbian, and Bosnian TV and radio broadcasts containing statements by leaders of these groups.

[35] There have been virtually no complaints from the Congress about the Macedonian deployment despite the fact that U.S. troops serve under UN command—a hot issue among conservatives. Of course, the support would probably disappear quickly if the troops in Macedonia appeared in danger of entering combat.

On the strategic level from the earliest days of the Clinton administration, U.S. leaders repeatedly threatened a deeper level of involvement in the conflict if Serb forces did not comply with various resolutions. The United States also deployed a considerable number of forces to the Adriatic and to Italian air bases, helping to enforce sanctions against Serbia and an arms embargo in Bosnia, as well as carrying out the limited strikes mentioned above. But the vagueness of the U.S. strategic threats encouraged Serb intransigence and continued Serb efforts to seize additional territory. The appearance of a lack of American resolve was compounded by clear indications that the Untied States was not willing to deploy ground forces to Bosnia and that the allies were willing to deploy troops but not to place them in danger, as would be required by any serious effort to compel Serb compliance with Western demands. Not until August 1995, following the atrocities in Zepa and Srebrenica and the successful Croat offensive against the Serbs, did the United States and its allies make a serious effort to pressure the Serbs into entering peace negotiations by carrying out repeated air strikes against a variety of targets. Soon thereafter, the Dayton talks were begun and the peace agreement now being implemented was concluded. Whether the Serbs were brought to the peace table by the Croat offensive, the new allied will to end the conflict suggested by the air campaign, or their own weariness with war and sanctions is anyone's guess. Whether the peace will last is an even greater unknown. In the post-Dayton phase, of course, the United States and its allies again used military force, deploying ground troops of the Implementation Force, or IFOR, throughout Bosnia to help keep the peace. IFOR was successful in ensuring that the parties observed the military aspects of the Dayton Accords and completed its mission in December 1996. It has been succeeded by a smaller force known as the Stabilization Force, or SFOR.

In the end, therefore, U.S. strategic threats appear to have been successful in persuading the Serbs to stop fighting and start talking, or at least were coincident with success. But this one success capped a long period of clear failure, consistent with the negative values of most of the enabling conditions in this case. All the contextual variables were negative: there was no precedent for U.S. involvement in the former Yugoslavia, the Congress and the American people were starkly divided as to the wisdom of U.S. involvement, and the allies were obviously reluctant to risk the lives of their soldiers. The credibility of the threat was strengthened by the deployment of forces, but the actual uses of these forces were so limited as to convey a message of reluctance and weakness rather than of strength. This is certainly the view of Undersecretary of Defense Walter Slocombe, who has said that "UNPROFOR's mistake was tolerating hostile behavior. It should have slapped down the people who were shooting at them."[36]

---

[36] Interview by Barry Blechman with Walter Slocombe, 27 January 1996.

Similarly, the enabling conditions pertaining to the final demand made of the Serbs were mainly negative. The U.S. demand to halt the war was not articulated clearly until the final air offensive, and no sense of urgency was conveyed until then. The U.S. objective was to compel participation in a peace process, rather that deter certain actions, requiring a positive and visible step by the target. And that target—Serbia's president—often was unable to deliver the Serb leaders in Bosnia even when he wanted to meet the U.S. demands.

The enabling conditions only turned positive, for the most part, following the massacres at Zepa and Srebrenica and the beginning of the massive NATO air strikes. As the air strikes continued, they not only raised the cost of noncompliance but also encouraged the development of a sense of urgency among Serb leaders. At this point, the choice became clearer to the Serbs—peace or destruction of the military infrastructure of the Bosnian Serbs. Given other conditions at the time, particularly the successful Croatian ground offensive that was changing the entire strategic situation and the evident weariness with the war in Serbia, the U.S. threats at last gained the potency necessary to achieve their objective. Then Secretary of Defense William Perry in fact believes that he can identify the defining moment: a visit by the chiefs of the U.S., British, and French armed forces to Bosnian Serb military leaders in Belgrade on 23 July 1995 to convey the new resoluteness of the NATO nations in the aftermath of the Srebrenica massacres.[37]

The picture that thus emerges with respect to the efficacy of U.S. military threats in Bosnia is mixed. For the most part the threats failed, mainly because the element central to their potency—a willingness to deploy U.S. ground troops and to utilize European forces already on the ground—was missing. Seeing the disarray in the United States and the dissension among the allies, the Serbs had little reason to comply. Only when the NATO allies, reacting to the murders in Srebrenica and the Croat offensive, made clear that they would be willing to act more forcefully did the Serbs perceive a real cost to their noncompliance and begin to take the allies' threats seriously.

Haiti, 1994–1996[38]

Haiti presents a similar picture: ineffective threats and excessively limited military actions showed U.S. irresoluteness for a considerable period of time but were followed by a potent threat that finally achieved its objective. The crisis in Haiti actually began in 1991, when a military coup expelled the country's first elected president, Jean Bertrand Aristide. The United States pursued a diplomatic strategy to reinstall the president, accompanied by sanctions for more than two years. Only when the Governor's Island agreement that would

---

[37] Interview by Barry Blechman with William Perry, 21 January 1997.

[38] Sources for this case study included Powell with Persico, *My American Journey*; contemporaneous U.S. news reports; and FBIS transcripts of Port-au-Prince Radio Metropole.

have permitted Aristide to regain office failed in the fall of 1993 and the Haitian military government turned back a U.S. ship delivering the lead element of a UN peacekeeping force, did the United States threaten to overthrow the military government and reinstall Aristide by force, if necessary.

The turning away of the U.S. ship followed closely on the defeat of U.S. forces in Somalia, a coincidence that was particularly harmful to the efficacy of U.S. threats.[39] For the next eight months the United States made numerous demonstrations of its military capabilities through deployments of Navy and Marine forces off the island and by staging exercises intended to show practice for an invasion. Yet the Haitian ruler, General Raoul Cedras, with virtually no means of defending himself if the United States did invade, refused to back down. Finally, President Clinton received authorizations to utilize military force from the OAS and the UN and set a deadline for the invasion. Still, the Haitian ruler refused to back down. It was only when he received word that U.S. airborne troops had left their bases and that the operation was actually under way that he accepted a U.S. offer, conveyed by a delegation chaired by former President Jimmy Carter, to step down with some semblance of dignity and a guarantee of safety.

It should have been easier to make effective threats in the Haitian case than in Bosnia. While U.S. opinion tended to oppose the use of American forces in both cases, there was ample precedent for U.S. interventions in Haiti and the Caribbean, and most other hemispheric nations were supportive. The demand was clear, the target could easily comply, the threat was potent relative to the demand, and U.S. military power was displayed with great visibility. There were also positive inducements for compliance: U.S. representatives offered to provide for the personal safety of the Haitian dictator and his family.

Why, then, was it so difficult to make a threat that worked? Why was it necessary to actually launch a huge invasion force before Cedras would believe that Clinton was truly committed to his ouster? Two factors relating to the context of the U.S. threat seem to have been essential. First, the opposition of much of the American public and Congress to invasion plans may have conveyed hope to Cedras that Clinton could not possibly go through with his threats. Indeed, knowing that he would be defeated, Clinton did not seek congressional authorization for the invasion. Second, particularly in view of this opposition, Cedras may have taken heart from the recent American behavior in Somalia, as well as from his success in compelling the ship carrying UN peacekeepers to withdraw.[40] He may have believed that even if the United States did invade, all

---

[39] D. Ribadeneira, "Life as Usual for Haiti Troops: At Military Headquarters in Capital, No Signs of Concern," *Boston Globe*, 15 May 1994; A. Downie, "U.S. Diplomats in Haiti Threatened, Ship Delayed," *Reuters*, 11 October 1993; A. Downie, "Tense Standoff in Haiti over U.S. Troopship," *Reuters North American Wire*, 12 October 1993.

[40] According to a wire service report, Downie, "U.S. Diplomats in Haiti Threatened," Haitian paramilitaries demonstrating in Port-au-Prince chanted, "We're going to make a second Somalia here!" and UN envoy Dante Caputo said that the Haitians were "trying to create an atmosphere where it would be a disaster, a blood bath, if foreign troops came."

his forces would have to do would be to inflict some casualties and the Americans would withdraw. If this is the case, the persuasiveness of the Carter mission,which made clear both the magnitude and commitment of the U.S. effort and provided positive inducements for compliance, was essential in increasing the potency of the U.S. threat and bringing Cedras to his defining moment.

Korea, 1994–1996[41]

The Korean case is probably the most successful use of military threats during this period. Essentially in this case, threats of military force were used as one element in a strategy that concentrated mainly on using economic instruments—both positive and negative—to halt the North Korean nuclear weapons program. While threats were not the most prominent element of the strategy, they clearly played a role, enforcing boundaries on Pyongyang's choices. According to Walter Slocombe, when Pyongyang tried to counter the U.S. threat to impose economic sanctions by stating that such an action would constitute an act of war, the United States made clear that it was willing to escalate along with North Korea through visible efforts to increase its readiness for war on the peninsula.[42]

The threats generally were vague in character and articulated indirectly. Neither the president nor other high-ranking U.S. officials threatened explicitly to destroy North Korea's nuclear facilities, but the administration let it be known that it was considering military options and reinforced the message by strengthening its presence in South Korea with air defense missiles and other items. Consultations with the U.S. commander in Korea to discuss military options were held with a fair amount of publicity. The fact that prominent Republicans, such as former National Security Adviser Brent Scowcroft, were calling for military strikes reinforced the message that the administration could not rule out direct military action if negotiations failed.

Enabling conditions in this case were generally positive for effective threats. The U.S. interest and willingness to use force in Korea had strong precedent, public opinion and the Congress supported the need to do something about North Korea's nuclear weapons program, the demand was clear, and the threat was supported by visible military actions. The major negative condition was that the U.S. ally, South Korea, was reluctant to see the crisis get out of control, as it faced the possibility of major casualties if combat resumed on the peninsula.

In the end, North Korea probably ended its nuclear program because it had gotten what it wanted—an economic payoff and, more importantly, the beginning of a dialogue with the United States that might lead eventually to normal

---

[41] Sources for this case study include North Korea, *The Public Perspective* 5 (July/August, 1994): 5; statements by President Clinton, Secretary of Defense Perry, and other U.S. officials; and contemporaneous news reports.

[42] Interview by Barry Blechman with Walter Slocombe, 27 January 1996.

relations. Still, U.S. officials believe that Pyongyang took the U.S. threats seriously and that they played some role in bringing about the so-far positive outcome.

Taiwan, 1996[43]

The final case is an odd one—more symbolic than real. In 1996, China staged a series of military exercises and missile tests near Taiwan as the latter moved toward an election in which opposition parties were campaigning on a platform that demanded independence from the mainland. The Chinese actions were apparently intended to intimidate the Taiwanese and to remind all other parties—particularly the United States—that China would not tolerate de facto Taiwanese independence indefinitely and especially would not tolerate overt steps toward a de jure sovereign status. In response, the United States sent an aircraft carrier task group through the straits that separate Taiwan from the mainland and later in the crisis deployed a second carrier near the island. The U.S. actions apparently were intended to remind China of the American interest in preventing Taiwan's unification with the mainland by force.

Both parties' actions, of course, were shadowboxing. China was probably not seriously contemplating invading Taiwan. It does not have the means to accomplish that goal, and Taiwan could probably defend itself against an invasion without U.S. help. Moreover, the fallout from such an action would set back China's economic development immensely, as well as antagonize neighboring states (especially Japan) and trigger massive armament programs on their parts—a counterproductive outcome from China's perspective.

But if China's threat was not serious, neither was that of the United States. Despite a great deal of hype in the news media, both countries apparently understood that they were playing on a stage, making points for world opinion and for domestic audiences. Both Chinese and American statements explicitly discounted any risk of a U.S.–Chinese military confrontation and anticipated continued relations in the future.[44] In this sense the U.S. threats were effective; the target, however, was not China but Taiwan and domestic U.S. audiences.

CONCLUSIONS

The results of the case studies discussed above are summarized in Table 1. The cases are arrayed in rows, moving chronologically from top to bottom. The outcomes of each case and a description of the enabling conditions constitute the columns.

---

[43] Sources for this case study include public statements by President Clinton, Secretary of State Christopher, and Secretary of Defense Perry; transcripts of State Department press conferences; and Chinese Foreign Ministry statements, including press conferences by Foreign Minister Qian Qichen.

[44] Burns, "Fallout from Taiwan Tensions: U.S. Cancels China Talks," *The Record*, 23 March 1996.

TABLE 1

Enabling Conditions and Outcomes

Case	Credibility				Tangible Military Action	Articulated	Degree of Difficulty		Positive Incentive	Potency	Outcome
	Precedent	Public Support	Third-Nation Support	Urgency			Content	Visibility			
Panama	+	+	+	–	+	–	3	–	–	–	YB
Iraq (Strategic Outcome)	–	+	+	+	+	+	2	–	–	–	YB
DS/DS[a]	–	+	+	+	+	+	2	–	–	–	YB
South No-fly	–	+	–	+	+	+	2	–	–	+	YB
Kurds	–	+	–	+	+	–	2	–	+	–	YB
Terror	+	+	+	+	+	+	1	+	+	+	S
VW[b]	+	+	+	+	+	+	1	+	+	+	S
Somalia	–	–	–	+	+	–	2	–	–	–	F
Macedonia	–	+	+	+	+	+	1	+	+	+	S
Bosnia (Strategic Outcome)	–	–	+	+	+	–	2	–	+	+	YB
Lift/No-fly	–	+	+	+	+	+	2	+	+	–	YB
Sanctions	–	–	+	–	+	+	2	+	–	–	YB
Safe/Weapons[c]	–	–	+	–	+	+	2	+	–	–	F
Dayton	–	–	+	+	+	+	2	–	+	+	S
IFOR	+	+	+	+	+	+	1	+	+	+	S
Haiti	+	–	+	–	+	+	3	–	+	+	YB
North Korea	+	+	+	+	+	+	1	–	+	+	S
Taiwan	+	+	–	–	+	+	1	+	+	+	S

[a] Desert Shield/Desert Storm.

[b] Valiant Warrior (1994).

[c] Safe Havens/Weapons Exclusion Zones.

Notes: The enabling conditions are generally labeled positive, meaning that they favored a successful outcome from the U.S. perspective, or negative, meaning the opposite. The one exception is the content of the demand made, which is ranked from 1 (least difficult for the target) to 3 (most difficult for the target).

Outcomes are categorized as a success (S), failure (F), or "yes, but" (YB), meaning that the outcome eventually favored the United States, but that getting there left a great deal to be desired. The Iraq and Bosnia cases are rated both for their strategic outcome and for specific uses of force within each case.

Overall, the use of military power by the United States clearly failed in only one of the cases—Somalia. U.S. threats to use military force clearly succeeded in three—Macedonia, North Korea, and Taiwan. In the four other cases—Panama, Iraq, Bosnia, and Haiti—the use of military power ultimately succeeded, but either success came only with great difficulty at considerable cost to other U.S. interests, or the United States was successful only in achieving its immediate objectives, not its longer-term strategic goals. In Panama, Bosnia, and Haiti, success came only after long periods of failure with high costs for the administration domestically and internationally; in Iraq each individual use of military power was successful, but the strategic situation remains unchanged and unsatisfactory from an American perspective; in Bosnia and Haiti the underlying political conflicts remain unresolved and easily reversible.

With respect to the enabling conditions, none alone appears to be a sufficient condition for success; nor can it be said for certain that any one condition—other than that the target indeed be able to fulfill the demand—is a prerequisite for success. Still, one noteworthy partial correlation can be seen between the difficulty of the demand and positive outcomes. In six of seven successes (counting individual uses of force within cases as well as overall cases), fulfillment of the U.S. objective demanded relatively little of the target. Typically, the actions required of the targets also tended to be less visible in these cases, with the exceptions of the action required of North Korea and of the Bosnian Serbs with respect to entering the Dayton negotiations. The U.S. posture in six of the seven successful uses of military power also included positive incentives, further reducing the difficulty of the demand as perceived by the target.

Enabling conditions pertaining to the credibility of U.S. threats, as determined by the context and character, present a less consistent pattern. There was precedent for U.S. action in only half of the cases, and the results were mixed in those cases with precedents and those without. Third-nation support and whether or not a sense of urgency was conveyed present no clear pattern. Tangible military actions were taken in all cases and hence shed no light.

The presence or absence of public support is more interesting. It was present in the three clear successes and absent in the one clear failure. The remaining four cases, which had mixed results, were also split with respect to public support. Public support for a threat evidently cannot guarantee its success, but an evident lack of public support apparently can make it difficult to make threats credibly. In Somalia and Haiti, as well as Bosnia for most of the conflict, the evident lack of public support in the United States for the policies being pursued by the administration seems to have given great comfort to the target of the U.S. action and encouraged him to attempt to stay the course. Evidence of public dissension was probably a factor encouraging Hussein to defy U.S. threats as well, and each of the former officials interviewed cited this factor as greatly complicating the use of military power by the United States.

Looking beyond the scoreboard of results to the cases themselves, the question of potency also appears to be especially important. Potent threats relative to the cost of noncompliance were made in each of the clearly successful cases (Macedonia, North Korea, and Taiwan) and were not made in the one clear failure (Somalia). In the case of Iraq, as in Panama and in all but the so-far-final stage of the Bosnian conflict, the unwillingness of the United States to make threats that would clearly offer the target the prospect of an unacceptable cost seems to have been an important reason for the failure of U.S. policy.

The problem that the United States faces, therefore, is very clear. It is rare that it can both make potent threats and retain public support. Potent threats imply greater risks. And the American public's aversion to risk, particularly the risk of suffering casualties, is well known; the legacy of Vietnam is real. This is particularly true in the types of conflict situations that have arisen since the end of the cold war—where there is little precedent for American action, where American interests are more abstract than tangible, where the battle lines are uncertain, and where none of the contending parties wears a particularly friendly face.

Recognizing this public aversion to casualties or predicting such opposition in particular cases, American presidents have been reluctant to step as close to the plate as has been required to achieve U.S. objectives in many post-cold war conflicts. They have made threats only reluctantly and usually have not made as clear or potent a threat as was called for by the situation. They have understood the need to act in the situation but have been unwilling or perceived themselves as being unable to lead the American people into the potential sacrifice necessary to secure the proper goal. As a result, they have attempted to satisfice, taking some action but not the most effective possible action to challenge the foreign leader threatening U.S. interests. They have sought to curtail the extent and potential cost of the confrontation by avoiding the most serious type of threat and therefore the most costly type of war if the threat were challenged.

The American public's sensitivity to the human and economic costs of military action is a clear legacy of the Vietnam experience. But it has been reinforced since then by sharp reactions by the public and elected officials to the suicide bombing of U.S. Marines in Beirut and to the deaths of U.S. soldiers in Mogadishu. Both Bush and Clinton have been keenly cognizant of this sensitivity, and their attempts to threaten to use military power have been hesitant as a result.

This syndrome would impair the effectiveness of U.S. coercive diplomacy under any circumstances, but its deleterious effects are magnified by the impact of those same historical events on foreign leaders. Vietnam syndrome is not solely an American disease: its symptoms are visible abroad, when potential targets of U.S. threats see the American public's sensitivity to casualties as a positive factor in their own reckoning of the risks and benefits of alternative courses of action. A review of the evidence reveals that Bosnian Serb leaders,

Haitian paramilitary leaders, Saddam Hussein, and Somalia's late warlord all banked on their ability to force a U.S. retreat by inflicting relatively small numbers of casualties on U.S. forces. That places American presidents attempting to accomplish goals through threats in a dilemma. Domestic opinion rarely supports forceful policies at the outset, but tentative policies only reinforce the prejudices of foreign leaders and induce them to stand firm. Vietnam's legacy abroad pushes foreign leaders' defining moments back, requiring greater demonstrations of will, greater urgency, more tangible actions by U.S. forces, and greater potency for threats to succeed. But Vietnam's legacy at home makes it much harder for U.S. presidents to take such forceful actions without significant investments of political capital.

As a result of this dilemma, American officials have often been unable to break through the preconceived notions of U.S. weakness held by foreign leaders to bring about a defining moment. Indeed, the cases in which decisive U.S. actions were taken only after long periods of indecision (especially Panama, Bosnia, and Haiti) may have only reinforced foreign leaders' preconceptions about America's lack of will. Until U.S. presidents show a greater ability to lead on this issue, or until the American people demonstrate a greater willingness to step up to the challenges of exercising military dominance on a global scale, foreign leaders in many situations will likely continue to see American threats more as signs of weakness than as potent expressions of America's true military power. As a result, they will likely continue to be willing to withstand American threats—necessitating either recourse to force to achieve American goals or embarrassing retreats in the pursuit of American interests abroad.

This suggests that American presidents have several options when considering potential uses of military power in support of diplomacy:

- They can pick their fights carefully, choosing to make public demands of other nations mainly in situations in which the actions they require will not be perceived by the target as excessively difficult and when they can leaven their threats with positive incentives to encourage compliance, as in the cases of Taiwan and North Korea.
- They can seek to "demilitarize" U.S. policy somewhat. Strategies close to those used in the Korean case may be more appropriate and more effective than the quick recourse to military threats seen in most of the other cases. Threats and limited military force have a clear role but more as reinforcing elements in policies dominated by economic, diplomatic, and political factors than as the primary policy instrument. In Haiti, ultimately a skilled diplomatic team backed by force, not the force itself, secured Cedras's removal from power. Given domestic constraints on U.S. ability to use military power in threats or in actuality, Presidents Bush and Clinton may have leaned too heavily on the armed forces to advance American interests in the immediate post-cold war world. Policies that deemphasize the role of force may be more appropriate more often.

- When nonmilitary instruments of policy seem likely to be ineffectual but the U.S. president still perceives an imperative to act, and the foreign leader seems likely to perceive compliance with U.S. demands as onerous, the president must act decisively. In these situations the demand must be clear and urgent, the demonstration of military power incontrovertible, and the threat itself potent relative to the target's alternatives. The ultimate achievement of U.S. objectives in Desert Storm and at the end of the Bosnian and Haitian scenarios demonstrates that presidential decisiveness can be effective, even at the later stages of a crisis. Most importantly, in Colin Powell's words, "The president himself must begin the action prepared to see the course through to its end. . . . He can only persuade an opponent of his seriousness when, indeed, he is serious."[45]

POSTSCRIPT

This article was prepared for publication in *Political Science Quarterly* at the midpoint of the second Clinton administration, precisely at a time when U.S. and British aircraft were carrying out an extensive bombing campaign in Iraq intended to weaken the Saddam Hussein regime and compel Baghdad to cooperate with UN inspectors seeking to verify destruction of Iraq's weapons of mass destruction. This massive air campaign was the direct consequence of the intrinsic difficulties faced by the United States in making military threats and using force in limited ways and of specific problems faced by the Clinton administration in its second term.

Saddam Hussein escalated Iraq's testing of U.S. resolve on the inspections issue in late 1997. The United States responded with threatening rhetoric and diplomacy, but stepped back from threatened air strikes on several occasions—the last in November 1998 when the aircraft were already enroute, minutes away from their targets. Hussein's strategy of probe and withdraw, test and comply, has been highly effective. It is costly for the United States in tangible terms to prepare for military action, and costly in political terms to appear indecisive and vacillating. After employing tough rhetoric, the administration has repeatedly ended by appearing anxious for any excuse not to undertake military action. As a result, support for a tough stance on the inspections issue declined internationally, even in the United States itself. Hussein clearly understood and took advantage of Clinton's reluctance to use decisive force, and no doubt was emboldened further by the president's increasing political problems stemming from the Monica Lewinsky affair.

Whether or not the December air strikes will achieve their objectives remains to be seen, but so far there is no evidence of any new willingness on Hussein's part to comply, rather the opposite. The United States has become more open in its support for groups seeking to overthrow the current government of

---

[45] Interview by Barry Blechman with General Colin Powell, 21 February 1997.

Iraq, but U.S. unwillingness to undertake clearly and unambiguously the only potent threat in this situation—to remove Hussein by force unless he complies—suggests that the Iraqi–U.S. conflict has not yet run its course.

What is clear is that the United States needs to strengthen its ability to threaten and use military forces in limited ways. It should be a high priority for any new administration to make clear that it recognizes the problems that have limited our effectiveness in the past and that it is charting a new course. To do otherwise would be to enforce the need for continued, long-term involvement in protracted conflicts, which over time impose costly financial and political burdens, and can only encourage adversaries in other nations to test American resolve. If the United States is to lead in world affairs, it must learn to use its military dominance in more adroit and more decisive ways.

A New Imperial Presidency?
Insights from U.S. Involvement in Bosnia

WILLIAM C. BANKS
JEFFREY D. STRAUSSMAN

In August 1995, President Bill Clinton caught a lucky break. A few days after Congress voted with veto-proof majorities to lift the arms embargo on Bosnia, the Croatian government launched an offensive against its dissident Serbian minority. Neither the Serb government in Belgrade nor Western nations responded, despite the fact that this Croatian operation was similar to the earlier Serbian "ethnic cleansing" that had received such negative attention in the Western news media. With the "clean" ethnic borders more or less in place, Serbia and Croatia appeared finally ready to move toward a settlement that had plagued the two countries since the breakup of Yugoslavia in 1991. However, when the Serbs continued to attack Muslim military positions in Sarajevo, Clinton was able to advance his alternative to congressional pressure to lift the arms embargo to the Western allies—namely, air strikes against the Serbs. The air strikes had the dual impact of blunting the efforts to override the vote on lifting the arms embargo and providing the military muscle to bring the warring sides in the Bosnian conflict to the bargaining table.

After several weeks of U.S.-sponsored negotiations at Wright-Patterson Air Force Base in Dayton, Ohio, the principals representing the three factions in Bosnia—Croats, Serbs, and Muslims—initialed a peace agreement on 21 November 1995. A few days after the formal signing of the Dayton Peace Accords in Paris on 14 December, President Clinton ordered the deployment of more than 20,000 United States troops as part of a NATO-led Implementation Force (IFOR) of 60,000, which was charged with patrolling and enforcing a cease-fire and a zone of separation between the newly created semiautonomous entities

WILLIAM C. BANKS is professor of law, College of Law, Syracuse University. JEFFREY D. STRAUSSMAN is professor of public administration and vice chair, Department of Public Administration, The Maxwell School of Citizenship and Public Affairs, Syracuse University.

in Bosnia—the Muslim-Croat Federation and the Serb Republic Srpska. More or less lost in all the attention given to the Dayton settlement was a missing and essential element of the U.S. participation in IFOR: there was neither congressional authorization nor an appropriation in support of the deployment of U.S. ground forces to Bosnia. How could such a commitment of U.S. troops to enforce the peace in Bosnia have been made unilaterally by the president?

This article explains how the Bosnia commitment was made, and it assesses its legality. Part one provides a primer on the defense appropriations power, emphasizing the evolution from the original understanding of the Constitution to the practical executive dominance in the post-Korean War era. Part two describes the events from the breakup of Yugoslavia to the creation of IFOR in the immediate aftermath of the Dayton Peace Accords. Part three assesses the funding dimensions of U.S. participation in IFOR. Part four notes the continuing U.S. presence in Bosnia and draws some lessons about the contemporary dynamics of the elected branches in planning and implementing national security operations.

A PRIMER ON THE POWER OF THE PURSE IN NATIONAL SECURITY AFFAIRS

In December 1995 hearings before the Senate Appropriations Subcommittee on Defense regarding the U.S. commitment to Bosnia, Chairman Ted Stevens (R–AK) stated: "I oppose this deployment, but . . . it is [not] our prerogative here to debate . . . with the President. . . . The President has ordered the deployment . . . we have no way to prevent that."[1] If James Madison or Thomas Jefferson could have witnessed Senator Stevens's remarks, they would have been puzzled at this position taken by a member of the Senate and the chairman of the Senate Appropriations Defense Subcommittee that opposition to the commitment of U.S. forces to a military operation abroad is not even a question for the Congress to debate, much less decide.

Jefferson or Madison would say that Stevens put it exactly backwards: the president would propose the military operation, debate in Congress would follow, and, depending on the outcome of a vote in Congress, the president would begin the operation or not. In 1789, Jefferson wrote to Madison that "[w]e have already given . . . one effectual check to the Dog of war by transferring the power of letting him loose from the Executive to the Legislative body, from those who are to spend to those who are to pay."[2]

Jefferson was referring, of course, to the Framers' decision to vest the power to declare war in the Congress. But he also was celebrating their strategy of cementing the congressional primacy over committing the nation to war through conferring on Congress the power of appropriating money for the ex-

---

[1] "Bosnia Costs and Funding Requirements," Hearing before a Subcommittee of the Committee on Appropriations, United States Senate, 104th Congress, 1st sess., 1 December 1995, S. Hrg. 104–286, 35.
[2] P. Ford, ed., *The Writings of Thomas Jefferson* (New York: G.P. Putnam's Sons, 1895), 123.

ercises of the war power, in the Spending, Army, Navy, and Necessary and Proper Clauses of the Constitution. The package of controls was completed in the Appropriations Clause and its prohibition on spending of public revenues without appropriation, and the Statement and Account Clause and its requirement of a periodic accounting of how public money is spent. Thus, the system put into place by the Framers separated the purse from the sword. The power of the purse supplemented the declaration power by allowing Congress to specify or restrict military spending ex ante. In the event that such controls failed, Congress was also given the power of supply, permitting Congress to determine through appropriations the magnitude and duration of U.S. involvement in military engagement.

The Framers' overarching national security objective was to make it difficult for the United States to engage in war. It was not that the Framers believed that the Congress would be more expert than the president in national security affairs. Rather, it was assumed that peace would more likely predominate if the Constitution placed obstacles in the path toward war. The Congress thus supplied a deliberative buffer to hasty action, while its role assured that the gravest decisions made by the nation would be made by those most accountable to the people. The process prescribed by the Framers in the Constitution, stated simply, requires presidents to request from Congress authority to commit the U.S. to a military operation where the use of force is likely. The commander in chief may act without congressional authorization only in defense of sudden attack or to effect a rescue of Americans.[3]

The history of how the United States made commitments to use military force abroad before 1950 was relatively consistent and mostly in keeping with the constitutional design outlined above. While there were occasional instances of unconstitutional engagements by commanders in chief, most involved minor skirmishes and none purported to usurp the congressional war power. The exceptional breach of the rules normally was based on a false claim of statutory authority and resulted in a contrite admission of error by the president.[4] Even President Franklin D. Roosevelt's pre-World War II sympathies toward the

---

[3] Although the "original understanding" of the Constitution is often obscure, the power to commit the nation to war, big or little, declared or undeclared, was clearly given to Congress. Only defensive actions where time does not permit deliberation by Congress may be lawfully conducted by the executive without congressional authorization. See Stephen Dycus, Arthur L. Berney, William C. Banks, and Peter Raven-Hansen, *National Security Law* (Boston: Little, Brown, 2d ed., 1997), 9–27.

[4] A Senate report stated: "[T]he practice of American Presidents for over a century after independence showed scrupulous respect for the authority of Congress except in a few instances." S. Rep. No. 797, 90th Congress, 1st sess., 1967, 23. While proponents of broad presidential power have developed various lists purporting to show instances in which the president has ordered military action without congressional authorization, these lists tend to mislabel an operation authorized by Congress, or the actions listed involve minor skirmishes with pirates or operations to rescue Americans abroad. See Frances Wormuth and Edwin Firmage, *To Chain the Dog of War: The Power of Congress in History and Law* (Urbana: University of Illinois Press, 2d ed., 1989); Dycus, et al. *National Security Law*, 334–341.

plight of Europe and his pre-declaration efforts to aid the allies were couched in the authorities Congress had granted. For example, Roosevelt answered the French appeal for military assistance this way: "Only the Congress can make such commitments."[5]

The constitutional design began to erode with President Harry Truman's unilateral commitment to send U.S. troops to fight a war in Korea. Commanders in chief following Truman cited their supposed independent constitutional authority (employing Korea as precedent) to deny the congressional primacy in initiating war, sometimes even denying that Congress is empowered to stop a president determined to act. They claimed that fast-breaking crises do not permit the luxury of congressional deliberation and cited the United Nations and other treaty-based obligations as authorization for their military actions. In addition, changes in the technology and speed of modern warfare have compromised the ability and perhaps the will of Congress to exercise its power over war before the use of force abroad. Precipitously, Congress has been relegated to the role of spectator in national security decision making.

As the actual power over national security shifted to the president after the Korean War and Congress increasingly ceded the initiative, the congressional role in deciding to commit the United States to war shifted from authorization to appropriations, from deciding in advance to grant the authority to act to ratifying or restricting ex post. The ex ante check on war making became an opportunity for ex post review and reaction. While some members of Congress carped about their subservience to unilateral executive decisions, occasionally national security commitments were influenced after the fact. In the Southeast Asia War, for example, appropriations restrictions were employed—first to limit the scope of the war through area and use restrictions, and later to bring it to an end.

In the waning years of the Southeast Asia War, Congress managed to beat back an already weakened President Richard Nixon and enact over his veto the War Powers Resolution (WPR) of 1973. Billed as a measure intended to restore congressional primacy in national security through requirements that the president consult Congress before and report to them after deploying troops where hostilities may be imminent, the WPR had no realistic chance of doing any such thing. First, the political compromises that shaped the final bill resulted in a statute that arguably enhanced rather than reined in presidential power. Second, once the weakened Nixon was gone, presidents since have routinely sidestepped its limited prescriptions while refusing to concede the act's constitutionality. Later attempts by Congress to curtail military operations through appropriations restrictions had mixed results, at best. These included U.S. operations in Angola through the Clark-Tunney Amendment, in Nicaragua through the Boland Amendments, and in Somalia through a compromise

[5] Edward Corwin, *The President: Office and Powers, 1787–1984* (New York: New York University Press, 1984), 246.

measure arrived at with President Clinton.[6] At other times, members of Congress tried but failed to muster the votes to curtail a military operation that they may not have authorized.

One reason that the president has assumed the dominant role in making national security commitments is that contemporary situations may present crises unimaginable to the Framers that call for prompt action; both the speed and destructive capacity of weaponry may justify some presidential discretion to act unilaterally, not after deliberation by 535 representatives. Indeed, if the president fails to act in a high stakes, contemporary national security crisis, unilaterally or as part of a multinational force, he may fail to meet his independent constitutional obligations as commander in chief and as chief executive to "preserve, protect, and defend" the Constitution. Although this justification for unilateral presidential action remains almost entirely hypothetical,[7] the possibility of such a crisis has facilitated the accretion of power to the president.

Another reason for presidential hegemony, however, has nothing to do with crises in a fast-moving world. Since Truman's move to deploy a massive force to Korea, Congress has demonstrated that it prefers not to take the risk of authorizing or forbidding risky national security ventures. If the president leads, Congress may remain silent and permit the president to act for the nation. Or, members may either applaud or chastise the president, short of making legislation, depending on how the operation pans out.

Today, national security commitments are not made pursuant to widely shared policy objectives. Indeed, allowing for the accretion of the power to the president over the past forty-five years, our nation's commitments of military forces are often not even made following policies clearly articulated by the president, much less those favored by the Congress. Instead deployments are made, no-fly zones are enforced, bombing raids are executed, peace is enforced—all generally following a pattern of vague, shifting, and imprecise policies, shaped to avoid alienating any important domestic or foreign constituency. A by-product of this process of nonpolicy making is the avoidance of accountability. What has developed is a sort of game, honed during the years of wrangling over the war in Southeast Asia and U.S. support for the Nicaraguan contras, now played with considerable skill by executive and legislative players.

In the contemporary crucible of the defense appropriations process, the policy questions of whether the United States should engage in this or that military operation become fiscal questions: How much should be spent in furtherance of an activity for which a commitment has already been made by the president? Thus, the national security commitments made by the United States in

---

[6] Department of Defense Appropriations Act, 1994, 107 Stat. 1475–77, §8151 (1993).

[7] The Constitution permits unilateral presidential action only to repel a sudden attack or to rescue Americans held abroad. Other unilateral uses of military force by the president in an emergency are best viewed as unlawful, permitting Congress to ratify the action after-the-fact if it believes the actions were justified. See Jules Lobel, "Emergency Power and the Decline of Liberalism," *Yale Law Journal* 98 (1989): 1385.

the former Yugoslavia have been made following a familiar pattern: The president decides to undertake a national security operation, be it a humanitarian relief in a dangerous setting; participation in peacekeeping, peace enforcement, or peacemaking; or the removal of a tyrannical leader or regime from power. The president does not seek authorization from Congress nor seek a specific appropriation to fund the operation.

According to the Framers' theory of appropriation, the commander in chief should be disabled from beginning the military operation because he lacks the appropriated funds. In fact, he has customarily claimed and exercised discretion to spend from large, lump sum accounts and to spend reprogrammed, transferred, emergency, and contingency funds without prior specific appropriation from Congress. From Nixon's use of such accounts to finance hostilities in and over Cambodia during the war in Southeast Asia, to President Ronald Reagan's use of them to finance the contras in Nicaragua, to President George Bush's employment of them to fund Operation Desert Shield until Congress made a specific appropriation, modern presidents have exercised what has in fact become a presidential spending power in national security.

From Yugoslavia to IFOR

The collapse of the socialist regimes in Eastern Europe and the former Soviet Union between 1989 and 1991 eventually reached Yugoslavia, which dissolved into five republics—Slovenia, Croatia, Bosnia-Herzegovina, Serbia and Montenegro, and Macedonia. Attempts by the Yugoslav federal army to prevent the breaking away of Slovenia and Croatia precipitated the first hostilities in the region after the end of the cold war. In December 1991, the Muslim Bosnian president asked the European Community to recognize Bosnia-Herzegovina as an independent state, an event that many expected to lead to civil war, given the religious and ethnic makeup of the region—44 percent Muslim, 31 percent Serb, and 17 percent Croat. In April 1992, shortly before formal recognition of the new state by the European Community and the United States, Serb and Yugoslav army forces seized over 70 percent of Bosnia's territory. Serb leaders stated that their goal was for all Serbs to live in either a small Serb-led Yugoslavia, or in a larger, independent Serbia. Serb attacks in the region were thus fashioned as "ethnic cleansing," and atrocities against civilian Muslims and Croats were reported in the international press. While Muslims and Croats also fought each other in the early rounds of the conflict, by March 1994, the Bosnian Croats and Muslims agreed to form a federation in Bosnia.

The response to Serbian aggression was effectively set in 1991, when NATO decided not to intervene in what it regarded as a Bosnian civil war. In August 1992, the UN Security Council adopted a resolution calling on nations to take "all measures necessary" to facilitate the delivery of humanitarian assistance to Sarajevo.[8] At about the same time, the Senate passed a resolution stat-

[8] United Nations Security Council Resolution 770, 13 August 1992.

ing that no U.S. military personnel should be introduced into hostilities without clearly defined objectives, and the House passed a resolution urging the Security Council to authorize measures, including the use of force, to ensure the delivery of humanitarian relief.[9]

The U.S. response to the events in Bosnia evolved slowly and unevenly. In 1993, Clinton ordered U.S. participation in UN and NATO-sponsored relief operations and enforcement of a no-fly zone and an arms embargo. His actions were modest and did not carry a significant risk of the loss of or injury to U.S. personnel; nor did they risk political fallout or failure in the eyes of any large constituency at home. In effect, the United States would act only as part of a multilateral force; ground forces would not be used; and the United States would not take sides in the conflict. Although the president talked of seeking congressional "support," he sought no authorization or appropriation for these actions.

Congress then considered but failed to enact restrictions on military initiatives in Bosnia. In September 1993, Senator Robert Dole announced his intention to offer a provision stating that no additional U.S. forces should be introduced into Bosnia without prior approval from Congress. Congress acted in the fiscal 1994 Defense Department appropriation, stating the "sense of the Congress" that defense appropriations should not be expended for a deployment in support of a peace settlement in Bosnia-Herzegovina "unless previously authorized by the Congress."[10] Clinton responded to the proposed restrictions by announcing that he would fight or ignore any attempts to interfere with his foreign policy prerogatives.

When air strikes were contemplated and then initiated in 1994, Clinton made no effort to seek congressional authorization. Instead, he simply noted in a report to Congress that U.S. forces "participate in these actions pursuant to my constitutional authority to conduct U.S. foreign relations and as Commander in Chief."[11] He further noted that the air strikes were "to support NATO's enforcement of the no-fly zone . . . as authorized by the U.N. Security Council."[12] Thus, the policy was made by the UN and NATO, not the United States, and the decision to commit the United States to the operation was made by the president, not Congress. The closest Congress came to making policy on Bosnia in 1994 was to say that if any of $12 billion in supplemental defense funds were spent on Bosnia, Department of Defense (DOD) operations were limited to "enforcement of the no-fly zone relating to Bosnia."[13]

Meanwhile, after considerable Western media attention and public revulsion at the scenes of genocide and stories of rape and barbaric prison camps

[9] S. Res. 330, 102d Congress, 2nd sess. (1992); H. Res. 554, 102d Congress, 2nd sess. (1992).
[10] Department of Defense, Appropriations Act for Fiscal 1994, Pub. L. No. 103–139, §8146, 107 Stat. 1476 (1993).
[11] William J. Clinton, 30 Weekly Compilation of Presidential Documents, 6 February 1994, 406.
[12] Ibid.
[13] Pub. L. No. 103–211, §302, 1994.

wrought by Serbian aggression, Congress voted in 1994 in "sense of the Congress" resolutions to lift the arms embargo on Bosnia to permit the Muslim government to defend itself more effectively. As the Defense Department appropriation and authorization bills were passed in the fall of 1994, the most that Congress could distill from its debates on the role of the United States in Bosnia was another nonbinding provision stating the "sense of Congress" that no U.S. funds should be spent on implementation of a peace settlement in Bosnia "unless previously authorized by the Congress."[14] In 1995, when Congress eventually required that the arms embargo be lifted, Clinton vetoed the bill, asserting that a U.S. decision to lift the embargo would cause the European allies to withdraw their forces from the conflict and, thus, actually make conditions more difficult for the Bosnian Muslims. In his veto message, the president berated Congress for attempting "to regulate by statute matters for which the President is responsible under the Constitution."[15]

As the negotiations toward a peace accord proceeded in Dayton in late summer and fall of 1995, Clinton indicated to Senate Majority Leader Dole that he would welcome a "strong expression of support" from Congress before committing U.S. forces to the implementation of an accord. While at first he phrased his request as one for "authorization," it was soon modulated to a request for "support" or "approval," all the while maintaining his "constitutional prerogatives in this area." In the weeks before and after the signing of the Dayton accords and leading up to the actual deployment of U.S. forces on 20 December 1995, both houses debated whether to support the introduction of U.S. ground forces in Bosnia. The House passed two measures: a nonbinding resolution stating that such forces should not be deployed without congressional approval, and then a flat-out prohibition of the deployment. In the Senate, the debate was heavily influenced by presidential candidate Dole's statements that the president had the authority to deploy the force to Bosnia. After the Dayton accords were reached, the Senate declined to approve the House prohibition, and it narrowly defeated a resolution expressing opposition to sending troops to Bosnia. As the peace agreement was being readied for signature in Paris, the Senate passed an unusually worded resolution that supported the troops but doubted whether it was wise to send them. Next, the House passed a nonbinding resolution expressing "serious concern and opposition to the President's policy," although it also expressed confidence that the U.S. forces would excel at their task.

On 15 December 1995, the day after the peace agreement was signed in Paris, the UN Security Council authorized the multilateral NATO-led implementation force under Chapter VII of the UN Charter. Based on his presumed authority under the Constitution and treaties, Clinton ordered the deployment of 22,000 U.S. ground troops to Bosnia, a decision he explained in a letter to

[14] Department of Defense, Appropriations Act for FY 1995, Pub. L. No. 103–335, §8100 (1994).
[15] 31 Weekly Compilation of Presidential Documents (11 August 1995), 1439.

Congress on 21 December as being based on his "constitutional authority to conduct the foreign relations of the United States and as Commander in Chief and Chief Executive."[16] Clinton vetoed the overall defense package a few days later—the fiscal 1996 Defense Authorization Act, which contained limitations on the president's use of ground forces in Bosnia and on his discretion to secure funds from operational accounts to pay for unbudgeted contingency operations such as Bosnia. He managed to cause the objectionable provisions to be dropped from the bill that he eventually signed.

FUNDING U.S. PARTICIPATION IN IFOR

The chronology of U.S. involvement in Bosnia summarized in the previous section emphasized presidential-congressional relations in the conduct of national security policy. A more focused attention on the funding dimensions of U.S. participation in IFOR shows how the Framers' conception of the relationship between Congress and the president has been radically altered in the post-Korea era. What we find is that significant big-picture policy questions concerning the efficacy of U.S. military activities are in fact resolved through arcane and low-profile spending decisions.

Beginning in summer of 1995, the Clinton administration was searching for creative ways to finance U.S. involvement in implementing a Bosnia peace agreement. One idea was to replicate the pre-Gulf War fundraising approach—a voluntary fund for contributions from governments toward implementing the peace in Bosnia. This, it was thought, would finesse Republican opposition in the congressional budget process and would exploit NATO support for U.S. participation in implementing an eventual agreement. The foreign contributions idea was abandoned, perhaps when the administration recalled that the possibility of financing a national security operation by U.S. forces with donated third-party funds was effectively eliminated by Congress in 1990. In response to the prospect of a "huge defense slush fund"[17] permitting President Bush to bypass Congress in funding Operation Desert Shield, Congress repealed previous authority permitting such gifts to be given to fund the nation's defense outside the appropriations process. In its place, a Defense Cooperation Account was created, where any contributions to national security activities of the United States must be placed, while the spending of such funds is subject to the requirement of an appropriation.

With the lack of support in Congress for the line of credit approach to funding peace operations and the unavailability of open-ended discretion to spend gifts from foreign governments, the Clinton administration was back to square one on the challenge of how to finance the operation in Bosnia. The obvious

[16] 31 Weekly Compilation of Presidential Documents (6 December 1995), 2144.
[17] Jefrey R. Smit and Ann Devroy, "Reduced Arms Sale to Saudis Discussed: Byrd Moves to Bar Pentagon 'Slush Fund,'" *Washington Post*, 21 September 1990.

path—seek a prior, specific appropriation for the operation from Congress—was politically unpalatable, based on the fear that the funds might not be approved at all. More likely, Congress would attach conditions to the spending that the commander in chief would find unacceptable. As a senior Pentagon official said, funding Bosnia was part of "the dance" with Congress, "forcing them to do something they do not want to do, and do it in a timely fashion."[18] But how and where would DOD find the money? Fortunately for the president, a combined accident of timing and luck presented a relatively painless path toward funding the operation.

Throughout fall of 1995, while the Dayton negotiations were on-going and members of Congress were debating proposals to restrict any U.S. operation in Bosnia, Congress was also engaged in its consideration and passage of the annual appropriation bills, including the bill for defense. Unrelated to the potential dispute over Bosnia, Congress and the president were locked in a battle over spending, primarily over new or expanded weapons systems favored by members of Congress and viewed as too costly by the president. When Congress passed a $243 billion defense appropriations bill on 16 November, Democratic leaders suggested that Clinton would veto the bill because it contained $7 billion more than he had requested, with the additional funds earmarked for several defense projects he had not requested. At the time, Republican leaders retorted that a veto would in turn produce a cut-off of funding for the Bosnia operation.

However, the Dayton accords were announced the following week, and testimony by Defense Secretary William Perry and Comptroller John Hamre on 1 December provided the first public budget estimate of $2 billion for a twelve-month Bosnia operation.[19] The president reconsidered his options. If he vetoed the spending bill and then requested the $2 billion separately, the Congress would be unlikely to approve the request for the Bosnia funds. If he offered to accept the $243 defense appropriation, he could seek to strike a political bargain with congressional leaders informally to funnel some of the defense funds to the Bosnia operation.

In effect, that is just what occurred when Clinton allowed the bill to become law without his signature on 1 December. Although House Appropriations Committee Chairman Robert L. Livingston stated that "there has been no agreement on where the [Bosnia] funds come from,"[20] it appears that the fat in the fiscal 1996 Pentagon appropriation provided the flexibility for the president to charge DOD officials with finding the funds for Bosnia from within fiscal

---

[18] Interview, 6 May 1997.

[19] William J. Perry, Prepared Statement, "Bosnia Costs and Funding Requirements," Hearing before a Subcommittee of the Committee on Appropriations United States Senate, 104th Congress, 1st sess., 1 December 1995, S. Hrg. 104–286, 21, 43.

[20] Donna Cassata, "Clinton Accepts Defense Bill in Bid for Bosnia Funds," *Congressional Quarterly Weekly Report*, 2 December 1995, 3672.

1996 accounts and thus avoid, temporarily at least, the need to ask Congress for funds for Bosnia.

When the Bosnia deployment was ordered by the president, Congress had thus neither specifically appropriated funds for the Bosnia initiative nor restricted the use of appropriated funds. As IFOR began, DOD relied on its discretion to draw down lump sum operations accounts. The administration's plan was to begin to spend for the Bosnia operation by depleting fiscal 1996 funds for operations and maintenance and personnel that would otherwise have been available for obligation later in the fiscal year. The enacted appropriation provided $81.6 billion for military operations and maintenance, $752 million over the president's request. Thus, the operation could have begun from accounts that were funded above the Department's request. However, because the drawdown from accounts where funds were added by Congress could conceivably affect specific projects favored by members of Congress, the administration required DOD to find all of the funds for Bosnia without diminishing the funds available for specific projects or activities added by Congress to the DOD budget request, and without the requirement of new funds. Thus, one apparent quid pro quo for the congressional leaders' commitment not to attempt to deny or formally condition funds for Bosnia in the DOD appropriation or otherwise was the administration's promise not to spend funds from within lump-sum accounts that had been earmarked for favored projects, and not to come asking for additional funds for Bosnia later in the fiscal year.

By their very nature, lump sums threaten the Framers' theory of the power of the purse: It was anticipated that the president would be disabled from acting without going to Congress first for specific appropriations. In effect, the use of lump-sum appropriations for national security eliminates the ex ante control over spending and sends Congress to the sidelines when any unanticipated national security operation comes along. However, lump-sum appropriations have been employed for some defense spending since the First Congress, because members found it impossible to estimate necessary expenditures without the help of the executive. Over time, the lump-sum practice replaced the tradition of line itemization in appropriations for defense, although the executive estimates were to some extent and at times incorporated into the statutory text.

If the first Congresses and presidents found lump-sum appropriations unavoidable for the military, no one would seriously contemplate line-item appropriations for a $250 billion defense budget today. Although DOD lump-sum accounts have historically been subject to nonstatutory understandings that sums would be spent in accordance with details in the itemized budget requests, the broad delegations in the statutes of hundreds of millions or even billions for "operations and maintenance, army" leave considerable room for the operation of spending discretion.

To facilitate obtaining replacement funds due to the costs of the Bosnia operation as early as possible and to take advantage of the availability of noncontroversial funding sources, the administration determined to request funding in three phases. IFOR operations in Bosnia (and logistical support in neighboring countries) fell primarily to the army. The army's estimated FY96 Operations and Maintenance budgetary requirements for Bosnia were $780.2 million. To offset the incremental costs of the Bosnia operation, the president submitted a request in January 1996 to reprogram $991 million in DOD funds, later revised downward to $876 million, financed by projected inflation savings resulting from revised economic assumptions. Thus, the claim was that no net costs would occur because the reprogramming would be "financed" by a downward revision of earlier inflation forecasts.

Reprogramming permits funds in an account to be used for different purposes than those contemplated when the funds were appropriated. In a reprogramming action, funds are shifted from one object to another or from one program element to another within an appropriation. It is thus different from the general discretion to spend from a lump sum account, although the differences are in degree, not kind, and often are based on informal arrangements between congressional committees and spenders. The authority to reprogram is implicit in an agency's discretion to manage its lump-sum appropriations. Typically, reprogramming is not authorized or prohibited by statute. However, by statute and DOD regulation, most of its requests require the approval of four congressional committees,[21] although this one anticipated no set costs to any program or activity, based on the administration's downward revision of its earlier inflation forecasts. Although statutes now limit DOD reprogramming to "higher priority items based on unforeseen military requirements," and by prohibiting the practice "where the item for which reprogramming is requested has been denied by Congress,"[22] reprogramming discretion is of central importance to DOD. Because the DOD appropriation builds in considerable discretion through large lump-sum accounts, and because Congress apparently expects contingencies to occur, reprogramming provides one of the mechanisms through which funding decisions are made as matters of judgment of DOD professionals and others in the political process. DOD also continues to comply with these "prior approval" reprogramming procedures as a courtesy to the congressional committees and as part of the politically powerful set of informal controls on the discretion to spend appropriated funds.

Operations and Maintenance (O&M) funds were reprogrammed first, because these funds make up a large part of the defense budget. Furthermore, if funding was not restored to these funds, there would be an adverse impact on military readiness. This was followed by military personnel costs that have a predictable outlays pattern. The overall strategy was to minimize congressional opposition by financing the Bosnia operations through inflation savings that were known when the operation commenced.

---

[21] These committee approval arrangements have no binding legal effect, in light of the Supreme Court's decision in *Immigration & Naturalization Service v. Chadha*, 462 U.S. 919 (1983).

[22] Department of Defense, Appropriations Act of 1992, Pub. L. No. 102–172, §8010, 105 Stat. 1173 (1991).

The second phase and next largest piece of the $2.5 billion was found through a virtual gift from the intelligence community—a proposed rescission of $620 million in previously appropriated funds located in an obscure National Reconnaissance Office fund. The NRO funds, substantially in excess of any needs for that agency, were rescinded from the NRO budget and were proposed to be added to DOD as a no-cost supplemental appropriation. Although the supplemental would require bicameral congressional approval, an affirmative appropriation of new funds for Bosnia would not be required.

As the initial reprogramming request was making its way through the four required congressional committees in January and February 1996, the NRO rescission grew from $620 to $820 million and then $858 million, when it was proposed that $200 million be included for civilian peace implementation programs, independent of IFOR. Even though the $820 million was not "new" money, an appropriation was nonetheless required before it could be spent by DOD for IFOR. By early March 1996, political compromises were reached whereby the entire $820 million of NRO funds would be spent on IFOR to assuage members of Congress who balked at spending DOD funds on civilian peace implementation programs, traditionally a State Department responsibility. A supplemental appropriation was prepared, including the $820 million for IFOR along with funding for several domestic programs at levels that Clinton may have vetoed if they were not bound together with the IFOR funds. By the end of March, both houses had approved the supplemental appropriation and the last of four committees had approved the reprogramming request, although not without some reservations. The Senate stipulated that its approval of the supplemental was contingent on not disbursing the funds until the Muslim government in Sarajevo cut its ties with Iran, and House National Security Committee Chair Floyd Spence (R–SC) wrote to Secretary William J. Perry that the practice of using inflation savings as a source of funds for reprogramming "allows the department and services unusually broad discretion to apportion what is in fact an undistributed reduction within each account."[23] Spence also said he remained concerned with the practice of the administration submitting proposals for funding based on savings from revised economic assumptions to fund unbudgeted activities.

By April, it was clear that the costs of IFOR would exceed DOD's first revised estimate of $2.2 billion for fiscal year 1996 and $.5 billion for fiscal year 1997. Another round of revised estimates were summarized by Under Secretary of Defense John J. Hamre in mid-April 1996 in a letter to Congressman C. W. Young, chairman of the Subcommittee on National Security, Committee on Appropriations, where he estimated that total costs for the twelve-month Bosnia operation for FY 1996/1997 would be $2.8 billion through December 1996. Some of the revisions were due to intelligence gathering and distribution, and environmental conditions that turned out to be harsher than expected.

---

[23] "Congress Oks Nearly $1 Billion for Bosnia," *Defense Daily*, 190 (22 March 1996): 440.

In the same letter to Chairman Young, Comptroller Hamre described an attached reprogramming request, the third of three phases of the DOD plan to finance the Bosnia operation. The 15 April request was for $659.6 million, primarily for Bosnia, although it also included modest amounts for contingency operations in Haiti and Cuba. The April request permitted DOD to incorporate its revised cost estimates for the operation in Bosnia. The phased timing also allowed DOD to take advantage of additional inflation savings as resources to fund the reprogramming. The inflation savings, along with some navy program sources, were used to fund the reprogramming for the balance of the anticipated fiscal 1996 costs for U.S. participation in IFOR, as well as some non-IFOR requirements for Bosnia and other non-Bosnia contingencies. The few navy program items reduced in the reprogramming—three Sea Cobra helicopters, the conversion of a few ships, reduced fleet support and maintenance upgrades, and the like—were lined out to make "funds available to finance higher priority items."

The funding flexibility enjoyed early in a fiscal year shrinks accordingly as the fiscal year enters the third and fourth quarters. As recently as 1995, congressional critics of peacekeeping spending had charged that such spending for unplanned operations was compromising combat-readiness accounts, including training exercises and equipment overhauls planned for the third and fourth quarters of the fiscal year. Although DOD Comptroller Hamre testified to a Senate panel that Clinton would ask Congress to authorize a "line of credit" that the services could use to pay for unbudgeted overseas missions, the administration's proposal was never given serious consideration.[24] As congressional consideration of the supplemental for DOD peacekeeping illustrated, many members of Congress face a dilemma when they vote on a proposal to fund a peacekeeping deployment in Bosnia, for example, when the spending has already occurred with "borrowed" funds from lump-sum or other accounts. The members who oppose the deployment are hard-pressed to vote against the supplemental, because of the obligation to support troops already in the field and the need to replace funds in the combat-readiness accounts to permit the possibly delayed training or equipment overhaul to be completed. Funding options thus change. While lump-sum spending discretion and reprogramming remain theoretically available as options, there are fewer unobligated funds late in the year.

A DEADLINE PASSES

The Dayton accords called for IFOR to enforce the peace and to provide a secure environment for other parts of the peace plan to take place. The United States was the major force provider to IFOR, and Americans held the key mili-

---

[24] Pat Towell, "Pentagon Seeks Money to Pay for Unscheduled Missions," *Congressional Quarterly Weekly Report*, 21 January 1995, 216.

tary leadership positions that conducted the operation. The principal military tasks for IFOR were to mark and monitor a four-kilometer-wide zone of separation between the three factions, patrol the zone of separation, and oversee the withdrawal of forces and weapons away from the zone and to containment areas. When the deployment was begun, DOD listed among "[m]ajor threats to IFOR"[25]

- Indirect fire against unprotected forces
- Landmines, civil disorder, snipers, noncombat losses
- Extremist elements
- Hostage taking for political goals
- Undisciplined local factions

Secretary Perry and General Shalikashvili testified that we "must be prepared for casualties."[26] Based on the prior deployment of UN Protection Force (UN-PROFOR) personnel in Bosnia, DOD estimated that there would be about fifty casualties in a year's deployment. Among the risks encountered by the troops were problems in identifying friends and foes, land mines (which claimed a U.S. casualty in February 1996), snipers, checkpoint control, and area and perimeter surveillance and protection. Military personnel deployed to Bosnia in IFOR were eligible to receive imminent danger pay. While no U.S. military were killed in combat in Bosnia during IFOR, the risk of casualties remained throughout the operation.

As the one year anniversary of the deployment approached, it became increasingly clear that it was not realistic to expect that the U.S. ground troops' presence in Bosnia would end in a year's time. The decision to delay municipal elections in Bosnia, an integral part of the Dayton accords, and the movement toward a sustained peace merely reflects that little progress has been made in transforming the war zone into some form of nation. Most of the political or economic structures necessary to nation-building are not yet in place in Bosnia, and the enmity and initiation of violence continues among the three factions. For example, in November 1996, the bloodiest postwar clash between Serbs and Muslims left at least one dead and ten people wounded, when a group of 600 Muslim villagers attempted to return to their prewar homes, located on what is now Serb land. NATO officials opined that Bosnian army officers forced the Muslims to return to the Serb-held village in an effort to provoke the Serbs. In an effort to punish both sides for their clash, U.S. troops raided a Muslim army brigade and a Serb police station and seized weapons and armored personnel carriers. Thus, in seeking to carry out the terms of the accords, a new conflict could easily reach a flash point in Bosnia.

---

[25] General John M. Shalikashvili, "Bosnia Costs and Funding Requirements," Hearing before a Subcommittee of the Committee on Appropriations United States Senate, 104th Congress, 1st sess., 1 December 1995, S. Hrg. 104–286, 22.

[26] Ibid., 33.

A report by the independent International Crisis Group concluded in November that the civilian provisions of the Dayton accords were in danger of collapse. Their report notes that indicted war criminals remain at large; leaders earlier held responsible for the outbreak of war have been given new mandates to govern after fraudulent elections; and repatriation of refugees has failed. The IFOR troops were not charged with resolving these problems, only promoting the stability thought necessary to make solutions possible. As the problems persist, however, the stability forced by armed forces is itself tenuous.

Although no firm commitments were made prior to the November 1996 election day, it seemed likely that only a continuing, probably long-term international ground force would be able to prevent the rekindling of war. The president had likely known that for a long time, as had his defense secretary, his military commanders, and most members of Congress. By contrast, the stated public policy was different. General Shalikashvili said in April 1996 that he was "absolutely convinced" that all U.S. forces would be out of Bosnia by year's end: "I cannot imagine circumstances changing in such a way that we would remain in Bosnia."[27] In May, DOD under secretary for policy, Walter B. Slocombe, said that "there's every reason to believe . . . that all IFOR forces will be out of Bosnia shortly after 20 December."[28] Secretary Perry played an additional semantic game with congressional leaders and the media by calling more recently deployed troops part of an "exit protection force."

In a 15 November 1996 speech, Clinton announced that in place of IFOR, a 8,500 strong Stabilization Force (SFOR) would "in principle" remain in Bosnia until mid-1998. Although Perry admitted that he was wrong one year before in recommending to the president that the objectives of the Dayton accords could be met in one year, he expressed confidence that the mid-1998 withdrawal target could be met. His convoluted explanation of his "error in judgment" in setting the exit deadline was, he said, "right in the sense that all of the specific tasks spelled out we did do in 12 months; it was not right in the sense that those tasks were enough to allow us to safely leave the country."[29]

Less than a month after the reelection of Clinton, the administration officially announced the extension of U.S. military involvement in Bosnia. In a letter to congressional leaders, Clinton wrote: "In order to contribute further to a secure environment necessary for the consolidation of peace throughout Bosnia and Herzegovina, NATO has approved, and I have authorized U.S. participation in, an IFOR follow-on force to be known as the Stabilization Force (SFOR). SFOR's tasks are to deter or prevent a resumption of hostilities or new threats to peace, to consolidate IFOR's achievements, to promote a climate in which the civilian-led peace process can go forward. Subject to this primary mission, SFOR will provide selective support, within its capabilities, to

[27] Michael Dobbs, "Bosnia Exit Deadline Crumbles," *Washington Post*, 28 November 1996.
[28] James Kitfield, "Six Months Down, Six More to Go," *The National Journal*, 25 May 1996, 1154.
[29] Elaine Sciolino, "Loosening the Timetable for Bringing G.I.'s Home," *New York Times*, 17 November 1996.

civilian organizations implementing the Dayton Peace Agreement."[30] The new NATO force includes 8,500 U.S. troops. This force was scheduled to stay until June 1998.

While Secretary of State Warren Christopher hinted in September 1996 that some form of international force would probably have to remain after IFOR completed its mission, many members of Congress were not pleased at both the timing and substance of the president's announcement. Tom Lantos, Democratic Congressman from California, commented: last year's talk about a "clear-cut exit strategy" was "an escape from reality. . . . This may have been the only way for [the administration] to get Congress to acquiesce in deployment."[31] Republican members were publicly less forgiving, and Senator John McCain (R–AZ) said that the credibility gap of administration officials on Bosnia is now "wide as the Grand Canyon."[32] Republican Senator Kay Bailey Hutchinson (R–TX) reacted to the president's postelection announcement of U.S. participation in a new peacekeeping force in Bosnia this way: "I don't think that the president has kept his word on the commitments he made to Congress last year. He said that he would keep the mission to a year. He didn't. He said he would arm and train the Bosnian Muslims. He hasn't. He said he would consult with Congress, and he hasn't." As for the administration's insistence that the original December 1996 "exit strategy" remained intact, because the original force will be withdrawn "on schedule," Senator Hutchinson's reaction was typical: "The President is playing with words."[33] Even some journalists voiced criticism. Writing in the *New York Times*, Thomas Friedman said, "Let's get right to the point: The Clinton Administration has not been candid with the American people about its intentions in Bosnia."[34] Two months later, Clinton's nominee to replace Perry—former Republican senator from Maine, William Cohen—tried to soften his former colleagues' criticisms of the administration's Bosnia policy by repeating the promise during his confirmation hearings that U.S. ground forces would leave in June 1998. In his words, "This is a signal, and a very strong message to our European friends. We are not going to be there [after the new deadline]. It was primarily a European problem to be solved, and it's time for them to assume responsibility."[35] He soon reiterated this position in early March 1997 on a trip to Germany, when he told reporters that the American forces will be out of Bosnia by the target date even if hostilities break out again. He also stated that any new peace force for Bosnia would not include

[30] William J. Clinton, "Letter to Congressional Leaders on Bosnia," 32 Weekly Compilation of Presidential Documents, 2535–36 (20 December 1996).

[31] Dobbs, "Bosnia Exit."

[32] Ibid.

[33] Ann Swardson, "Bosnian Presidents, Western Powers Renew Dayton's Promises; U.S. Peacekeepers Seize Weapons from Muslim Army," *Washington Post*, 15 November 1996.

[34] Thomas Friedman, "The Fudge Factor," *New York Times*, 3 November 1996.

[35] Pat Towell, "Cohen, in Confirmation Hearing, Vows Timely Bosnia Pullout," *Congressional Quarterly Weekly Report*, 25 January 1995, 247.

U.S. troops, even though some European officials were already planning for that eventuality.

The administration's fiscal 1997 budget contained only the previously identified $542 million in DOD funds for Bosnia, earmarked as part of the originally anticipated costs of a twelve-month operation. Given the timing of the president's announcement of U.S. participation in SFOR, it was not practically possible to request SFOR funds in the regular DOD appropriation. Thus, the administration faced the same situation and followed the same strategy as in fiscal 1996 in budgeting for SFOR—find the funds from within the fiscal 1997 DOD accounts, and do not ask for new money. One difference between the fiscal 1996 and 1997 budgeting strategies, however, was that the planners and cost estimators within DOD had a better chance to come up with a budget closer to actual needs. First, they had the 1996 IFOR actual spending experience to work with. Second, they had more time to prepare the spending plans the second time around. Even though the president did not announce that the U.S. forces would stay beyond December 1996 until November 1996, behind the scenes, the planners were anticipating the expected contingency.

Another difference from fiscal 1996 was that the fiscal 1997 DOD appropriation included the Overseas Contingency Operations Transfer Fund for the first time.[36] Any contingency fund would, of course, supply additional obligational authority, to be used when unanticipated circumstances or needs arise. In such instances, the need to obligate funds is determined by the agency officials, consistent with the underlying appropriation act. However, despite its title, this $1.1 billion fund, available for transfer only to operation and maintenance accounts in DOD, was envisioned as a funding source for known contingencies, such as Bosnia. It did not signal any acquiescence on the part of Congress to give DOD a blank check for new Bosnia costs or for other peacekeeping operations.

Less than two months after announcing SFOR, Pentagon Comptroller Hamre testified that Bosnia costs, as of late February 1997, would total $6.5 billion, more than three times the original cost estimates. A $2 billion supplemental appropriation for fiscal 1997 would be required, largely to fund U.S. participation in SFOR. By mid-April 1997 funding sources for the supplemental were identified. About $1 billion was proposed for rescission from specific programs; $246 million from unobligated balances; $307 million from revised inflation estimates; and $308 million related to fluctuation in foreign currency rates.[37]

Meanwhile, DOD once again played its readiness card. Hamre said that if Congress did not act on the fiscal 1997 supplemental before its mid-April recess, the army and the air force would have to cancel selected training exer-

---

[36] Department of Defense Appropriations Act, Fiscal 1997, Pub. L. No. 104–208, §618 (1996).

[37] "House Defense Appropriators Mark Up Bosnia Supplemental," *Defense Daily*, 18 April 1997, 195.

cises.[38] At the same time, Marine General John Sheehan, head of the Atlantic Command, told the House National Security Committee in March that the army would start cutting back on tank miles, flight hours, and training.[39]

As DOD was emphasizing the exigencies of the funding situation for SFOR and the need for Congress to enact the supplemental expeditiously, Republican leaders in Congress decided to join the DOD supplemental to a supplemental for disaster relief and then to encumber the larger supplemental with unrelated riders. The supplemental was, in terms of its $6.5 billion and publicity, dominated by funds for disaster relief for flood victims, primarily in North Dakota. In the face of an explicit veto threat by Clinton, Congress added to the disaster relief/peace operation supplemental two politically charged provisions—one prescribing an automatic continuing resolution in the event that the regular appropriations were not enacted by the end of the fiscal year, and the other forbidding the use of statistical sampling techniques in compiling census data for the next biennial census.[40] As expected, Clinton exercised his veto, and Republican leaders were embarrassed by the obvious realization that they lacked the votes to override the veto and that public opinion would not look favorably upon delays in forwarding disaster relief to flood victims as a pawn in political battles with the president.[41] After a few more days of wringing hands and political posturing, a new bill was passed, stripped of the objectionable riders. It was signed by the president on 12 June 1997,[42] almost two months after it was scheduled for passage.

The enacted supplemental provided funds for Bosnia in part through replenishing the Overseas Contingency Operations Transfer Fund with $1.4 billion, thus permitting DOD to transfer the infusion of funds into such of the operations accounts as, in the Department's view, should have the new budget authority, or to pay for the costs of drawdown.[43] The balance of funds for Bosnia was earmarked for personnel accounts. In keeping with the pattern of paying for peace operations with existing funds, the president proposed and Congress accepted a cancellation of $2 billion of unidentified appropriations from the fiscal 1997 Appropriations and Military Construction Acts. The secretary of Defense was authorized to determine which programs, projects, and activities should be rescinded to attain the $2 billion amount.[44] The secretary was thus not even required to adhere to his proposed list of rescissions.

[38] Ibid.

[39] Tom Breen, "Sheehan: Atlantic Command Faces Cutbacks Without Supplemental," *Defense Daily*, 7 March 1997, 194.

[40] James Bennet, "As Promised, President Vetoes Bill on Flood Aid," *New York Times*, 10 June 1997.

[41] Jerry Gray, "Flood Relief Bill Passes As G.O.P., in Turmoil, Yields," *New York Times*, 13 June 1997.

[42] Ibid.; Supplemental Fiscal 1997 Appropriations Act, Pub. L. No. 105–18,—Stat.—(1997). See also Andrew Taylor, "Clinton Signs 'Clean' Disaster Aid After Flailing GOP Yields to Veto," *Congressional Quarterly Weekly Report*, 14 June 1997, 1362.

[43] See H.R. Rep. 105–119, 105th Congress, 1st sess. (1997).

[44] H.R. Rep. 105–83, 105th Congress, 1st sess. (1997).

LESSONS

The commander in chief has acquired his own spending power, eroding the congressional power of the purse and the check it gives on executive national security initiatives. At a minimum, the Bosnia deployments to IFOR and SFOR show that the ex ante check resulting from the on-going need for military supply and the inevitability of unanticipated military operations have been substantially undercut by the accretion of discretionary spending authority in the commander in chief. The Bosnia operation illustrates that drawdown options—lump sum spending authority, along with special discretion to reprogram, transfer, and spend for contingencies—have given the commander in chief a formidable short-term national security spending cushion without the need for prior specific appropriations. As Bosnia demonstrates, however, the discretionary mechanisms also permit the president to undertake long-term, large-scale operations, which may leave Congress little practical choice but to appropriate specifically for their continuation.

In addition, once an unauthorized operation begins without an explicit appropriation, members may balk at being seen as unwilling to support troops in the field. In the throes of the Bosnia deployment debate, on 30 November 1995, Senate Majority Leader Bob Dole said: "It is time for a reality check in Congress. If we would try to cut off funds, we would harm the men and women in the military who have already begun to arrive in Bosnia."[45] Senator Dole's response merely recognizes a dilemma that Congress itself created through its inability to enact an authorization, appropriation, or restriction on the Bosnia operation. Nonetheless, this justification for congressional acquiescence has recurred often, at least since the Vietnam War.[46]

Because the president committed U.S. forces to a potentially hostile environment, risking at least limited involvement in hostilities and ensuing casualties, the deployment was, in our opinion, an unconstitutional usurpation of congressional power over war. Congress itself recognized the legal and policy problem in 1995, when the conference report on the DOD supplemental appropriation stated that military deployments "in support of peacekeeping objectives both merit and require advance approval by Congress."[47] Ironically, when Secretary Perry was asked by Senate Appropriations Committee members whether IFOR was empowered to arm and train Bosnian Muslim forces, Perry demurred: "I do not believe the Defense appropriations bill gives me the authority to use [funds appropriated for DOD] to buy equipment for the Bosnian

[45] Pat Towell, "Congress Reluctantly Acquiesces in Peacekeeping Mission," *Congressional Quarterly Weekly Report*, 2 December 1995, 3668.

[46] See *Mitchell v. Laird*, 488 F. 2d 611, 615 (D.C. Cir. 1973) ("This court cannot be unmindful of what every schoolboy knows . . . that a Congressman wholly opposed to the war's commencement and continuation might vote for . . . appropriations . . . because he was unwilling to abandon without support men already fighting.")

[47] H. Rep. No. 104–101, 104th Congress, 1st sess. (1995), 25.

army. . . . There has to be some enabling legislation for that to happen. . . . If the cost is to be paid by an American taxpayer, there has to be an authorization. . . ."[48] Thus, according to the secretary, more than 20,000 troops may be deployed into a hostile environment at a cost of more than $2 billion with neither an authorization nor appropriation for that purpose, but the deployed forces cannot undertake a politically controversial operation that bears little dollar costs. Too little attention has been paid to this mischaracterization of Congress's role.

In addition, the president's efforts to rely on NATO or the UN as authority for U.S. participation in IFOR are wide of the mark. First, NATO is a defensive treaty, intended to contain the Soviet Union through "collective defense" and resistance to "armed attack." The treaty does not authorize offensive actions generally or peacekeeping in particular. Second, the provisions of the treaty were to be carried out "in accordance with [the parties'] constitutional processes." This language, like a parallel provision in the UN Charter, reminds us that, for operations like Bosnia peacekeeping, the treaty provisions are not self-executing. Thus the treaties grant the president no unilateral power to use the military to enforce the peace in the Balkans.[49]

At the same time, the Bosnia deployment followed a familiar script. Neither the president nor Congress ever articulated a clear or consistent set of policy objectives for Bosnia, certainly not before the Dayton accords. And when the proposal was made by the president to commit U.S. ground troops to enforce the peace, the proposal was not made to Congress. Instead, the president relied on NATO and the UN, and he came to Congress only as a reporter and huckster, selling a done deal. Factions and individuals within Congress tried but failed to get Congress to take a principled up or down vote on Bosnia, either through the authorization or appropriation processes. At the same time, members of Congress and the administration knew that the discretionary spending devices permitted the operation to occur without further action required by Congress. To implement the discretionary spending, the president made political deals to free up the funds, while he sent the secretary of Defense and chairman of the Joints Chiefs to congressional hearings to brief members of Congress on the details on an operation that had already begun. Members of Congress thus remained free either to criticize or applaud the operation and the president; no institutional position or risk was taken by Congress. The presi-

---

[48] Transcript: DoD News Briefing, Secretary William J. Perry with press, 20 December 1995, http://www.dtic.dla.mil/cgi-bin/wa.

[49] While treaties become part of "the supreme Law of the Land" pursuant to the Supremacy Clause, U.S. Constitution Article VI, the domestic legal effect of treaties may turn on whether their provisions are consistent with other constitutional limits, such as the Declaration Clause. See Louis Fisher, *Presidential War Power* (Lawrence: University of Kansas Press, 1996), 92–97, 188–189. In addition, "if implementing legislation is constitutionally required" by a treaty, it is non-self-executing and thus does not permit the President to act alone. *Restatement (Third) of the Foreign Relations Law of the United States* §111(4) (1987).

dent continued to call the shots, and if things did not go well, he could choose to blame the Congress for insufficient support.

The case of financing U.S. military involvement in Bosnia highlights the relationship between budget execution and public policy, particularly in the area of national security. More than twenty years have past since Louis Fisher wrote: "Public policy is not so easily apportioned into watertight compartments. Policy-making is a dynamic, ongoing phenomenon, beginning with the inception of an idea and carrying through to its enactment and implementation. . . . If Congress is to play the role of major policy-setter, it must avoid situations where budget execution becomes a controlling factor, locking Congress into commitments and decisions ahead of time."[50] Fisher's study documented the use of budget execution procedures throughout the nineteenth and twentieth centuries. It is instructive to recall that the secret bombing of Cambodia in 1972-1973 was financed through a transfer of funds that was approved after the fact.[51] A more recent account of the use of budget execution devices to finance national security activities by William Banks and Peter Raven-Hansen documents several interventions from the Vietnam War period through Operation Desert Shield.[52] This case study of Bosnia is consistent with these earlier assessments in the overall conclusions about the changing institutional dimensions of financing national security activities in the post-cold war era.

From time to time, Congress has rescinded some of the commander in chief's discretionary spending authority—such as the authority to fund operations from third-party funds outside the appropriations process. But the longevity of the remaining sources suggests that Congress believes that the flexibility this discretion affords in matters of national security is worth the cost in congressional control and the risk of abuse by the executive. Or, as we believe, the continuation of the discretionary spending devices is best explained as facilitating a sort of accountability-avoidance game, played by Congress and the president. For members of Congress who do not wish to play the game and who seek to force votes on authorization and appropriation for operations like Bosnia before-the-fact, these discretionary spending devices are potentially maddening. They permit, as House National Security Chairman Floyd D. Spence (R–SC) put it, "[t]he proverbial train [to leave] the station, [with] our troops . . . already on board."[53] Comments like this highlight the frustration created by the ad hoc nature of peacekeeping activities like Bosnia, the political opposition generated by a commitment of this type, and the fear that it will take valuable resources away from more important missions. At the same time, while the absence of U.S. casualties in the Bosnia operations to date has weakened the political opposition, the perceived need on the part of the administration

[50] Louis Fisher, *Presidential Spending Power* (Princeton: Princeton University Press, 1975), 258.

[51] Ibid., 111–12.

[52] William C. Banks and Peter Raven-Hansen, *National Security Law and the Power of the Purse* (New York: Oxford University Press, 1994).

[53] Towell, "Congress Reluctantly Acquiesces," 3668.

to avoid casualties may have weakened the effectiveness of the operations and protracted the length of the U.S. commitment. When asked if there is anything that can be done to reduce the conflict between the branches when funding for unplanned contingencies like Bosnia arise, John Hamre said when he was the comptroller of the Defense Department: "This is a fault line in the Constitution."[54] In other words, from the Pentagon perspective, contingencies such as Bosnia will likely continue to occur, funded ad hoc and without prior approval from Congress. From the constitutional perspective, the fault line has a different purpose—to insure congressional control over the purse strings. That this fundamental piece of our system of separated powers has failed is due to actions of both of the elected branches.

[54] Interview with the authors, 6 May 1997.

Public Support for Peacekeeping in Lebanon and Somalia: Assessing the Casualties Hypothesis

JAMES BURK

Among the many lessons that the U.S. military and political leaders drew from the Vietnam War, one was that the military could not deploy effectively or for very long without public support. Another was that public support for military deployments had declined quite predictably (one is tempted to say invariantly) in response to the accumulation of casualties.[1] In principle, it is nothing but wise counsel that rulers ignore the deadly consequences of military deployments only at their peril.

Recently, however, a new lesson has been taught that resembles but should be distinguished from these. Based on accumulating experience with peacekeeping operations, it holds that the public will not support peacekeeping deployments if they lead to the loss of American lives. This lesson is a source of worry and concern for those who believe armed forces are an essential instrument of national security policy, and it is taken very seriously. Since the barracks bombing that killed 241 Marines in Beirut in 1983, national security doctrine has required that there be "some reasonable assurance" of public support before combat forces are committed abroad.[2] The worry is that public support for missions, which seems sufficient, will quickly evaporate when faced with American casualties. It is often noted, for instance, that public support for

[1] On the issue of support for deployment, see Harry G. Summers, *On Strategy: A Critical Analysis of the Vietnam War* (New York: Dell, 1984); and Lewis Sorley, *Thunderbolt* (New York: Simon and Schuster, 1992). The key source on the relation between accumulation of casualties and trends in support for war is John E. Mueller, *War, Presidents and Public Opinion* (New York: Wiley & Sons, 1973).

[2] This is the fifth element of the so-called Weinberger doctrine. See Caspar W. Weinberger, *Fighting for Peace* (New York: Warner Books, 1990), 442.

JAMES BURK is professor of sociology at Texas A & M University. His most recent book, an edited collection, is *The Adaptive Military: Armed Forces in a Turbulent World.*

63

American participation in the peacekeeping mission to Somalia was strong. But immediately following the deaths of eighteen soldiers in the streets of Mogadishu, negative public reaction forced President Bill Clinton to withdraw U.S. forces.[3] As John Mueller observed, "when Americans asked themselves how many American lives it was worth to save hundreds of thousands of Somali lives, the answer came out rather close to zero."[4] The concern is that public intolerance of casualties radically constrains the government's ability to use armed force effectively to defend national interests and to maintain a more peaceful world order.[5] Quick reversals of public support ignore the long-range goals of foreign policy, jeopardize mission accomplishments, and underestimate the logistical difficulties or political costs of rapid withdrawal. Under these circumstances, military and political leaders are understandably wary of undertaking any military action.

The question is whether these worries and concerns are warranted. How reliable is the evidence that the public is so reluctant to accept even minimal casualties that it is fickle in its support of military missions and hamstrings political decisions about the use of force?[6] Is the public so intolerant of casualties that it will only approve peacekeeping operations that are virtually casualty free? And, in any case, does public opinion about casualties wield so much influence over political and military elites that it controls or constrains national security policy making?

In this article, I consider these questions in light of trends in public opinion about American peacekeeping in Lebanon from 1982 to 1984 and, ten years later, in Somalia from 1992 to 1994. The cases are not directly comparable. The intervention in Lebanon occurred during the cold war in an area of the world

[3] See, for example, Donald C. F. Daniel, "The United States" in Trevor Findlay, ed., *Challenges for the New Peacekeepers* (Oxford, England: Oxford University Press, 1996), 94–95; and Ioan Lewis and James Mayall, "Somalia" in James Mayall, ed., *The New Interventionism 1991–1994* (Cambridge, England: Cambridge University Press, 1996), 94–124, esp. 118.

[4] John E. Mueller, "Policy Principles for Unthreatened Wealth-Seekers," *Foreign Policy* 102 (Spring 1996): 31.

[5] General John Shalikashvili, when chairman of the Joint Chiefs of Staff, voiced this concern in testimony before the Senate Armed Forces Committee, as reported by Williams Matthews, "Shali Warns Against Myth of Nonviolent War," *Navy Times* (2 October 1995), on-line edition. He is not the only one to have done so. See Benjamin C. Schwarz, *Casualties, Public Opinion, and US Military Intervention* (Santa Monica, CA: Rand, 1994); Eric V. Larson, *Ends and Means in the Democratic Conversation* (Santa Monica, CA: Rand, 1996); Charles J. Dunlap, "The Origins of the American Military Coup of 2012," *Parameters* 22 (Winter 1992–93): 2–20; and A. J. Bacevich, "The Use of Force in Our Time," *Wilson Quarterly* 19 (Winter 1995): 50–63.

[6] In the current debate over civil-military relations, this question has also been raised the other way around by Deborah D. Avant, "Are Reluctant Warriors Out of Control?" *Security Studies* 6 (Winter 1996/97): 51–90. Wondering about the influence of military leaders over foreign policy, she asks: "Are civilian decisions [to employ force] hamstrung by a reluctant military?" Her answer is "not quite" (52). Her analysis and mine, while oriented differently, are not unrelated. We both argue that the decision to use force rests with civilian elites and is substantially affected by whether elites are unified or divided in their outlooks.

in which the United States thought it had (and still thinks it has) vital security interests. The intervention in Somalia had no such justification. Somalia was important to the United States as part of its cold war rivalry with the Soviet Union, but afterward American interest in the country flagged. The decision to intervene in Somalia in late 1992 was fairly disinterested, in sharp contrast to the intervention in Lebanon. Nevertheless, these cases are alike in key respects, important for present purposes. They were both highly visible peacekeeping missions attracting public attention, unlike for instance the American peace-keeping mission in the Sinai. They were both peacekeeping missions in which combat casualties unexpectedly occurred. And they were both popularly re-garded as missions that failed. For these reasons, these cases may help us to see whether casualties cause the public to withdraw its support of the missions and whether, in fact, the withdrawal of public support drives political leaders to abandon the missions earlier than they might otherwise have done. My argu-ment is that public support for military deployments was neither as unsteady nor as uncritically contingent on the absence of casualties as many have claimed. Nor was it obvious (although it is difficult to prove conclusively) that public worry over casualties was a key factor affecting government decisions about normal security policy.

Before turning to these empirical claims, however, we need to examine more closely the logic of what may be called, the "casualties" hypothesis. It seems perfectly plausible to say that the public is concerned when foreign policy pursuits cause bloodshed and that in a democracy public concerns carry weight. But what reasons do we have to believe it? It matters what we say. To my knowledge, Edward Luttwak has offered the only comprehensive defense of the hypothesis.[7] His argument is provocative, especially its recommendations about how best to frame current military strategy. Yet it is not entirely persua-sive. His contention that public intolerance of casualties is a new phenomenon, resulting from recent changes in family structure, is at best historically mis-leading. Moreover, he offers no reasons for believing that public opinion will exert a determining influence over national security policy. That is a surprising omission given the accumulation of evidence in recent years that relationships between public and elite opinion are extraordinarily complex and that the in-fluence they have on one another defies summary by any single simple rule.[8]

---

[7] See Edward N. Luttwak, "Where Are the Great Powers?" *Foreign Affairs* 73 (July/August 1994): 23–28; "Toward Post-Heroic Warfare," *Foreign Affairs* 74 (May/June 1995): 109–122; "A Post-Heroic Military Policy," *Foreign Affairs* 75 (July/August 1996): 33–44.

[8] On this, see Michael X. Delli Carpini and Scott Ketter, *What Americans Know about Politics and Why It Matters* (New Haven: Yale University Press, 1996); Benjamin I. Page, *Who Deliberates?* (Chi-cago: University of Chicago Press, 1996); Benjamin I. Page and Robert Y. Shapiro, *The Rational Public* (Chicago: University of Chicago Press, 1992); John R. Zaller, *The Nature and Origins of Mass Opinion* (Cambridge, England: Cambridge University Press, 1992); and Bruce Russett, *Controlling the Sword* (Cambridge, MA: Harvard University Press, 1990).

INTOLERANCE OF CASUALTIES

Put simply, the casualties hypothesis states that American public opinion at present will not support the deployment of military forces abroad if that deployment results in the lives of American soldiers being lost. It is a strong claim and should be distinguished immediately from a related but substantively weaker claim that public support for military operations takes the risks of casualties into account.

We have strong evidence that Americans think the risk of casualties is a crucial, perhaps the most important, factor affecting their support of a decision to use armed force. In an Americans Talk Security survey done in 1988, well over 80 percent of the respondents said that the cost in American lives was an important factor to consider before deploying military force. No other factor ranked higher. The second most important consideration, at just under 80 percent, was the likely cost of civilian deaths in the area of combat. Other factors were mentioned, but were thought less important and some, like the possibility of failure or the cost in dollars, were thought much less important.[9] This is not the first or the only evidence we have on this score. John Mueller deserves credit for systematically documenting the strong negative relationship between the accumulation of casualties and public support for the Korean and Vietnam Wars. His analysis is well known and requires no detailed retelling here. It is enough to recall that in both cases a ten-fold increase in casualties led to a significant drop of 15 percentage points in support of these wars. More recently, Mueller studied public support for the Persian Gulf War. In this case, the ground war was mercifully short, American casualties were remarkably few, and support for the war while the war was going on "soared." It was lower before the fighting began. Nevertheless, Mueller concludes on evidence from polls querying the matter that this support was not unconditional. It was contingent on the level of casualties. "[A] drop off of support," he thought, "would have followed a logarithmic pattern as in Korea and Vietnam."[10] This judgment cannot be tested but is probably accurate given the divided state of public opinion on the eve of the war with Iraq, a division that was not evident when the country initially faced war in Korea and Vietnam.

This evidence, however, shows that public support for military deployments erodes as casualties accumulate and that erosion takes time. It does not speak directly to the hypothesis we are interested in. It does not say that the public will only support what are virtually casualty-free military deployments, a claim that lies at the center of the casualties hypothesis. And it does not hint that

[9] Eugene R. Wittkopf, *Faces of Internationalism: Public Opinion and American Foreign Policy* (Durham, NC: Duke University Press, 1990), 228–229.

[10] For the original analysis, see Mueller, *War, Presidents and Public Opinion*, 60. Analysis of the Persian Gulf War is found in John E. Mueller, *Policy and Opinion in the Gulf War* (Chicago: University of Chicago Press, 1994), 77. See also Benjamin C. Schwarz, *Casualties, Public Opinion, and US Military Intervention*, 17.

public opinion will quickly abandon support for an operation in midstream if casualties are taken. This stronger claim has been made by military and political leaders in private and public, and has affected their willingness to undertake peacekeeping operations short of war. Drawing on U.S. experience in Somalia, for instance, General John Shalikashvili, then chairman of the Joint Chiefs of Staff, noted the public's unwillingness to support military operations as soon as casualties were incurred. He worried that insistence on casualty-free operations may have a deleterious effect on the judgment of young military leaders. Some might say that his was a defensive posture adopted to prevent the military from being sent on deployments where for a variety of reasons the risk of failure may be high. Obviously, no institutional leader wants to preside over failure.[11] But we should not rush to dismiss the hypothesis as a rhetorical exaggeration rather than an empirical claim to be taken literally and seriously.

Luttwak's Defense of the Casualties Hypothesis

Recently, Edward Luttwak, a noted scholar of national security affairs, incorporated the casualties hypothesis into a larger argument about what strategic posture the United States should adopt in the post-cold war environment.[12] His argument runs as follows. Historically, great powers, like the United States, have been willing to project force beyond their own borders to secure their own interests. And they have been willing to accept causalities as the price of success. "To lose a few hundred soldiers in some minor probing operation or a few thousand in a small war or expeditionary venture," he says, "were routine events for the great powers of history."[13]

Not now. Whether we look at the United States or Britain or France or even the Soviet Union before its downfall, we find societies "so allergic to casualties that they are effectively debellicized, or nearly so."[14] In this situation, Luttwak fears, lesser powers will be quick to flex their muscle, unworried that the resulting violence will be checked by great power interventions. His primary concern, therefore, is to find some means of reorienting great power strategy that respects the public's disinclination to accept casualties and yet permits

[11] See Avant, "Are Reluctant Warriors Out of Control?"; Stevenson, "The Evolving Clinton Doctrine"; Matthews, "Shali Warns Against Myth of Nonviolent War"; and Colin L. Powell, "Why Generals Get Nervous," *New York Times*, 8 October 1992.

[12] I focus on the argument of Luttwak, because it is the most fully developed one I know. For references to his argument see above note 7. But the central hypothesis is repeated uncritically in other places. For instance, Bacevich, "The Use of Force," 60, writes: "An enterprise that yesterday seemed expedient is today not worth the blood of a single American soldier. In the case of Somalia, such thinking led the United States to abandon its commitment altogether." And Daniel Yankelovich, *Coming to Public Judgment* (Syracuse: Syracuse University Press, 1991), 62 writes: "Sooner or later public opinion makes itself felt, sometimes directly as in the public pressure that . . . persuaded President Reagan to withdraw the Marines from Lebanon after a number of Marines had been killed by a terrorist bomb."

[13] Luttwak, "Where Are the Great Powers?" 27.

[14] Ibid.

great powers to use force to limit violent conflicts while they are still small and more easily contained. This can be done, he thinks, if force structures, presently organized (if necessary) to fight large-scale war are redesigned to wage something like siege warfare, following the model of ancient Rome and relying on advanced technology "to use force remotely, yet accurately and with discrimination."[15]

Luttwak may or may not be correct in his prescriptions for strategy and force structure. That is not our present concern. More important here are the reasons for believing that casualty-free warfare is required. His rationale is sociological. In preindustrial and early industrial societies, there was greater tolerance for casualties than in the advanced postindustrial societies of the present day.[16] That greater tolerance was founded on a family demography that was vastly different from the family demographics of today. In the past, families were larger, and it was "normal to lose one or more children to disease." So "the loss of one more youngster in war had a different meaning than it has for today's families." While always tragic, "a death in combat was not the extraordinary and fundamentally unacceptable event that it has now become." This changed attitude toward the death of young family members in combat reflects a widely shared expectation that children born into post-industrial families, fewer in number, will survive to old age and that each will consume "a larger share of the family's emotional economy." That is why parents and adults generally (to include decision-making elites) "react with astonishment and anger when their children are actually sent into combat situations. And they are apt to view their wound or death as an outrageous scandal, rather than as an occupational hazard."[17]

Luttwak does not say when this change in outlook occurred. Presumably it is relatively recent. And its influence was shown, he believes, in the decision to withdraw U.S. forces from Somalia after the lives of eighteen soldiers were lost, in the reluctance of the United States to send troops into Haiti to overturn its military dictatorship, and in the reticence of European powers to risk ground troops to counter aggression in the former Yugoslavia.[18]

Criticisms of Luttwak's Argument

There are at least three difficulties with the logic of this argument. First, we must suppose, if Luttwak is right, that earlier generations were more tolerant of casualties than ours. Is that really the case? It may be true that great powers incurred more casualties in earlier times. But that is not evidence for his argument. Perhaps the chief difference between then and now is that the public today is better able than it was to hold elites to account for the consequences of

---

[15] Luttwak, "A Post-Heroic Military Policy," 43.
[16] Luttwak, "Toward Post-Heroic Warfare," 115.
[17] Luttwak, "Where Are the Great Powers?" 25.
[18] Ibid., 23–24; Luttwak, "Toward Post-Heroic Warfare," 115.

their security policy. If so, their ability might stem from an earlier intolerance of casualties. It is not improbable that public revulsion and unrest over the casualties incurred during World War I forced political and military elites since then to take greater care of the lives of soldiers in their command. We know with certainty that soldiers objected to being thrown into battle without regard for their survival; it was not only Russian soldiers who engaged in mutiny.[19] Jay Winter's recent study of that war documents the extensive grief that civilians felt for the death of loved ones and strangers. Attempts by government officials to assuage or channel those feelings in support of their policies were not always successful. Tellingly, while war memorial art recognized the sacrifice by citizens, the message was "expressed in terms of sacrifice that must never be allowed to happen again."[20] Birth rates in Britain, France, and Germany were on average much higher from 1910 to 1920 than they are today.

Second, Luttwak attributes a complex change in the pattern of public opinion to just one factor, the decline in birth rates with all that implies for family structure and the emotional economy of family life. But single factor theories, for all their luster, dim as we imagine how many other factors might explain the same result. Luttwak does briefly consider and dismiss the possibility that the changed attitude toward casualties is explained by the growth of democracy or the publicity of mass media.[21] Even if we accept these dismissals, other possibilities remain. A major conclusion of Winter's study, for example, is that our traditional language for justifying death and consoling the bereaved, revived during World War I, lost its persuasive power after that war and has not been replaced by any other. The modernist culture dominant since then, as shown in the work of Paul Fussell, can express anger and despair at war's casualties, but it does not console or heal. Military actions may still be justified, but there is no shared theodicy to explain away the losses.[22] Unwillingness to endure casualties may also rest on the perception that there are alternatives to putting armed forces at risk.[23] In his study of public opinion and the Persian Gulf War, John Mueller suggests that before the war began, support for it was divided, in part because many believed sanctions could force Iraq's withdrawal from Kuwait. Public willingness to support resort to force weakens when a range of nonmilitary options are available.[24]

[19] See S. P. MacKenzie, *Politics and Military Morale* (Oxford, England: Oxford University Press, 1992), 12–13.

[20] Ibid., 95.

[21] Luttwak, "Where Are the Great Powers?" To support this claim he draws attention to Soviet conduct of its war with Afghanistan. The Soviet Union was no democracy and yet, he asserts, authorities adopted "inordinately prudent tactics" in order "to avoid casualties at all costs" (24). Moreover, they "never allowed its population to see any television images of the war;" nevertheless, "the reaction of Soviet society to the casualties of the Afghan war was essentially identical to the American reaction to the Vietnam war" (25).

[22] Winter, *Sites of Memory*; see Paul Fussell, *The Great War and Modern Memory* (New York: Oxford University Press, 1975); and Fussell, *Wartime* (New York: Oxford University Press, 1989).

[23] I am grateful to Ben M. Crouch for suggesting this possibility.

[24] Mueller, *Policy and Opinion*, 62; and Wittkopf, *Faces of Internationalism*, 181–186.

Third, turning from causes to consequences, Luttwak argues that in consequence of the public's intolerance of casualties, great powers now avoid resort to force; they are effectively "debellicized." It may be true that public tolerance of casualties is low and that great powers are reluctant to use force in pursuit of foreign policy. It remains to be said how these states of the world are linked. Is there evidence that public intolerance has the causal power to affect (to debellicize) great power policy? Surely, it is a plausible hypothesis. But that is not enough. The causal process must be specified and evidence must be provided to show that it produces the predicted effect. Failing to do that, Luttwak's predicament is formally similar to the one Arnold Toynbee faced when he argued that war weariness causes peace. His "evidence" was the "long peace" that followed the Napoleonic Wars. But, as Geoffrey Blainey asks, what caused the "long peace" from 1870 to 1914, when there was no war weary generation? Or what caused the outbreak of World War II, which war weariness should have prevented?[25] The problem, however, is not only a formal omission to state the causal mechanism at work. It is substantive as well.

Recent studies of public opinion reject simple models of influence between the public and policy makers, no matter whether the direction of influence attributes dominant power to the public or to the policy-making elite.[26] The relationship between them is highly mediated by experts through systems of mass communication and so is more complex than either simple model would suggest. Public opinion, to include knowledge about foreign affairs, is shaped (literally mediated) by the views of elites (public officials, intellectuals, and journalists) whose judgments and opinions are broadcast electronically and reported in print.[27] That does not mean, however, that elites can manipulate and dominate public opinion. Much depends, as the work of John R. Zaller and Benjamin I. Page has shown, on whether elites agree or are divided among themselves about the appropriate policy and on the relative complexity of the policy issues under debate. In general, the more complex the issue and the more unified elites are about the appropriate policy response, the less likely public opinion will oppose and constrain the policy-making elite. But when the facts of the issue are relatively easy to grasp and elite opinion is divided, then public opinion may wield significant influence and operate as an important constraint on policy making. Most important is elite disagreement. As Zaller has argued, "resistance to [elite] persuasion depends very heavily on the availability of countervalent communications, either in the forms of opposing information or of cueing messages from oppositional elites."[28]

[25] Geoffrey Blainey, *The Causes of War*, 3rd ed. (New York: Free Press, 1988), 7–9.

[26] See Russett, *Controlling the Sword*, 87–118; also Page, *Who Deliberates?*; and Zaller, *The Nature and Origin of Mass Opinion*.

[27] As Benjamin I. Page observed in *Who Deliberates?* 107: "Research has indicated that experts' views, as presented in the media, have a significant impact on public opinion: when experts speak in favor of a policy proposal, public opinion tends to move toward supporting that proposal."

[28] Ibid., 267.

Applying these findings to our problem suggests an alternative to the casualties hypothesis: namely, that public support of particular peacekeeping deployments depends on the degree of elite consensus that the deployment is justified or required. Expectations of consensus and dissensus must be framed in relative terms, of course. Since the Vietnam War, elites have been divided over whether U.S. involvement in world affairs should be, in Wittkopf's words, "cooperative" or "militant."[29] Indeed, on some accounts, elite opinion has divided over the wisdom of foreign "entanglements" ever since the country's founding. We may, nevertheless, attempt to weigh the preponderance of elite opinion. Recently, for example, Eric V. Larson examined the relative unity of public and elite opinion for American wars from World War II to the Gulf War and for the less intense deployments to Panama and Somalia. Based on that half-century of analysis, he concluded that public support for military deployments— to include toleration of casualties—"is influenced heavily by consensus (or its absence) among political leaders."[30] Given his findings, we have reason to expect that mass support for peacekeeping operations and tolerance of casualties are bolstered by evidence of a favorable elite consensus and eroded by evidence of elite disagreement. This elite consensus hypothesis offers a complex alternative to the casualties hypothesis for understanding public support for peacekeeping. It does not preclude considering the effects of casualties on any determination of support for a mission. But it rejects the view, supposed by the casualties hypothesis, that policy makers are virtual hostages to the public's recoiling from the loss of American life. It suggests that there is room for political leaders to shape public opinion and create a forum for public deliberation and debate.

In sum, the first two difficulties cast doubt on Luttwak's argument that public opinion is somehow less tolerant of casualties today than it has been. Those difficulties do not allow us to reject the claim. But they render it suspect. The third difficulty is more serious. It shows the inadequacy of Luttwak's argument that public opinion about casualties constrains decisions made by the policy-making elite. The difficulty is only formal and might be overcome by specifying the connection between mass and elite opinion. When this is done, however, we are led not only to doubt the casualties hypothesis but to consider an alternative, elite consensus hypothesis that is apparently better grounded in current public opinion research. In the following section, we examine public reaction to the Lebanon and Somali deployments to consider which hypothesis has greater support.

---

[29] Wittkopf, *Faces of Internationalism*; see also Ralph B. Levering, "Public Opinion, Foreign Policy, and American Politics since the 1960s," *Diplomatic History* 13 (Summer 1989): 383–393.

[30] Eric V. Larson, *Casualties and Consensus* (Santa Monica, CA: Rand, 1996), xv.

SUPPORT FOR PEACEKEEPING IN LEBANON AND SOMALIA

American peacekeeping missions in Lebanon and Somalia were preceded by a radical deterioration of social order caused by civil war. Neither country had an effective government able to exert its authority across the territory.[31]

In 1982, Lebanon was a country occupied by no fewer than six indigenous armed forces. In addition, Lebanon had been occupied since 1976 by a large Syrian force, dispatched formally by the Arab League to end the civil war. In the early 1980s, it was occupied also by Libyans, Palestinians, Israelis, and a small number of Iranian Revolutionary Guards. In addition, the United Nations (UN) had peacekeeping forces (UNIFIL) in southern Lebanon to monitor a cease-fire in that area. The complexities posed by this military situation reflected the difficult politics of the Middle East, heightened by the tensions of cold war. Following Israel's invasion of Lebanon in June 1982 to destroy Palestinian Liberation Organization (PLO) strongholds, the United States quickly intervened to arrange a cease-fire and help guard the withdrawal of PLO forces from Lebanon. In late September—following a massacre of Palestinians by the Phalangist Lebanese Forces, under the eye of the Israeli Defense Force—the United States intervened again as part of a multinational peacekeeping force that aimed to restore the authority of the legitimate government in Lebanon. U.S. Marines were deployed around the Beirut airport. French, Italian, and a small number of British troops were deployed elsewhere in the city. In the spring of 1983, U.S. and Italian troops began to patrol Beirut in support of the official, but contested, government and its army. At that point, they met armed attacks from opposing Muslim forces. In April, the U.S. embassy in Beirut was blown up by a car bomb. In August, U.S. Marines were under mortar attack from Druse militia forces (killing two). Then, on 23 October, 241 Marines were killed in a suicide terrorist attack in which a truck bomb was used to blow up the Marine barracks at the Beirut airport. President Ronald Reagan threatened to retaliate; but sporadic fighting continued without result. In January 1984, despite rising concern over escalating the conflict, President Reagan argued against sudden withdrawal of the multinational force. Nevertheless, the French announced that they would begin to withdraw some of their forces. In February, U.S. forces were also withdrawn to ships off shore and, on 30 March 1984, Reagan formally ended the U.S. role in the multinational peacekeeping force.

In 1991, Somalia too was wracked by a civil war. The military situation in Somalia was less complex than in Lebanon. There were no foreign forces to contend with, and the cold war was no longer available to intensify and in some ways to restrain the conflict. But in human terms, it was no less serious. The fighting disrupted economic life and led to a severe food shortage that threatened starvation for millions of Somalis. Concern for their straits led the UN

---

[31] Unless otherwise noted, facts about these two cases are drawn from *Facts on File Yearbook* (New York: Facts on File, 1983–1985, 1993–1995); *Keesing's Record of World Events* (London: Longman, 1982–1984, 1992–1994).

Security Council in 1992 to monitor a cease-fire of the conflict and to facilitate delivery of humanitarian aid for the country's relief (UNOSOM I). Relief efforts, however, were seriously hampered when rival clans attacked the relief convoys and stole the food. In December 1992, President George Bush sent U.S. troops to Somalia for peacekeeping duty. They were to protect the relief efforts from armed attack by rival clans, a goal that required proactive peace enforcement from the beginning. In February 1993, the United States declared that security in Somalia was "substantially restored." It prepared to transfer control of the peacekeeping and humanitarian mission to the UN (UNOSOM II) in May. This was done despite ongoing demonstrations (sometimes violent) against U.S. and French forces by followers of the Somali warlord, Mohammed Farah Aidid, who complained that the peacekeepers favored his rival. Shortly after the UN took over, its forces too were attacked, but more seriously. On 5 June 1993, over twenty Pakistani soldiers serving as UN peacekeepers were ambushed and killed, allegedly by Aidid's supporters. The UN Security Council condemned the incident and called for the arrest and punishment of those responsible. This began military operations to capture Aidid. Unfortunately for the UN, these operations were not successful. They only increased the number of casualties taken on both sides. On 8 August, four Americans were killed while patrolling streets in Mogadishu. On 24 August, President Clinton sent 400 U.S. Army Rangers to Somalia to capture Aidid. Their efforts were mired in difficulty. On 27 August, U.S. troops conducted a raid in which they mistakenly "captured" UN aid workers. Worse, on 9 September, when crowds turned on UN troops fighting Somali militia, U.S. helicopter fire killed about 200 Somali civilians. The Rangers did apprehend four of Aidid's close aides; but Aidid remained at large. On 3 October, eighteen Rangers were killed, over seventy were wounded, and one was captured in a fifteen-hour firefight with Aidid's forces. Television pictures showed Aidid's men dragging dead American soldiers through the streets of Mogadishu. Four days later, Clinton announced that he would send reinforcements to Somalia immediately, but he also promised to withdraw most troops by 31 March 1994.

Public response to the Somali debacle, we have seen, is frequently cited as evidence for the casualties hypothesis. The perception is that the public supported the deployment so long as there were no casualties, but once the Rangers were killed, support collapsed; and political elites without public support were forced to withdraw the forces, whether or not it was sound policy to do so. Put generally, the argument breaks down into three claims. First, public opinion in support of peacekeeping missions is volatile; rather than a stable foundation on which to base national security policy, it is subject to quick reversal. Second, the most important cause of the erosion of public support for force deployments is the taking of casualties; the loss of eighteen U.S. soldiers precipitated the debacle in Somalia. Third, rapid erosion of public support for a peacekeeping mission causes political elites to suspend the deployment.

Assessing the Casualties Hypothesis

Are these three claims borne out by what we know of the public's response to peacekeeping missions in Lebanon and Somalia? To answer this question, I identified the population of poll items dealing with these two missions and carefully examined all questions asking about public approval, decisions to remain or withdraw, and assessments of the missions' success.[32] Ideally, a number of questions with variant wording for each topic would be asked repeatedly over the entire course of both peacekeeping missions. Moreover, the questions asked during the Lebanon mission would be very much like the questions asked during the Somali mission. That ideal is rarely met in public opinion analysis, and it is not met here. Nevertheless, to answer questions about change, trend data are required. And to check the effect of casualties, the trend data must begin before the truck bombing in Beirut or the unsuccessful Ranger attack in Mogadishu and then continue somewhat beyond. While few questions met these criteria, fortunately some did, and they refer to the critical issue of public support for the two missions. Public support is measured here by questions that asked whether the respondents approved or agreed with the decision to send troops on the mission and by questions that asked whether troops should withdraw or stay in the area.

To assess whether public support for these missions was stable or changing, I followed the conventions outlined by Benjamin I. Page and Robert Y. Shapiro in their study, *The Rational Public*.[33] Public opinion is *stable* if it has not changed significantly over time. To determine whether public opinion has changed, they first recalculate poll responses to exclude don't know, not sure, and no opinion responses from the results.[34] After that, any movement in re-

---

[32] I collected all public opinion poll data on deposit with the Roper Center that mentioned either "Lebanon" in the years 1982 through 1984 or "Somalia" in the years 1992 through 1994. I conducted this search on line, accessing the Roper Center through CompuServe, and downloading the results. The Roper Center has public opinion poll data back through 1960 available for such on-line searches. I also searched for items before and after the years of focal interest. A few items were found, but there were virtually no items of any relevance to the present research. There were substantially more poll items reported for Lebanon (n=671) than for Somalia (n=267). Many of the items relating to Lebanon dealt with public reaction to Israel's invasion of Lebanon begun in June 1982, an important topic beyond the scope of this article. Otherwise, almost all of the items for both Lebanon and Somalia related directly or indirectly to the U.S. involvement in peacekeeping. Unfortunately, very few questions were asked repeatedly over the course of either operation, so trend data are not as numerous as we would like.

[33] Page and Shapiro, *The Rational Public*, 44–53.

[34] The rationale for excluding these data is that it clarifies tracking changes "in the balance of opinion among those people who express opinions," which is of course what we are interested in doing here. Page and Shapiro illustrate why with the following example. Take two data points. In the first, responses are 20 percent favor, 40 percent oppose, and 40 percent have no opinion. In the second, responses are 30 percent favor, 60 percent oppose, and 10 percent no opinion. The apparent increase in public favoring or opposing the policy issue, caused by including no opinion data masks that on balance at both points in time, 33 percent of those with opinions favored the policy. It is that kind of masking that their methodology aims to avoid. See *The Rational Public*, 423–424. The don't know, not

TABLE 1

Public Approval of U.S. Peacekeeping Mission in Lebanon, 1982–1984 (in percentages)

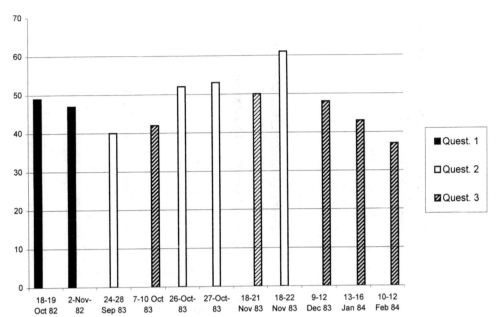

Questions: (1) *NBC News/Associated Press:* Do you approve or disapprove of President Reagan's decision to send American troops to Lebanon? (2) *CBS/NY Times:* U.S. Marines went to Lebanon as part of an international peacekeeping force to try to prevent fighting there. Do you approve or disapprove of the government sending troops to Lebanon for that purpose? (3) *Gallup:* Do you think the U.S. made a mistake sending the Marines to Lebanon or not? (To ensure comparability across all questions, "not a mistake" responses were coded "approve" and "mistake" responses were coded "disapprove."

Note: Percentages were recalculated to eliminate "don't know," "not sure," and "no answer" responses.

sponses from one time to another of six percentage points or more constitutes *significant change*. If the change is twenty percentage points or more, it is *large*; and if the change occurs at a rate of ten or more percentage points a year, it is *abrupt*. Public opinion *fluctuates* when it reverses itself within a given time interval, operationally defined to mean two or more significant changes in opposite directions within two years or three or more over four years. Change is *gradual* if it is neither abrupt nor fluctuating.

Applying these conventions to the data reported in Tables 1 and 2, we can say that public support for U.S. peacekeeping missions in Lebanon and Somalia was definitely not stable. In Lebanon, before the truck bombing of 23 October 1983, opinion was divided over whether to approve or disapprove of the mission, with most disapproving (Table 1). It is impossible to say with certainty whether the level of approval declined from the fall of 1982 to early fall 1983. The 1982 question (1) is not repeated in 1983 and the closest parallel questions

---

sure, and no opinion responses for the trend data reported here never exceeded 10 percent and ranged most often between 4 percent and 7 percent.

TABLE 2

Public Approval of U.S. Peacekeeping Mission in Somalia, 1992–1993 (in percentages)

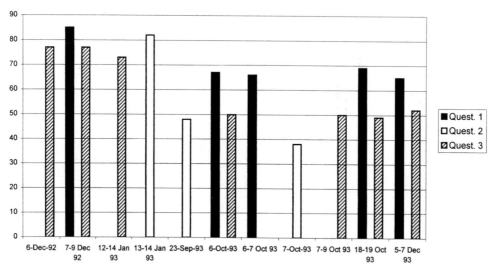

Questions: (1) *CBS/NY Times:* Do you think the United States is doing [did] the right thing to send U.S. troops to Somalia to try and make sure shipments of food get through to the people there, or should U.S. troops have stayed out? (2) *Times/CNN/Yankelovich:* In general do you approve or disapprove of the presence of U.S. troops in Somalia? (3) *CBS/NY Times:* Given the [possible] loss of American lives and the other costs involved, do you think sending U.S. troops to make sure food gets through to the people of Somalia is worth the cost or not? (To ensure comparable interpretation across all questions, "worth it" responses were coded "approve" and "not worth it" responses were coded "disapprove."

Note: Word in brackets in questions 1 and 3 represents variant wording. Percentages were recalculated to eliminate all "don't know," "not sure," and "no answer" responses.

(2 and 3) are worded too differently for us to attribute exact meaning to the different levels of approval and disapproval. We can say that from September through November 1983, approval of the mission rose abruptly from 40 percent to 61 percent in question 2 and that the change is evident immediately after the truck bombing in October. A similar but less abrupt rise in mission approval is shown in the data for question 3. Interestingly, that rise in approval reversed itself by January 1984. In early 1984, the level of support for the mission was not significantly different from what it was in early October 1983, before the truck bombing occurred. In brief, in this case, opinion change is significant, large, abrupt, and fluctuating.

Almost the same can be said about support for the peacekeeping mission in Somalia (see Table 2). From the winter of 1992–1993 to early fall 1993, there is a significant, large, and abrupt decrease in public approval of the peacekeeping mission. One cannot say how large or abrupt the change was. Taken together the three questions used to measure this movement give widely different estimates. Higher levels of approval generated by question 1 may well be caused by asking whether it was the "right thing" to send troops to provide food relief, which was always a popular rationale for the mission. Question 2 asked simply whether one approved "in general" of the presence of troops in Somalia. This question enabled the respondent to take more factors into account. It is quite conceivable that one could believe both that it was right to send troops for food relief and disapprove of U.S. presence in Somalia on other grounds. Question 3 linked mission approval of the humanitarian purpose with the costs, and that depressed levels of support attained when purpose alone is mentioned. Nevertheless, the pattern is the same in each instance. Opinion certainly changed over the period, and the change was, by the conventions adopted here, large and abrupt. There are, however, two differences worth noting between the patterns here and in Lebanon. First, the Somali data show no tendency toward fluctuation. Once the public changed its mind, no later than the fall of 1993, its mind stayed changed. This conclusion is supported by other poll data for 1994 collected at single points in time. Second, perhaps more important, in Lebanon opinion changed in the first place toward greater support for the mission and then by winter returned more or less to its original position. In Somalia the change withdrew support for the mission. Note too that, unlike the Somali mission, support for the Lebanon mission even in the beginning was not very high; opinion was closely divided.

Can we say that these changes in opinion resulted from the unexpected and unwelcome experience of casualties to American soldiers? Obviously, the public did not ignore and was not indifferent to the loss of life in these deployments. Nevertheless, I am hard-pressed to find support in either case for the supposed public unwillingness to support operations because casualties were incurred. At best the data are conflicting. In Lebanon, public reaction to the truck bombing increased support for what never was a very popular peacekeeping operation. Two months later, support began to decline. One might explain the decline as a cooling off of tempers raised by the initial terrorist attack or as recognition that the conflict was continuing without hope of resolution. In either case, support for the operation in February 1984, when Marines were pulled out of Beirut, was not significantly different from what it was in early October 1983, before the truck bombing occurred. One cannot conclude that the loss of 241 Marines, tragic as it was, eroded support for this peacekeeping mission.

In Somalia, support for the mission did erode, and there is evidence that support eroded further and substantially (dropping ten percentage points) after eighteen Rangers were killed in Mogadishu. But even here, one hesitates before concluding that these casualties are the reason why support for the mission declined, increasing support for an early withdrawal. The trend data for question 2 in Table 2 show that by September support for the mission had already declined precipitously (by thirty-four percentage points) from its January high. In short, 77 percent of the decline in public approval of the mission occurred before the Rangers lost their lives. Casualties may still have played a role in the erosion of support for the mission. Throughout the summer of 1993, the UN force faced Somali resistance and suffered casualties. On 9 September, a U.S. helicopter opened fire on a crowd of Somalis, killing about 200 people, including women and children. The UN claimed that those killed were combatants or were being used by combatants as human shields. This incident may also have played a role. Recall the data reported above, from the Americans Talk Security Survey, showing that the public opinion does consider the likelihood of civilian deaths in the area second only to the likely death of American soldiers when deciding to use force in foreign affairs.

Conceding this, one still cannot confidently conclude that casualties had the predicted strong effect. The reason why is that the U.S. Somali peacekeeping operation, which people approved in the winter (Operation Restore Hope), was not the same peacekeeping operation in which the United States was involved in the summer and fall (UNOSOM II). Although the questions remained the same, the mission they referred to in reality had changed. Quite possibly, public support for U.S. involvement in UNOSOM II was never very high. From its beginning, in late spring 1993, that operation aimed more at using force to end the civil war than at providing humanitarian relief. But peacekeeping to end the civil war in Somalia was not as popular as famine relief. A Gallup poll taken in December 1992 asked whether the U.S. role in Somalia should be "limited to delivering relief supplies" or widened "to bring a permanent end to the fighting." Only 31 percent thought the United States should attempt to end the fighting; 59 percent thought the role should be limited to delivering relief supplies.[35] Most thought that their preferences were being acted on. A *Times Mirror News* poll taken in January 1993 showed that 81 percent believed the principal objective of American forces in Somalia was "to restore enough order so that famine relief can take place." Only 10 percent believed it was "to disarm the gangs of Somali gunmen"; 9 percent were not sure.[36] In late March and early April, when asked to rank various possible missions in Somalia, 62 percent of the respondents thought the use of the military for humanitarian purposes was "very preferable."

In contrast, 45 percent thought it very preferable "to arrest leaders of warring factions." Just 19 percent thought it very preferable to use "overwhelming force to defeat the primary aggressors."[37] In June, about two-thirds of the public did approve of U.S. actions to retaliate against Aidid for attacking UN forces. Yet many (42 percent) worried that these actions would cause the United States to be "bogged down in Somalia."[38] By mid-September, only 36 percent believed

[35] Gallup Organization, Question ID: US GALLUP.121192 R2 (Storrs, CT: Roper Center, 1995).

[36] Times Mirror News Interest Index, Question ID: USPSRA.011393 R11 (Storrs, CT: Roper Center, 1995).

[37] Americans Talk Issues, Question ID: USMS.ATI121 R40-42 (Storrs, CT: Roper Center, 1995).

[38] These data come from two sources. Over 18–21 June, Gallup pollsters asked, "Last week, the United States participated in a military operation with the United Nations against one of the warlords in Somalia. Do you generally approve or disapprove of that decision?" 65 percent approved, 23 percent disapproved, and 12 percent had no opinion (Question ID: USGALLUP.062393 R6 [Storrs, CT: Roper Center, 1995]). Over 21–24 June, CBS News/*New York Times* pollsters posed a broader question. It read: "Mohammed Farah Aidid is the leader of a Somali clan whose troops killed United Nations peacekeepers. UN troops are trying to capture him. Do you think this is a good idea because it shows that violence against the UN will not be tolerated, or do you think this is a bad idea because this gets

that the mission there was "under control." Most (52 percent) thought the United States was "too deeply involved in Somalia." The reason they thought so is tied plausibly to their still strong belief, held by 69 percent, that U.S. troops should "only be responsible for making sure that food is delivered." Few (22 percent) believed the troops should "be responsible for disarming the rival warlords there."[39] While we would prefer repeated questions to assess the trend, these various questions asked before (some long before) the Mogadishu fire-fight show that the public never supported the more aggressive mission of UN-OSOM II, as they did the mission of famine relief. Admittedly, this argument is more complex and the evidence less telling than in the Lebanon case. Still, on balance it is difficult to find strong support for the casualties hypothesis in the data for Somalia. That is striking, as this case is often supposed to provide clear-cut evidence in favor of the hypothesis.

Given this analysis, it is difficult to conclude that changing public opinion had the predicted effect on political decisions to suspend the peacekeeping missions. Once the putative link between eroded support and casualties is broken, the entire logic of the analysis breaks down. Nevertheless, in both cases, public opinion favored withdrawing U.S. forces from the regions before the president announced a decision to withdraw. In Lebanon, public sentiment for withdrawal increased markedly from 39 percent to 61 percent between October 1983 and January 1984 (Table 3). Over the same period, support for sending more troops, never strong, fell below 10 percent. President Reagan did not announce his decision to remove Marines from Beirut until February 1984. Only a limited number of trend data are available for Somalia (Table 4). They all follow the 3 October firefight and show an unvarying and high proportion—nearly two-thirds—favoring withdrawal from Somalia. The first of these polls was taken the day before President Clinton announced his decision to withdraw from Somalia in six months. Examination of these and other poll data taken at single points in time suggest that the public accepted the president's proposal for a gradual withdrawal; support for immediate withdrawal was limited.

---

the UN involved in Somalia's civil war?" 66 percent thought it a good idea, 23 percent thought it a bad idea, and 11 percent had no opinion (Question ID: USCBSNYT.62893A R69 [Storrs, CT: Roper Center, 1995]). But, in the same poll, when asked, "When United Nations peacekeepers are killed in Somalia, should United States troops retaliate, or is that likely to get the United States bogged down in Somalia?" 41 percent thought US should retaliate, 42 percent though retaliation would bog down the United States, and 17 percent did not know (Question ID USCBSNYT.62893A R68 [Storrs, CT: Roper Center, 1995]).

[39] The NBC News/*Wall Street Journal* pollsters asked "are you concerned that the United States is too deeply involved in Somalia, or do you think that our efforts in Somalia are under control?" (Question ID: USNBCWSJ.93SEPT R19B [Storrs, CT: Roper Center, 1995]). One week later, Time/CNN/Yankelovich pollsters asked "do you think the US troops in Somalia should be responsible for disarming rival warlords there, or should the U.S. troops only be responsible for making sure that food is delivered to the areas affected by the famine?" (Question ID: USYANK.092493 R41 [Storrs, CT: Roper Center, 1995]).

TABLE 3

Public Pressure to Remove Troops from Lebanon, 1983–1984
(in percent)

| Date | Deploying Troops | | | |
	Remove Troops	Same Number	Send More	n
22–26 Sep 83	42	51	7	1430
23 Oct 83	53	23	23	454
25 Oct 83	41	27	32	588
26 Oct 83	48	35	17	686
26–28 Oct 83	44	38	18	1184
28 Oct 83	39	43	18	491
3–7 Nov 83	42	44	14	1400
8–13 Dec 83	51	40	9	1431
3 Jan 84	63	32	5	571
4 Jan 84	61	30	9	478
12–17 Jan 84	60	32	7	1463

Question: *ABC News/Washington Post:* Would you say the US should send more troops to Lebanon, leave the number of troops about the same, or remove the troops that are there now?

Notes: Percentages and sample sizes were recalculated to eliminate all don't know, not sure, no answer responses. Not all rows add to 100 due to rounding.

It is certainly likely that both Reagan and Clinton were aware of the poll numbers before they made their decisions. But other factors than these weighed in the balance. Reagan faced increasing opposition to the Lebanon deployment, especially to his announced policy to retaliate against terrorist attacks, from European allies including Margaret Thatcher and, at home, from congressional leaders. In late December 1983, even Robert Michel, the Republican House minority leader, urged Reagan to remove troops from Beirut, an opinion joined in January 1984 by Republican Senator Charles Percy, who chaired the Senate Foreign Relations Committee. Clinton faced similar pressures in Somalia. In August 1993, the Italians withdrew from UNOSOM II, re-

TABLE 4

Public Pressure to Remove Troops from Somalia, 1993
(in percent)

| Date | Deploying Troops | | |
	Withdraw	Remain	n
6 Oct 93	65	35	483
6–7 Oct 93	65	35	1027
18–19 Oct 93	65	35	831
5–7 Dec 93	64	36	1193

Question: *CBS News:* What should the United States do now? Do you think the United States should keep its troops in Somalia until the situation in Somalia is peaceful, or should the United States withdraw its troops as soon as possible?

Note: Percentages and sample sizes were recalculated to eliminate all don't know, not sure, no answer responses.

deploying their forces in Somalia under their own command. They, along with other allies, objected to the "Rambo methods" of the UNOSOM commander. At home, congressional opposition to the Somali mission mounted as well. In September 1993, two days before the helicopter incident, the Senate passed a nonbinding resolution urging Clinton to outline the goals of the mission by 15 October and to seek congressional approval for further involvement. The House followed with a similar resolution on 28 September. In this context, it is difficult to conclude that public opinion—and especially that public reaction against the unexpected casualties—played a powerful determining part in shaping policy.

Overall, examination of the evidence for Lebanon and Somalia lends some, but not much, support to the hypothesis that public intolerance of casualties renders it a changeable and untrustworthy basis for deciding whether to launch or sustain peacekeeping deployments. Opinion was changeable. But it is not clear that casualties (or casualties alone) affected the change. Sudden, unexpected casualties did not cause the public to withdraw its support for either peacekeeping mission. In Lebanon, support for the mission rose, albeit briefly, after the truck bombing, which killed so many Marines. In Somalia, support for the U.S. deployment did fall in reaction to the firefight in Mogadishu that killed eighteen Rangers. But we must remember that public support for the mission had declined significantly even before the Rangers were killed. This evidence makes it difficult to believe that the public withdrew its support for either peacekeeping mission simply because of these tragic incidents or that its withdrawal was a decisive cause forcing political leaders to abandon the missions.

Assessing the Alternative Elite Consensus Hypothesis

If not by casualties, how can we explain the changing patterns of public support for peacekeeping missions? It is possible, of course, that we cannot. Studies of public opinion that point to the orderliness and interpretability of public beliefs have been based on examinations of long-term trends.[40] Opinion about peacekeeping missions form and change and turn into history in a matter of months. Perhaps that is not time enough to become aware of, work through, and reach a settled judgment about the complex issues that most peacekeeping initiatives raise. Or, perhaps, short-term changes over a period of months are due to the random shock of particular events beyond the reach of generalization. Such fluctuations may mask a more stable and orderly pattern that is only evident when we average observations over a period of years, as daily market fluctuations may mask the long-term trend in stock prices. They are interpreted at one's peril.

[40] See Ronald Ingelhart, *Cultural Shift in Advanced Industrial Society* (Princeton: Princeton University Press, 1990); Wittkopf, *Faces of Internationalism*; Yankelovich, *Coming to Public Judgment*; and Page and Shapiro, *The Rational Public*.

The issue, of course, is not so easily disposed. When criticizing the casualties hypothesis, we noted there was a significant alternative to it—the elite consensus hypothesis. Put simply, this hypothesis holds that when political elites (or, more generally, the "experts") agree on the course of policy, then public opinion, especially over the short term, is likely to go along; but when elites disagree, so will the public. Following this logic, we expect the public to withhold or withdraw its support from peacekeeping deployments when there is division among elites about the necessity for the deployment or the availability of alternatives to military action; and this will occur even if there are no casualties. At the same time, we expect the public to continue support for a deployment, despite casualties, if elite opinion is solidly behind it. How well does this hypothesis explain the observed patterns of public response to the deployment in Lebanon and Somalia?

Consider Lebanon. The first deployment, in August 1982, to protect the withdrawal of the PLO was not controversial. It was limited in scope, incurred no casualties, and was a quick success, ending early. Notice too that the president notified Congress of the deployment, acting consistently with the War Powers Resolution. That resolution requires the president to consult with Congress and gain its authorization for deployments of armed forces into hostile situations or situations where hostilities are imminent. Presidents have been reluctant to grant that they are subject to that resolution; they see it as an encroachment on their powers as commander-in-chief of the armed forces.[41] It remains a source of friction between the two branches of government. That any notice was sent suggests that the president expected no strong opposition to the deployment. The second deployment in late September 1982, following the Phalangist massacre of Palestinians, was quite different. It was always controversial, even within the administration that proposed it. It was strongly opposed by Secretary of Defense Caspar W. Weinberger and the Joint Chiefs of Staff, who thought the mission was vaguely defined. With no certain objective to achieve, it was difficult to define appropriate force size, equipment, rules of engagement, etc.[42] Yet Secretary of State George P. Shultz was equally strong in his support for the deployment and, most important, so was the president.[43] This time, however, President Reagan did not act consistently with the War Powers Resolution; no notification was sent to Congress, and Congress did not authorize the deployment.

In early 1983, elite divisions over this issue deepened and broadened. Marines were attacked while on patrol in Beirut and, on 18 April, the U.S. embassy was bombed, leaving dozens dead and many more wounded. The next day, congressional objections to the deployment were strongly stated. Senator Barry Goldwater (R-AZ) was blunt: it was time, he said, to withdraw the Marines

[41] See Louis Fischer, *Presidential War Power* (Lawrence: University Press of Kansas, 1995); and John Hart Ely, *War and Responsibility* (Princeton: Princeton University Press, 1993).

[42] Weinberger, *Fighting for Peace*, 151–152.

[43] George P. Shultz, *Turmoil and Triumph* (New York: Charles Scribner's, 1993), 107–110.

from Lebanon. The Foreign Affairs Committees of both houses approved sending additional aid to Lebanon, but only on condition that any expansion of U.S. forces in Lebanon had congressional approval. Agreement on this forestalled an effort by Senator Claiborne Pell (D-RI) directly to apply the War Powers Resolution to Lebanon. It did not silence congressional criticism of the deployment, which continued through the summer and never subsided entirely.

By late August 1983, when fighting in Beirut killed two Marines—the first American combat casualties—members of Congress renewed calls to review troop commitments as required under the War Powers Resolution. Reagan resisted, creating a dispute between Congress and the administration. Finally, a compromise was reached. Congress passed a resolution that placed the Marines' involvement in Lebanon under the War Powers Resolution, but also authorized the administration to keep Marines there for another eighteen months. Reagan signed the resolution, but asserted "that he felt no constitutional obligation to seek congressional authorization" to extend the deployment.[44]

In short, long before the barracks bombing, political leaders were divided over the wisdom and conduct of this mission, and their divisions grew deeper and more vocal over time. Nor were they silenced by the barracks bombing. Although the House defeated a proposal to end funding for the peacekeeping effort by March 1984, congressional criticism of the deployment intensified through the fall. Division over this issue was also found in newspaper editorials. Immediately after the barracks bombing, the *Wall Street Journal* argued that it was "time for retaliation" against military targets in Syrian-occupied Lebanon, even if those responsible for the bombing were not positively identified. Action was necessary to demonstrate U.S. resolve against terrorists.[45] The *New York Times*, in contrast, argued that America was once again being held hostage in the Middle East in pursuit of a "murky diplomatic cause"—removing Syrian backed forces from Lebanon—that is "not a vital American interest." It asked bluntly what purpose U.S. forces served in Lebanon and under what conditions would they finally depart.[46]

Given elite dissensus, it is hardly surprising that public support for the Lebanon operation was divided from the beginning and remained divided until early 1984, when opinion finally crystallized to favor removing the troops (Tables 1 and 3). What is surprising is that public support for the operation rallied briefly in the fall following the barracks bombing, despite casualties and in the face of elite dissensus. The explanation for that rise in support remains matter for speculation. Perhaps it reflected collective anger and frustration with the terrorist attack, so different from acts of war. Perhaps it represented a rally effect associated with the successful invasion of Grenada, which was launched

[44] Fischer, *Presidential War Power*, 141.

[45] "Time for Retaliation," *Wall Street Journal*, 25 October 1983, 28.

[46] "America Held Hostage," *New York Times*, 24 October 1983.

two days after the Beirut bombing. Whatever the cause, the rally was short-lived. By early December, public pressure mounted in favor of withdrawal from Lebanon. Again surprisingly, at this point, public opinion was to some degree in front of (it certainly was not following) the opinion of the still-divided political elite. In this case, the domestic public pressure joined with the pressure of foreign elites to urge a change in U.S. policy. As the year ended, House Speaker Tip O'Neill (D-MA) called for a meeting of Democratic leaders to review their support for the mission, and House Minority Leader Bob Michel (R-IL) called for the Marines to be withdrawn. Administration leaders still defended policies they hoped would unify the country in support of the Lebanon mission. But they failed to do this before the barracks bombing. They were unlikely to succeed, as conditions in Lebanon grew worse, following the barracks bombing.[47] With violence continuing in the region and opposition mounting in Congress, the president's policy to stay and perhaps retaliate for losses was not sustainable. On 1 February 1984, the caucus of House Democrats called on the president to withdraw the Marines from Lebanon. One week later, he did.

In Somalia, initial support for the humanitarian relief effort was high not only among the public (Table 2) but among political leaders as well. And support was bipartisan. In fact, although it was Bush's decision to intervene, Congress took the initiative in the summer of 1992 to promote intervention.[48] Nevertheless, as shown by hearings held by the House Foreign Affairs Committee in December 1992, members of Congress were in no mood to write blank checks. Their support was for a humanitarian relief effort to relieve the famine and nothing more. Once that was done, U.S. forces were to withdraw. A similarly restrictive understanding of the mission to Somalia was embodied in the Senate Joint Resolution 45 (SR 45). Passed in February 1993, SR 45 authorized the use of American armed forces in Somalia, as required under the War Powers Resolution, but it prescribed a narrow humanitarian mission for them.

It was not long before continuing clan warfare showed that sticking to limited aims would be difficult. In March, the new administration under President Clinton declared a victory for Operation Restore Hope and turned the problem back to the UN for a new operation to begin in May. The new operation, however, had an expanded mission. Beyond humanitarian relief, it was to end civil war and begin democratic nation building. It was, moreover, to require continuing commitment of U.S. forces, although many fewer than before. As the terms of this transition were negotiated at the UN, the House of Representatives de-

---

[47] This argument is elaborated in Larson, *Casualties and Consensus*, 96–97.

[48] The facts in this and the next several paragraphs come from the account of Harry Johnson and Ted Dague, "Congress and Somalia" in Walter Clarke and Jeffrey Herbst, eds., *Learning from Somalia*, (Boulder, CO: Westview Press, 1997), 191–204. Both were participants in the events. Johnston is a member of Congress (D-FL). He is the senior member of the House International Relations Committee and formerly chaired the Subcommittee on Africa. Dague is a foreign affairs analyst for the Congressional Research Service and served as a professional staff member for the subcommittee on Africa when Johnston was its chair.

bated its version of SR 45 to authorize the troop deployment to Somalia. Here is the earliest evidence of elite dissensus over the peacekeeping mission. The House resolution adopted a broad definition of the mission, akin to that assigned to UNOSOM II. But expanding the mission beyond what Bush initially outlined and the Senate had approved was strongly opposed, largely along partisan lines, both in committee and on the House floor. Although it passed on 25 May, by a vote of 243–179, it was never "taken up by the Senate because Senate majority leader [George] Mitchell [D-ME] would not allow debate."[49]

What has most to be explained in this case and what the casualties hypothesis left in doubt was the sharp drop in support for the mission between January and September 1993. It is possible, but by no means certain, that public support eroded in the spring with erosion of elite consensus in Congress about what the mission in Somalia was supposed to be and disagreement over who was competent to authorize and define it—the president or Congress. Yet, as we learned from our analysis of the casualties hypothesis, the public never expressed much support for a peacekeeping mission that had other than humanitarian purposes. The public's mood was captured in SR 45 rather than in the broader resolution passed by the House. The strength of elite support for the broader resolution would be tested when the mission in Somalia changed radically in June 1993 to include a quest to bring Aidid to justice for the massacre of Pakistani peacekeepers. Surprisingly, one looks in vain for evidence in June that elites were divided over this shift to a more aggressive policy. *New York Times* editorials strongly supported action against Aidid, suggesting that "Mr. Clinton dare not flinch" and that "threatening General Aidid with arrest seems a minimal way of expressing international condemnation."[50] The *Wall Street Journal* was less effusive but also supportive. After the peacekeepers attacked Aidid, with more attacks sure to follow, it editorialized that the UN's mission must so far be regarded a success and that attacks against Aidid showed that UN troops cannot be murdered with impunity.[51] Indirect evidence is also revealing. Strikingly absent from reports about Somalia filed in June and broadcast on the network evening news are any interviews with public figures or leaders from the United States who opposed the actions taken. Protests by Somalis against the more aggressive UN actions were aired.[52] On the surface, public opinion accepted the new policy. We noted earlier that about two-thirds of the public approved of U.S. participation in UN military operations against Aidid, though they were worried that the action might cause the United States to be bogged down in Somalia's civil war. Here perhaps is evidence that the public may suspend its doubts when elites agree that a given policy should be pursued. By September many minds had changed.

[49] Ibid., 199.

[50] "Bloody Sunday in Somalia," *New York Times*, 15 June 1993; and "Drawing the Line in Somalia," *New York Times*, 20 June 1993.

[51] "Somali Awakening," *Wall Street Journal*, 14 June 1993.

[52] Based on my own analysis of abstracts held in the Vanderbilt Television News Archive.

As the United States became more actively involved in efforts to capture the warlord Aidid, the mission was subject to heightened scrutiny and criticism in Congress. In July 1993, Senator Robert Byrd (D-WV) spoke against the mission on the Senate floor, objecting to the expense of the peacekeeping mission—he chaired the Appropriations Committee—and noting that the Senate never authorized use of American troops in Somalia for peace enforcement purposes. As peace enforcement was not contemplated by SR 45, the senator had raised an important constitutional question about which branch of government should authorize foreign deployments of American armed forces. Hostilities intensified through the summer and, though U.S. casualties were low (fewer than eight), Congress returned from its summer recess ready to pick up the cudgel that Senator Byrd had thrown down. Disillusioned with the peace enforcement effort, on 9 September the Senate voted 90–7 to require President Clinton to seek congressional authorization before 15 November to continue the mission in Somalia. The House passed an identical measure on 28 September by a vote of 406–26. Congress was controlled by the president's party. Still, it would not follow the president's lead in this matter. Moreover, we know from Eric Larson's work that the mass media widely reported congressional concerns with administration policy.[53] Elite disagreement was not kept from the public view. Yet, as public support for peace enforcement was never high, we cannot say that decreased public support for the mission resulted from the resurgence of elite opposition in September.

We can say that the October firefight in Mogadishu brought elite disagreement to a climax, making it inevitable that Clinton would not try to expand or to extend the expanded mission in Somalia. It sealed the doom of a policy already so unpopular among congressional leaders that it would probably have been sharply modified or discontinued in any event. In this context, it is perhaps surprising that public opinion favoring withdrawal from Somalia remained the same (at 65 percent throughout the fall). It did not rise as elite disagreement gave way to consensus over what the policy should be. This may be an artifact of the polling, as the first poll on this issue was not conducted until 6 October. By this time, there was already a clear elite consensus favoring gradual withdrawal from Somalia. Alternatively, public skepticism about the mission in Somalia may have exerted pressure on elite opinion to favor withdrawal. But, if so, public opinion was not behaving as predicted by the elite consensus hypothesis. The most we can say is that public support for the mission eroded as elite consensus eroded, that public disillusionment, already strong, grew stronger when casualties were taken, and that public support for gradual withdrawal was unwavering once political elites agreed to limit the mission and leave Somalia by March 1994.

In sum, we cannot conclude with certainty, on the basis of evidence here, exactly how elite and public opinion are interrelated. Our expectation, based

[53] Eric Victor Larson, *Ends and Means in the Democratic Conversation* (Santa Monica, CA: RAND Graduate School Dissertation Series, 1995), 272–296.

on current public opinion theory and research, was that patterns of elite opinion were the guiding force and that public support for peacekeeping missions would be high when elite opinion agreed on the missions and then drop as elite opinion about them became more divided. But neither case offers much support for that hypothesis. Some evidence in the Somali case suggests that when elites agreed on the policy to pursue, the public did suspend disbelief and go along. In both cases, however, it was most often the case that elite and public opinion were divided. Yet when opinion was divided, there was no certain relation between elite and public opinion. In the Lebanon case, at least, elite division did not invariably predict an erosion of public support. We would stand on shaky ground to conclude that public opinion is patterned after elite opinion. What we encountered rather was a highly mediated situation in which presidents and other leaders decided on policies that elites and the public evaluated and then accepted or rejected as their deliberation on the matter led them to believe. The causal order, if any, that explains the influence of one judgment on the other remains unclear.

Conclusion

We began by asking whether there was reliable evidence to support the central claims of the casualties hypothesis. These were, first, that the public will not support military deployments which result in casualties; second, that public support for a deployment would be abruptly withdrawn if casualties unexpectedly occurred; and, finally, that public opinion on this issue is so powerful that it constrains the use of force by—indeed, effectively debellicizes—great powers. Based on this article's analysis of public and elite opinion during U.S. peacekeeping deployments to Lebanon and Somalia, we may conclude with confidence that evidence for this hypothesis is lacking. While public opinion was not insensitive to the deaths of American soldiers, public approval or disapproval of both missions was, in fact, largely determined before casualties occurred. Opinions about the missions did change. The changes were sometimes large and abrupt. In the case of Lebanon, public opinion fluctuated back and forth in response to the terrorist bombing that killed so many Marines. But when opinion fluctuated about the bombing, it moved in a direction opposite to what the casualties hypothesis predicts. It moved to continue rather than end the deployment. In Somalia, support for the mission had withered already in response to the changing mission before the firefight in Mogadishu.

Stating the matter strongly, patterns of public support for peacekeeping missions reveal no irrational or knee-jerk reactions based on a putative unwillingness to tolerate casualties. They reveal no immature demand for a casualty-free security policy, both wrong to promise and impossible to deliver. They reveal a public prudently cautious about what to expect from the use of force. They are willing to risk it for humanitarian purposes, but they are risk averse with respect to the more complex and often partisan peace enforcement missions.

In light of these findings, why have so many found the casualties hypothesis persuasive, especially within the political elite? One reason may be, as Donald C. F. Daniels suggests, that members of Congress place more credence in what their constituents tell them than what national polls show, and that patterns of constituent contacts might actually support something like the casualties hypothesis.[54] This is a valuable suggestion. Taken seriously, it means that clear specification of the relation between elite and public opinion requires a different kind of study than undertaken here. Local studies are needed to compare public opinion within congressional districts with opinions expressed through constituency contact and to examine whether these influence or are influenced by the policy positions taken by members of Congress. Alternatively, rhetoric about public intolerance of casualties and its influence over policy may simply mask an intra-elite struggle, still unresolved, about the distribution of warmaking powers between the president and Congress. In both Lebanon and Somalia, elite opinion about the deployments divided most often over the application of the War Powers Resolution. The resolution asserts that the president's power over force deployments is not unilateral, but must be shared with Congress whenever forces are deployed in situations where hostilities are imminent. Presidents may say a situation is not hostile, of course. But hostilities are hard to deny once casualties are taken. On this account, casualties are a hot issue, because they trigger intra-elite conflict. Both of these ideas require further research.

Note, finally, a key assumption of democratic theory—namely, that the public is competent to decide what public policy should be, including national security policy. The casualties hypothesis may seem to share this assumption. It does not. It certainly holds that public opinion is powerful. But by supposing public support for peacekeeping deployments rests on the utopian condition that military operations be casualty free, the casualties hypothesis lays a groundwork for discrediting the quality of public judgment, for denying its competence. By supposing that elites are unwittingly constrained to desire whatever public opinion at the moment desires, the casualties hypothesis adopts the view that democracy is prone to corruption, as Aristotle and others long after have feared. In short, the casualties hypothesis undermines confidence in the public to govern itself wisely and well, at least in the area of foreign affairs. This study suggests that there is no reason to undermine confidence. The claims of the casualties hypothesis lack support and should be laid to rest.*

---

[54] Daniels, "The United States," 94–95.

* Earlier versions of this paper were presented at the Pontignano Seminar on Public Opinion, Democracy and Defence Policy, Siena, Italy, 7–10 October 1996, funded in part by the United States Information Agency, and at the biennial meetings of the Inter-University Seminar on Armed Forces and Society, in Baltimore, October 1995. I am grateful for comments received from the conference participants and from Christopher Dandeker, Robert Goldich, Maria Bina Palmisano, Richard Wells.

The Panama Invasion Revisited: Lessons for the Use of Force in the Post–Cold War Era

EYTAN GILBOA

The 1989 U.S. invasion of Panama was the first American use of force since 1945 that was unrelated to the cold war. It was also the first large-scale use of American troops abroad since Vietnam and the most violent event in Panamanian history. It ended with the unusual capture of Manuel Antonio Noriega, Panama's head of state, who was then brought to the United States and tried for criminal drug operations. Despite the end of the cold war, dictators such as Noriega, Saddam Hussein, and Serbian leaders Slobodan Milošević and Radovan Karadzić will continue to exist and to challenge the international order. How should the United States, the only remaining superpower, deal with these kinds of authoritarian leaders? What lessons can we learn from the Noriega challenge and the means employed by the United States to handle him?

Noriega was a corrupt dictator heading an efficient narcomilitaristic regime in Panama. He was involved in drug trafficking, arms smuggling, money laundering, and the ruthless oppression of his people. He also systematically violated the American–Panamanian Canal treaties and harassed U.S. forces and institutions in Panama. But were all these violations sufficient to justify a massive military intervention to remove Noriega from power? In the last forty years, the United States intervened in Latin American countries but always in connection with perceived communist threats and the cold war. Noriega was not a communist and did not plan to move Panama into the Soviet sphere of influence. On the contrary, he played a key role in American efforts to contain the spread of

EYTAN GILBOA teaches international politics at the School of International Service, The American University, Washington, D.C. He is the author of numerous articles and books including *American Public Opinion Toward Israel and the Arab-Israeli Conflict*. He is currently writing a book on American use of force since Vietnam.

communism in Central America. Historically, Panama was strategically important to the United States because of the Panama Canal. By the mid-1980s, however, the canal had lost much of its strategic value.[1] In 1978 President Jimmy
Carter recognized this change and negotiated an agreement to transfer control
of the canal to Panama by the end of the century.[2]

Why then, in the absence of cold war considerations, did the United States
consider a relatively insignificant dictator a major challenge whose removal from
power required full-scale military intervention? To answer this question, one must
examine a combination of factors: escalation in the conflict, domestic priorities
including the war on drugs, George Bush's leadership difficulties, and America's
new global responsibilities as the sole remaining superpower.

The Noriega problem began in 1985 as an internal Panamanian affair. Between
1985 and the 1989 U.S. invasion, it went through a series of five minicrises. A
turning point occurred in February 1988, when the United States declared drugs
to be the major threat to American society at the same time that Noriega was
indicted in Florida for drug trafficking and money laundering. Following the
indictments, the United States sought to remove Noriega from power. The Reagan
and Bush administrations hoped for and preferred a Panamanian solution, like
a coup d'etat, an election that would end Noriega's rule, or a popular uprising
of the kind that removed from power dictators such as Anastasio Somoza of
Nicaragua and Ferdinand Marcos of the Philippines.

The two administrations used overt and covert operations to help start popular
uprisings and coups and also assisted the opposition in the 1989 Panamanian
elections. None of these efforts were successful, and the United States decided
to use other measures to remove Noriega such as negotiations, economic and
diplomatic sanctions, and military threats. These measures also failed, mainly
due to underestimation of Noriega's ability to survive, bureaucratic infighting,
mixed messages, congressional–White House feuds, operational restrictions, and
incompetent American implementation of policies and plans. The failure of these
measures strengthened Noriega's position in Panama, as he defiantly withstood
superpower pressure. Thus, as his political position became stronger, it became
more important to the United States to remove him from power.

Throughout the confrontation, Noriega felt immune to American reprisals
or punishment. One author claimed that "the United States sent clear signals,
which if evaluated correctly, could have provided warning [to Noriega] of a U.S.
attack."[3] But even hours before the actual attack, Noriega did not believe the

[1] David Parker, "The Panama Canal Is No Longer Crucial to U.S. Security," *Armed Forces Journal*
125 (December 1987): 54–60.

[2] Walter LaFeber, *The Panama Canal: The Crisis in Historical Perspective* (New York: Oxford
University Press, 1989); Michael J. Hogan, *The Panama Canal in American Politics: Domestic Advocacy and the Evolution of Policy* (Carbondale: Southern Illinois University Press, 1986).

[3] Susan Horwitz, "Indications and Warning Factors" in Bruce Watson and Peter Tsouras, eds.
Operation Just Cause: The U.S. Intervention in Panama (Boulder, CO: Westview, 1991), 49.

United States would use force to capture him.[4] His failure was not only the result of faulty evaluation. The evidence presented in this article shows that over a long period of time, the United States sent him mixed and confusing signals. Thus, a tougher and more unified U.S. policy that was clearly articulated and communicated from the beginning could have obviated the need for the Panama invasion.

THE EARLY U.S. MESSAGES

Noriega had been an intelligence officer under General Omar Torrijos before he became the commander of the Panamanian Defense Forces (PDF).[5] He had been a corrupt official involved with illegal smuggling of drugs and arms.[6] Yet he was considered a close ally of various American governmental agencies. He cooperated with the Drug Enforcement Administration (DEA), had allies in the Department of Defense (DOD), and was on and off the CIA payroll as early as 1971.[7] In addition, he was a source of intelligence for and a channel of communication between the United States and Fidel Castro. Most importantly, however, during the civil war in Nicaragua, he provided access and assistance to the contra campaign against the Sandinistas.

Despite his involvement with drugs, at least until his indictment in 1988, Noriega was considered by the United States both as an asset and a liability. When he committed crimes and abused his power, Washington looked the other way. In 1979, for example, senior officials in the Carter administration blocked federal prosecutors from bringing drug-trafficking and arms-smuggling indictments against Noriega, because they preferred to continue receiving the intelligence information he was providing them. Following the conclusion of the canal treaties, they did not want to upset the political situation in Panama.[8] With the United States continually ignoring his abuses, Noriega may have been encouraged to continue or even increase his drug-related activities.

Washington also looked the other way during the 1984 elections in Panama. In May 1984, Panama held its first free elections in sixteen years. The official vote count showed Noriega's hand-picked candidate, Nicolas Barletta, winning

[4] Margaret Scranton, *The Noriega Years* (Boulder, CO: Westview, 1991), 202.

[5] Noriega created the PDF in 1983 by merging the National Guard, the police, and the immigration forces.

[6] R. M. Koster and Guillermo Sanchez, *In the Time of the Tyrants, Panama 1968–1990* (New York: Norton, 1990).

[7] George P. Shultz, *Turmoil and Triumph: My Years as Secretary of State* (New York: Charles Scribner's Sons, 1993), 1052; Frederick Kempe, *Divorcing the Dictator: America's Bungled Affair with Noriega* (New York: G. P. Putnam's, 1990), 83; Kevin Buckley, *Panama: The Whole Story* (New York: Simon and Schuster, 1991), 14; Scranton, *The Noriega Years*, 13–14.

[8] Linda Robinson, *Intervention or Neglect: The United States and Central America Beyond the 1980s* (New York: Council on Foreign Relations, 1991), 111; and Jim McGee and Bob Woodward, "Noriega Arms Indictment Stalled in '80," *Washington Post*, 20 March 1988.

by 1,713 votes. But rumors of fraud appeared on election day and persisted in subsequent days. Eventually it became clear that the PDF had doctored the election results in order to produce a victory for Noriega's candidate.[9]

The fraudulent May 1984 elections set back the chances for democracy in Panama and demonstrated Noriega's ability to undermine the political process. They might have also served as a warning to the United States about Noriega. But instead of viewing Noriega's manipulations as a threat to democracy in Panama, Washington chose to ignore them. Barletta was well known in Washington and had good connections with several senior officials. He had studied economics at the University of Chicago when Secretary of State George Shultz was a professor there, was a former vice president of the World Bank and ex-director of the Department of Economic Affairs at the Organization of American States (OAS). Shultz legitimized the elections by attending Barletta's inauguration as president of Panama.

Finally, American actions in an undercover drug operation sent Noriega a message that his involvement in drug trafficking would be overlooked if he assisted the United States in the battle against the Sandinistas. In 1984, the DEA conducted a major undercover operation in Colombia designed to arrest and convict druglords, including Pablo Escobar.[10] In June, Barry Seal, a DEA agent, took a rare picture of Escobar and Sandinista officers loading cocaine into an airplane. A few weeks later Oliver North, on the staff of the U.S. National Security Council, leaked the photo to American newspapers, hoping that the evidence on links between the drug cartel and the Sandinistas would encourage Congress to vote in favor of aid to the contras. The disclosure of the photo ruined the covert operation and the chance to indict Escobar and his allies. Noriega thus understood that the United States cared more about fighting the contras than about waging war against drugs.

Thus, during the first two years of Noriega's rule, the United States ignored his criminal activities and abuses of the political process in Panama. The U.S. messages may have shaped a belief system that encouraged Noriega to continue the same policies and may have distorted his ability to correctly interpret further U.S. reactions to his behavior. This phenomenon was clearly visible in five American–Panamanian crises.

CRISIS 1: THE MURDER OF HUGO SPADAFORA

Dr. Hugo Spadafora was a physician but also a romantic revolutionary, a guerrilla fighter, and a political activist. He first confronted Noriega and accused him of illegal activities when both were serving in General Torrijos's government. In September 1985, Spadafora announced that he would expose Noriega's involve-

---

[9] Scranton, *The Noriega Years*, 75–77; Buckley, *Panama: the Whole Story*, 74.
[10] Details about the operation appeared in Buckley, *Panama: the Whole Story*, 59–60.

ment in drug trafficking and arms smuggling.[11] But before he could reveal his evidence, he was captured, severely tortured, and murdered in a manner intended to send a message to Noriega's opponents. His body was found decapitated, a punishment reserved for traitors.[12]

The brutal murder of Spadafora created a crisis in Panama. The media, the Spadafora family, and leaders of the opposition demanded an immediate investigation and punishment of the murderers. Noriega and the PDF were the obvious prime suspects, but they had the power to block any attempt to discover the truth about the murder. President Barletta condemned the murder and insisted on investigating the case, but Noriega forced him to resign. Elliot Abrams, the new assistant secretary of state for Inter-American Affairs, encouraged Barletta to stand firm.[13] Despite his effort, Barletta announced his resignation and was replaced by Vice President Eric Delvalle.

Spadafora's murder and Barletta's dismissal concerned the State Department, but Abrams thought that a tough American message would modify Noriega's behavior. Therefore, U.S. embassy officials visited the offices of *La Prensa*, the local newspaper that had implicated Noriega and the PDF in the murder, and received members of the Spadafora family. The U.S. ambassador in Panama, Everett Briggs, also declared in a public speech that true democracy requires supremacy of civilian authority over the military.[14] Later, in a highly symbolic measure, the Department of State diverted $14 million in aid from Panama to Guatemala, where a new civilian president had just taken office.[15]

At the same time, however, the CIA and the DEA continued to view Noriega as a vital asset and sent him the opposite message. CIA Director William Casey summoned Noriega, still on the CIA payroll, to a meeting on 1 November 1985 in the CIA headquarters. The State Department expected Casey, whom Noriega highly respected, to warn him. Casey, however, did not raise any of the disturbing questions about the Spadafora murder and the forced resignation of Barletta, and even assured Noriega that the Reagan administration would continue to support him.[16] The DEA also continued to send Noriega thank-you letters for his cooperation in drug enforcement efforts.[17]

A few weeks later, the White House and the State Department attempted to correct the positive messages the CIA and the DEA had delivered to Noriega. In mid-December, new National Security Adviser, Admiral John Poindexter, Elliot Abrams, and other U.S. officials met Noriega in Panama. Poindexter criticized Noriega for his illegal activities and "PDF brutality," a coded reference to the murder of Spadafora. Noriega denied all the charges, however. Poindexter

[11] Kempe, *Divorcing the Dictator*, 126–142.

[12] Buckley, *Panama: The Whole Story*, 27.

[13] Ibid., 34.

[14] Scranton, *The Noriega Years*, 89–91.

[15] Buckley, *Panama: The Whole Story*, 46.

[16] Kempe, *Divorcing the Dictator*, 169–170.

[17] David N. Miller, "Panama and U.S. Policy," *Global Affairs* 4 (Summer 1989): 139.

did not press him any further and chose not to warn him.[18] Noriega manipulated the meeting, and the State Department plan to send him a tough message did not materialize.

Bureaucratic infighting, mainly among the State Department, CIA, and DEA, produced a mixed message. This allowed Noriega to conclude that his status in Washington was well protected. He believed that he had only a few opponents in the State Department who did not realize the valuable contributions he had made to U.S. interests and that his friends in the CIA and DOD would defend and protect him against these opponents.

CRISIS 2: THE HERRERA CONFESSIONS

According to an internal secret plan signed after the death of Torrijos, Noriega was supposed to retire in 1987, when his deputy, Colonel Roberto Diaz Herrera, was supposed to replace him as PDF commander. However on 5 June 1987, Noriega announced that he would remain PDF commander for another five years and assigned Diaz Herrera to an unattractive diplomatic position, leaving him bitter and frustrated. The next day Diaz Herrera retaliated against Noriega by publicly revealing details about Noriega's crimes.[19] He accused him of orchestrating the murder of Spadafora and rigging the 1984 elections. He even blamed Noriega for the death of Torrijos in a 1981 mysterious plane crash, claiming that Noriega had placed a bomb in his plane.

Herrera's charges inspired massive protests against the government. On 8 June 1987, nearly 100,000 people, close to a fourth of the population of Panama City, demonstrated against Noriega. The opposition formed a new coalition and demanded the immediate resignation of Noriega and other individuals named by Diaz Herrera. Demonstrations and strikes continued for several weeks in both cities and rural areas. Noriega responded by charging Diaz Herrera with treason and by cracking down hard on the demonstrators, destroying and damaging property belonging to political opponents and shutting down the media.

On 26 June 1987, the U.S. Senate approved a nonbinding resolution by an overwhelming vote of 84 to 2 (S. Res. 239) calling upon Noriega and his principal officers to step down pending a "public accounting" of Herrera's charges. Noriega struck back by sending government workers to demonstrate near the American Embassy. The demonstration turned into a riot, with workers throwing rocks,

---

[18] Seymour Hersh, "Panama Strongman Said to Trade in Drugs, Arms and Illicit Money," *New York Times*, 12 June 1986; Buckley, *Panama: The Whole Story*, 46. According to one source, at this meeting Poindexter may have tried to convince Noriega to train the contras in Panama. This could explain Poindexter's reluctance to deliver Noriega a tougher message. John Weeks and Andrew Zimbalist, "The Failure of Intervention in Panama: Humiliation in the Backyard," *Third World Quarterly* 11 (January 1989): 14.

[19] John Dinges, *Our Man in Panama, The Shrewd Rise and Brutal Fall of Manuel Noriega* (New York: Random House, 1991), 265; Scranton, *The Noriega Years*, 107–108; Kempe, *Divorcing the Dictator*, 212.

smashing windows, and overturning and damaging employees' cars. This incident reminded Shultz of the 1979 Iranian attack on the American Embassy in Teheran, and it led him to tell Arthur Davis, the U.S. ambassador in Panama: "If that's the kind of relationship they [Noriega and the PDF] want, that's the kind of relationship they'll get."[20] Shultz quickly clarified what he meant by a new kind of relationship. The State Department suspended military aid to Panama, the DOD reduced military contacts between the U.S. Southern Command (SOUTH-COM) and the PDF, and, most importantly, the CIA removed Noriega from its payroll. The real U.S. goal, however, was to remove Noriega from power either by negotiating his resignation or by encouraging a PDF coup against him.

In a speech given to the World Affairs Council in Washington on 30 June 1987, Elliot Abrams called on the PDF leaders to "remove their institution from politics, end any appearance of corruption, and modernize their forces to carry out their large and important military tasks." Abrams's aides explained to reporters beforehand that "corruption" referred to Noriega's involvement in drug trafficking and that the rest of the statement was intended to encourage the PDF to remove Noriega from its ranks.[21] On 2 July the *Washington Post* reported on the speech with the explanations and clarifications of the code terms and the intended messages.

Between August and December 1987, the United States also used three negotiating channels to present Noriega with several plans and deals for his resignation. The first channel involved Jose Blandon, the Panamian consul general in New York, who was a close associate of Noriega. The second channel was initiated by Noriega, who invited retired Admiral Daniel J. Murphy to meet with him in Panama in August and November 1987. Finally, on 30 December 1987, Richard Armitage, assistant secretary of defense for International Security Affairs, met with Noriega in Panama.

The first channel produced the Blandon Plan, which called for the retirement of Noriega and his inner circle of PDF officers by April 1988 at the latest, the establishment of a transition regime under President Delvalle that would rule the state until the May 1989 elections, an independent media, and the resumption of U.S. aid.[22] The circumstances behind the Murphy mission are still in dispute. Prior to his retirement in 1985, Murphy held important governmental positions including chief of staff to Vice President George Bush. It is not yet clear whether this was a private mission or another unofficial channel for communications and negotiations.[23] In any case, Noriega acted as if Murphy represented the official American position. Murphy repeated the Blandon terms but revised one critical component—the time-table. Murphy told Noriega he had until the May 1989 elections to resign. Noriega concluded that the American timetable was not as

---

[20] Cited in Kempe, *Divorcing the Dictator*, 223. Also see Miller, "Panama and U.S. Policy," 140.
[21] Buckley, *Panama: The Whole Story*, 90.
[22] Scranton, *The Noriega Years*, 118–119.
[23] Buckley, *Panama: The Whole Story*, 106–108.

tough as Blandon had originally presented. On 21 December 1987, Noriega rejected the Blandon Plan and a few weeks later fired Blandon.[24] Blandon then accused Murphy of undermining his plan by giving Noriega extra time to depart.

On 30 December 1987, Armitage went to Panama to send Noriega a "tough" message and to tell him that all the branches of the Reagan administration had adopted a unified position seeking his departure. Armitage may have offered Noriega an incentive to resign, such as agreeing to stop the investigation into his drug trafficking activities.[25] It is not clear, however, whether Armitage carried out this mission. The press briefings in Washington on the meeting conveyed a tough American stand, but according to one source, "Armitage never asked Noriega to leave."[26] Even if he did, the message became blurred when Noriega and Armitage appeared before PDF officers laughing and drinking Old Parr scotch together.[27]

Why did all these negotiating channels between the United States and Noriega fail to resolve the crisis? The main problem was that there were too many different channels transmitting too many confusing messages, causing Noriega to believe there was a split in the Reagan administration over his removal. He may also have thought that as the U.S. terms got better for him, time was on his side. He may have rejected deals offered to him, hoping at every point in time that a new deal would provide him with more concessions and better conditions. However, it is also probable that he only wanted to confuse and frustrate the United States and never had any intention of negotiating a settlement. The United States should have taken such motivation into consideration and should have used more aggressive bargaining techniques to uncover Noriega's real intentions.

CRISIS 3: THE FLORIDA INDICTMENTS

The next major crisis in the continuing saga erupted in February 1988, when Noriega was indicted by two federal grand juries in Miami and Tampa.[28] The Miami indictment included twelve counts of racketeering, drug trafficking, and money laundering. More specifically, it accused Noriega of assisting the Colombian Medellin cartel in transporting more than two tons of cocaine to the United States via Panama in return for a payment of about $4.5 million. He was also accused of allowing the cartel to build a cocaine processing plant in Panama and of providing shelter for drug traffickers. The Tampa grand jury charged Noriega on three counts of assisting American-based operatives to smuggle 1.4 million

---

[24] See "Panamanian Chief Dismisses Aide Seeking Political Deal," *New York Times*, 19 January 1988.

[25] Robinson, *Intervention or Neglect*, 114; Scranton, *The Noriega Years*, 126–127.

[26] Buckley, *Panama: The Whole Story*, 112.

[27] Dinges, *Our Man in Panama*, 288; Kempe, *Divorcing the Dictator*, 233.

[28] See Philip Shenon, "Noriega Indicted by U.S. for Links to Illegal Drugs," *New York Times*, 6 February 1988.

pounds of marijuana into the United States in return for a payment of more than $1 million.

The indictments exposed a major breakdown in Reagan's foreign policy making. Clearly, indicting any foreign leader, especially indicting the leader of a close ally for drug trafficking, should have been carried out in close consultation with the White House and the State Department. The Justice Department, however, acted as if this was a domestic case. Despite the obvious significance of the indictments, Reagan and Shultz learned about them only after the fact.[29] It was clear that the indictments would create an entirely new situation in the Noriega continuing crisis, but the administration was surprised and unprepared to deal with this situation.

The public disclosure of Noriega's involvement in drug trafficking was an embarrassment for the United States. It became clear that U.S. officials had tolerated these activities at a time when antidrug sentiment was at an all time high.[30] Because public concern about drugs was so prominent, "the [U.S.] Government could not afford to be seen as coddling a dictator-druglord after its own courts called for his prosecution."[31]

The indictments created a new crisis in Panama. After days of hesitating, President Delvalle finally fired Noriega on 25 February 1988 and appointed Colonel Marcos Justines as the new PDF commander. But the attempt to dismiss Noriega failed. Immediately after he was fired, Noriega restricted Delvalle to his home, cut his telephone lines, closed the independent print and electronic media, and ordered the PDF to disperse demonstrators. Justines remained loyal to Noriega and refused to assume the commander position. Under Noriega's instructions, the National Assembly voted to oust Delvalle and replace him with the education minister.

The United States had hoped a popular uprising would support Delvalle over Noriega, but one never developed. The administration denounced the ouster of Delvalle, recognized him as Panama's legitimate leader, and brought him to the United States. But this was not enough; the Reagan administration had to devise alternative means to remove Noriega. Throughout 1988 the Reagan administration encouraged a PDF coup, offered Noriega deals in return for his resignation, imposed sanctions on Panama, authorized covert actions against him, dispatched additional forces to the U.S. bases in Panama, and debated a military intervention to capture Noriega.

On 16 March 1988, Panamanian Chief of Police, Colonel Leonidas Macias, organized a coup against Noriega. The coup failed, however, either because of bad planning or because some coup participants double-crossed their leaders and

---

[29] Shultz, *Turmoil and Triumph*, 1052; Kempe, *Divorcing the Dictator*, 250.

[30] In July 1988, 27 percent of the respondents to a Gallup poll named drugs as the most important problem facing the country – greater than the percentage of respondents who cited all economic problems combined (24 percent).

[31] Linda Robinson, "Dwindling Options in Panama," *Foreign Affairs* 68 (Winter 1989–1990): 192.

informed Noriega of the plot. Despite this outcome, the Reagan administration continued to encourage the PDF to topple Noriega. On 22 March 1988, the White House issued the following statement: "The United States favors the integrity of the PDF as a professional military institution, and we look forward to the PDF playing an important and constructive role under a civilian regime."[32] In this statement, the United States distinguished again between the PDF and Noriega, promising to preserve the PDF if it removed Noriega and obeyed civilian authority.

Because of Macias's failure, it was unlikely that another PDF coup would be attempted in the near future. Since other means had been unsuccessful in persuading Noriega to retire and congressional and public pressure to remove him was mounting, administration officials raised and debated the military option. White House spokesperson Marlin Fitzwater indirectly acknowledged this when he said on 29 March 1988 that the United States was now "willing to take a look at all the hard options."[33] On 25 April, however, Treasury Secretary Jim Baker said, "There are other things that you can do but they all involve putting our military assets into play, and we're not going to do that."[34]

The Reagan administration was split on the military option. The State Department supported military intervention but Defense and the Joint Chiefs of Staff (JCS) opposed it. In March 1988, Elliot Abrams suggested a limited use of force — a commando raid to capture Noriega and to bring him to trial in the United States, accompanied by 6,000 American soldiers to defend Delvalle against any PDF retaliations. But the Pentagon raised many practical and legal questions about such an operation. JCS Chairman William Crowe was concerned that the PDF might take American hostages. Others pointed to casualties and operational difficulties with any "Rambo"-type commando raid. One officer even raised legal and moral issues: "Kidnapping is a crime. Under what international law would you have us do that?" he asked.[35]

Abrams thought that the Pentagon was doing its best to avoid using force and considered the obstacles raised by officers ridiculous.[36] He considered Pentagon opposition an example of the Vietnam Syndrome, namely fear of the consequences of what could become an unpopular intervention. Senior military officers also invoked the Vietnam War experience to criticize their opponent. They viewed Abrams as a civilian official who too enthusiastically suggested and advocated

---

[32] Cited in Scranton, *The Noriega Years*, 146.

[33] Bill McAllister, "US Patience Not Unlimited Noriega Warned," *Washington Post*, 30 March 1988.

[34] The statement was published without specific attribution, Peter Kilborn, "U.S. Preparing to Relax Some Panama Sanctions," *New York Times*, 26 April 1988. Shultz revealed that Baker made the statement in a background briefing, *Turmoil and Triumph*, 1057.

[35] Buckley, *Panama: The Whole Story*, 138–139.

[36] Bob Woodward, *The Commanders* (New York: Simon and Schuster, 1991), 84–86.

violence with little understanding of the consequences.[37] Fearing that Reagan would somehow adopt the Abrams strategy, the Pentagon mounted a public attack on Abrams, including leaking some of his "harebrained" ideas to the press.

A similar debate over military action in Panama also took place in Congress. Speaker of the House Jim Wright, for example, said that "obviously we don't want to go [to Panama] with the force of military arms—that's ridiculous."[38] But in a telephone conversation with Reagan's new Secretary of Defense Frank Carlucci, Senator Alfonse D'Amato accused the Department of Defense and the JCS of being "cowards" for their lack of military decisiveness in Panama.[39] After Carlucci had sent him a letter of protest, D'Amato claimed he had been misunderstood, but he still continued to favor the use of force in Panama.[40] Noriega could have concluded that the split in the administration and Congress was too wide for U.S. military action to be employed.

Since Reagan rejected military intervention, his administration tried again to negotiate a deal with Noriega.[41] In March 1988, Deputy Assistant Secretary of State Michael Kozak offered Noriega a chance to retire on 12 August 1988, the fifth anniversary of his command, and to take a long vacation abroad, at least until after the May 1989 elections in Panama. In return, the United States would agree to drop the Florida indictments. On 11 May 1988 the White House officially announced that if Noriega retired, the indictments would be dropped.[42] The announcement drew severe criticism from Congress and also from Vice President Bush, who publicly opposed the negotiations and the proposed deal with Noriega.[43] Bush was then in the middle of his presidential campaign and for him, "the prospect of letting a drug-dealing dictator out of the indictment looked like political suicide."[44] On 17 May the Senate passed a nonbinding amendment to the 1989 Defense Authorization Bill that read: "No negotiations should be conducted, nor arrangement made by the United States Government with Noriega, which would involve the dropping of the drug-related indictments against him." The amendment passed by a vote of 86 to 10.[45] Although Senate Minority Leader Robert Dole thought that Noriega should be removed from power, Dole

[37] Interesting details about the debate between Abrams and the military were revealed more than a year later in an exchange of op-ed articles Abrams and Crow published in the *New York Times*, respectively on 3 and 16 October 1989.

[38] Cited in Scranton, *The Noriega Years*, 147.

[39] Buckley, *Panama: The Whole Story*, 137.

[40] See his criticism of a *Washington Post* editorial, published in the same paper on 13 August 1988.

[41] See Shultz, *Turmoil and Triumph*, 1062–1079.

[42] Joe Pichirallo, "Noriega Given Offer to Drop Drug Charges," *Washington Post*, 12 May 1988.

[43] David Hoffman, "Bush Splits with Reagan on Handling of Noriega," *Washington Post*, 19 May 1988.

[44] Thomas Donnelly, Margaret Roth, and Caleb Baker, *Operation Just Cause, The Storming of Panama* (New York: Lexington Books, 1991), 35. Also see Michael L. Conniff, *Panama and the United States: The Forced Alliance* (Athens: The University of Georgia Press, 1992), 158–159.

[45] Lou Canon and Helen Dewar, "Senate Opposes Ending Noriega Case," *Washington Post*, 18 May 1988.

defended the amendment by arguing that the United States should not "send him off with a legal golden parachute."[46]

Despite this criticism, Reagan did not back off and approved the deal. In several stormy policy sessions, Reagan argued that the only alternative to get Noriega out of power was the use of force and he opposed this option.[47] The diplomatic effort, however, failed to produce an agreement. Reagan and Shultz let Noriega know that the deal must be concluded by 25 May. That was the day they were scheduled to travel to Moscow for an important summit with Mikhail Gorbachev. Hours before the expiration of the deadline, Noriega accepted the deal but wanted two weeks to persuade PDF officers to accept it as well. Shultz, who delayed his travel to Moscow, decided to withdraw the U.S. offer.

Even before the failure of this round of negotiations, the United States imposed harsh economic sanctions against Panama.[48] The sanctions consisted of freezing Panamanian assets in the United States, suspending canal payments to the Panamanian government, revoking Panama's most favored trade status, and banning all payments from American individuals and companies. The main purpose of the sanctions was to erode Noriega's base of support, primarily in the PDF and among government officials. The idea was to squeeze him financially to the point where he could no longer pay the salaries of his own loyalists so that they would turn against him. In addition, the sanctions were expected to hurt the Panamanian people, who would then blame Noriega for their hardship and demand his resignation. Finally, the sanctions were intended to provide the American negotiators with additional leverage against Noriega.

The sanctions did in fact succeed in damaging Panama's economy; Noriega failed to meet his financial obligations to the PDF and government workers. Reagan's new National Security Adviser Colin Powell said that the sanctions were having a "telling effect."[49] Elliot Abrams declared that Noriega was "clinging to power by his fingertips."[50] But the pressure was not strong enough to bring Noriega down. The Treasury Department made too many exceptions to the sanctions, which helped mostly Noriega and his supporters. Thus, "the sanctions were the economic equivalent of the neutron bomb: they destroyed the economy but left the leader standing."[51] Once again, the United States underestimated Noriega's remarkable survival power.

In crisis situations, states sometimes use armed forces for political purposes. They mobilize and deploy military forces and conduct military exercises in order

---

[46] Helen Dewar, "Dole Warns against Dropping Noriega Case," *Washington Post*, 17 May 1988.

[47] Shultz, *Turmoil and Triumph*, 1070–1079.

[48] Robinson, *Intervention or Neglect*, 117–119; Scranton, *The Noriega Years*, 132–140.

[49] Lou Canon, "Anti-Noriega Sanctions Are Having 'Telling Effect,'" *Washington Post*, 6 April 1988.

[50] Robert Pear and Neil Lewis, "The Noriega Fiasco," *New York Times*, 30 May 1988.

[51] Larry Berman and Bruce Jentleson, "Bush and the Post-Cold War: New Challenges for American Leadership" in Colin Campbell and Bert Rockman, eds. *The Bush Presidency First Appraisals* (Chatham, NJ: Chatham House, 1991), 110.

to scare opponents and make them do things that they would otherwise not do.[52] The political use of force can be effective only if an opponent understands the message and believes the threat is genuine. The United States already had bases and forces in Panama. The political use of force in this case, therefore, meant the redeploying of existing forces, dispatching additional troops, and carrying out exceptional military exercises.

In March 1988 the Reagan administration considered dispatching additional troops to bases in Panama to send a message to Noriega. SOUTHCOM chief, General Frederick Woerner, opposed this step, because he knew that Noriega would think that the United States was merely bluffing and did not intend to intervene at this time. Because he felt that Reagan did not seriously intend to launch a military action, Woerner said the policy was not credible and would not achieve its goal.[53] Despite Woerner's objections, Reagan decided to send approximately 1,300 troops to Panama on 6 April 1988. Woerner was right. If the purpose of the dispatch was to scare Noriega, it failed. Noriega was unmoved and did not alter his defiant behavior.

In addition to all of the preceding means, the United States conducted covert operations to remove Noriega. Very little information is available on the first two operations—Panama 1 and Panama 2.[54] In July 1988, Reagan authorized Panama 3 to help Eduardo Herrera Hassan, an exiled rival of Noriega, mount a coup. The CIA presented the plan to the Senate Select Committee on Intelligence on 26 July 1988. The next day, the *Washington Post* published an article ironically titled "Covert Action on Noriega Is Cleared." The White House accused the committee of leaking information about the plan. The committee, in turn, accused the White House of doing the same thing.[55] The White House may have wanted to discredit the committee as part of a debate over the right of Congress to receive information about any covert operation plan in advance. Regardless of who leaked the information, the publication of the story killed the operation.

All the efforts of the Reagan administration to remove Noriega failed, mainly because of bureaucratic infighting, which resulted in the United States sending confusing messages. Shultz commented that the outcome of the negotiations "could well have been different if President Reagan had been supported in his decisions and if the execution of his decisions had been firm and accelerated.[56] Credible military threats could have affected Noriega's behavior and, perhaps, even his willingness to accept one of the deals offered to him. But Reagan ruled out military intervention, and the other methods the United States used to try to remove Noriega were ineffective. However, Bush's victory in the 1988 presidential elections created an opportunity to develop new ideas to deal with Noriega.

---

[52] Philip Zelikow, "The U.S. and the Use of Force: A Historical Summary" in George Osborn et al., *Democracy, Strategy and Vietnam* (Lexington, MA: Lexington Books, 1987), 31–81.

[53] Buckley, *Panama: The Whole Story*, 139.

[54] Scranton, *The Noriega Years*, 152–158.

[55] *Washington Post*, 29 July 1988.

[56] Shultz, *Turmoil and Triumph*, 1079.

CRISIS 4: THE ELECTIONS IN PANAMA

Reagan and Bush held different opinions about Noriega. One of Bush's main themes in the 1988 presidential campaign was the War against Drugs. Bush, therefore, strongly opposed a deal with Noriega that would result in dropping the charges against him. Thus, Bush ruled out the deal favored by Reagan. Compared to Reagan, Bush's leadership image was much weaker, and he was more vulnerable to Noriega's provocations. On the other hand, with the changes in the makeup of his cabinet, Bush had the opportunity to impose one clear strategy on the various branches of his government. From the beginning of his term when referring to Noriega, he used tough language and set the stage for a major confrontation with the Panamanian leader.

On 22 December 1988, after a meeting with Reagan and Delvalle, Bush's spokesperson said: "There must be no misunderstanding about our policy. . . . Noriega must go."[57] Bush hoped Noriega would be defeated in the May 1989 elections in Panama, as this would have been an exclusively Panamanian solution to the long conflict. However, the Bush administration was concerned with two problems: the ability of the Panamanian opposition to mount a serious campaign against Noriega and the PDF's possible falsification of the election results. Bush decided upon measures to deal with both problems. First, Bush approved a new covert plan (Panama 4) to help the Panamanian opposition; and second, he encouraged many individuals and organizations to monitor the elections in Panama.

After much deliberation and Bush's personal pleading, Congress approved Panama 4 and allocated $10 million to cover opposition expenses for printing materials, advertisements, transportation, and communication.[58] However, the operation was hindered by failures and setbacks. About a month before the election, Noriega captured a CIA operative who was using some of this $10 million allocation to run a clandestine anti-Noriega radio network.[59] Shortly afterward, Carlos Eleta Alamaran, a Panamanian entrusted by the CIA to distribute the rest of the $10 million to the opposition, was arrested in the United States and charged with a conspiracy to import cocaine.[60] The case showed both deficiencies in the selection of agents and a complete lack of coordination between the CIA and drug enforcement agencies.

Recalling how Noriega rigged the 1984 elections, American officials made an effort to prevent fraud by calling for various organizations and monitoring groups to send observers to Panama. Former President Jimmy Carter led one of these teams. Yet, the monitoring teams did not deter Noriega and the PDF from rigging the elections. According to the official results, Noriega's candidate, Carlos Duque, won the elections by a 2 to 1 margin. Exit polls conducted on

---

[57] Bill McAllister, "Bush Vows to Press Noriega," *Washington Post,* 23 December 1988.
[58] AP Report, "Bush Directs Noriega Foes," *Washington Post,* 23 April 1989.
[59] Buckley, *Panama: The Whole Story,* 176.
[60] Scranton, *The Noriega Years,* 158.

election day, however, revealed a clear victory for the opposition: 55.1 percent for Guillermo Endara compared to 39.5 percent for Duque.[61] An exit poll conducted by the Catholic Bishops Conference found an even larger margin of about 3 to 1 in favor of Endara. The PDF managed to "win" the election by seizing ballot boxes, destroying tally sheets, and manipulating the counting process. All the observer teams agreed that the elections were fraudulent. Jimmy Carter accused Noriega of "robbing the people of Panama of their legitimate rights." Carter said he hoped there would be a "worldwide outcry of condemnation against a dictator who stole this election from his own people."[62]

Noriega's response to international criticism of the election process was to nullify the elections and appoint one of his high school classmates to serve as provisional president. This led to mass protests, which were violently put down by Noriega's paramilitary squads called Dignity Battalions. Television cameras worldwide showed Noriega's men brutally beating up Endara and his running mates—Ricardo Arias Calderon and Guillermo "Billy" Ford. The beatings were broadcast repeatedly on American television, and "the image of the white-haired Ford, robbed of his elected post, bloodied and temporarily blinded, became an instant symbol of the state of lawlessness and chaos in Panama."[63]

On 11 May 1989, Bush made a major statement on the situation in Panama and announced a seven-point plan designed to remove Noriega through a combination of threats and incentives.[64] In the introduction to the plan, Bush characterized the crisis as "a conflict between Noriega and the people of Panama, with the United States siding with the people." He indicated to the PDF that the United States hoped it would stand with the people and defend democracy. By ousting Noriega, Bush implied, the PDF "could have an important role to play in Panama's democratic future." This was again, not only a call for a PDF coup, but an attempt to separate Noriega from the PDF.

Then Bush announced seven specific measures:

- *Regional Diplomacy.* Supporting and cooperating with initiatives taken by OAS members to address the crisis.
- *Diplomatic Sanctions.* Recalling U.S. Ambassador Arthur Davis from Panama and reducing embassy staff to essential personnel only.
- *Safety Measures.* Relocating U.S. government employees and their dependents living outside of U.S. military bases or Panama Canal Commission housing areas, either to areas outside of Panama or to secure U.S. housing areas.
- *Safety and Preventive Measures.* Encouraging U.S. businessmen in Panama to send their dependents back to the United States.

---

[61] Ibid., 161.

[62] Lindsey Gruson, "Noriega Stealing Election," *New York Times*, 9 May 1989.

[63] Woodward, *The Commanders*, 84.

[64] *Public Papers of the Presidents of the United States: George Bush, 1989*, Book 1 (Washington, DC: U.S. Government Printing Office, 1990), 536–537.

- *Economic Sanctions.* Continuing economic sanctions.
- *Panama Canal Treaties.* Affirming U.S. obligations and enforcing U.S. rights under the Panama Canal Treaties;
- *Military Actions.* Dispatching a brigade-size force (between 1,700 and 2,000 soldiers) to augment military forces already stationed in Panama.

Bush did not rule out further steps beyond these seven such as invasion, but said "an honorable solution" was still possible. The combination of a call for a PDF coup, the announcement of safety and preventive measures, and the dispatching of additional forces to Panama all raised speculations about U.S. military intervention, at least to support a coup. The administration, however, did not speak in one voice. On the same day that Bush announced his new strategy, Secretary of Defense Richard Cheney said on the *MacNeil–Lehrer Newshour* that U.S. troops would not intervene in Panama. The purpose of the troops, said Cheney, "is not to be involved with deciding who governs Panama." Moreover, DOD dispatched the troops slowly and again confused the intended message. The State Department wanted a quick show of force and the rapid dispatch of the additional forces, but Cheney slowed down the process.[65] He may have been influenced by Pentagon and JCS officials who opposed the action on the grounds that it could endanger American civilians living in Panama.

The change from Reagan to Bush did not correct the basic flaws in U.S. policy. Although Bush was more determined than Reagan to remove Noriega and was more willing to use force to achieve this goal, the results of his policy remained the same. Noriega continued to doubt the credibility of the American military threats and felt free to pursue his domestic abuses and to challenge the United States. Again, this happened mainly because of the continuing mixed and confusing messages coming from the administration.

CRISIS 5: THE GIROLDI COUP

On 1 October 1989, the wife of Moises Giroldi, a member of Noriega's inner circle who had crushed the 1988 Macias coup attempt, informed SOUTHCOM officers that her husband was planning a nonviolent coup against Noriega and that he wanted limited U.S. help.[66] She said her husband wanted the United States to block two roads and to provide sanctuary for her and her children. Cheney approved these requests and told SOUTHCOM they could arrest Noriega in case the rebels turned him over to the American forces in Panama.

Giroldi's coup took place on 3 October 1989. Mrs. Giroldi and her children were given shelter, and the U.S. forces blocked the two requested roads. For a few hours Noriega was a prisoner in the hands of Giroldi, who tried unsuccessfully

---

[65] Richard Halloran, "U.S. Troops to Go Slowly into Panama," *New York Times*, 12 May 1989.

[66] For details about the coup, see Scranton, *The Noriega Years*, 185–192; Buckley, *Panama: The Whole Story*, 197–218; Kempe, *Divorcing the Dictator*, 369–397.

to persuade him to retire. Apparently several rebel leaders, but not Giroldi, were then prepared to turn Noriega over to U.S. authorities. The rebels approached SOUTHCOM officers, but it was too late; Noriega was able to call for help from his special unit, Battalion 2000. This battalion used air transportation to circumvent the U.S. roadblocks and joined other Noriega loyalists in crushing the rebellion. When the original plan of blocking two roads did not work, the U.S. forces did nothing to prevent the loyalists from rescuing Noriega. Giroldi was severely tortured and killed as were several other coup leaders. Following this coup attempt, Noriega began to purge the PDF of dissident elements and to crack down even harder on civilian dissent. The PDF harassment of Americans intensified, and it became very dangerous for them to venture into downtown Panama City.

The American inaction during the coup raised a stormy debate in Washington. Congressional leaders from both parties, reporters and commentators, and even anonymous White House officials criticized the administration for missing an opportunity to capture Noriega and for failing to follow Bush's own strategy to encourage and help a PDF coup against Noriega. Senator Jesse Helms called the administration "a bunch of Keystone Kops" and bitterly predicted that, "after this, no member of the PDF can be expected to act against Noriega."[67]

Representative Les Aspin, then chairman of the House Armed Services Committee and later secretary of defense, said the United States should be "ready at any opportunity to use the confusion and the uncertainty of a coup attempt . . . to do something about Mr. Noriega." Others, such as Democratic Congressman Dave McCurdy, chairman of the House Select Committee on Intelligence, went so far as to ridicule Bush: "Yesterday makes Jimmy Carter look like a man of resolve. There's a resurgence of the wimp factor." Commentator George Will called the Bush administration "an unserious presidency," and Harry G. Summers, a highly respected military expert, wrote in his syndicated column: "Our national security decision-making process . . . was revealed to be in chaos."[68]

The administration countered the criticism by first denying prior knowledge of and involvement in the coup. It accused Giroldi of being as "mischievous" as Noriega and therefore did not deserve U.S. support. The administration also claimed that it did not miss an opportunity, since Giroldi had not intended to turn in Noriega anyway. And finally, senior officials used the casualty factor, suggesting that military intervention to save the coup would have been too costly. In a press conference held on 13 October 1989, Bush asserted that there was no inconsistency between his call for a PDF coup and his inaction during the Giroldi coup. He said he wanted to see Noriega thrown out of office and brought to

---

[67] David Hoffman and Ann Devroy, "U.S. Was Caught off Guard by Coup Attempt" and Molly Moore and Joe Pichirallo, "Cheney," *Washington Post*, 6 October 1989.

[68] David Hoffman and William Branigin, "Key Queries Never Put to Bush," *Washington Post*, 7 October 1989.

justice, but that did not mean the United States would support every coup against him.[69]

The official explanations for the U.S. inaction were quite confusing. The argument that Giroldi was no better than Noriega was particularly strange. Whom did the Bush administration think could or would strike against Noriega? The PDF leadership was brutal and corrupt, but Giroldi was relatively less corrupt than the others. If administration officials thought that he was unlikely to serve American interests in Panama, why then did they promise him assistance. And when the coup did occur, why did they give shelter to Giroldi's family and block certain roads?

American policy towards the Giroldi coup was chaotic and inconsistent. One of the main reasons for the confusion was a simultaneous change in two top military positions. Shortly before the coup, the JCS Chairman and the SOUTHCOM chief were replaced. On 30 September 1989, three days before the coup, General Maxwell Thurman replaced Woerner as SOUTHCOM chief. One day later, General Colin Powell took over the JCS chairmanship from Admiral Crowe. Crowe and Woerner opposed the use of American troops to solve the Noriega crisis.[70] Powell and Thurman were willing to use force under certain conditions, but felt that these conditions did not characterize the Giroldi coup.

Thurman suspected that Noriega was using Giroldi to set up a trap to undermine and destroy his credibility during his first days as SOUTHCOM Chief.[71] He knew Giroldi had been very loyal to Noriega, and he thought the coup operational plan was too simplistic with too many details left out.[72] In addition, the execution of the coup had been delayed twice. Thurman communicated his concerns to Powell, who reportedly said "getting rid of Noriega was something that had to be done on a U.S. timetable." Powell said he did not like the idea of "a half-baked coup with a half-baked coup leader."[73]

Powell wanted a coup with no direct American intervention, or at the most with some limited assistance such as blocking roads. He thought that if the United States decided to use force in Panama, the objective would have to change from merely capturing Noriega to destroying and replacing his entire regime.[74] Since Powell came to office only a few days before the coup, he did not have time to develop the idea and to persuade the president and the other branches of the national security bureaucracy to adopt it. The result was a highly confusing policy toward the coup.

The U.S. response to the Giroldi coup exposed a conceptual confusion in the administration's policy toward Noriega. Powell and Thurman adopted stra-

---

[69] David Hoffman, "Bush Attacks Critics of Response to Coup," *Washington Post*, 14 October 1989.
[70] Robinson, *Intervention or Neglect*, 126.
[71] Woodward, *The Commanders*, 120; Buckley, *Panama: The Whole Story*, 199.
[72] Donnelly, *Operation Just Cause*, 67.
[73] Woodward, *The Commanders*, 121.
[74] Donnelly, *Operation Just Cause*, 66; Scranton, *The Noriega Years*, 190.

tegic and tactical concepts that determined their interpretations of the coup and consequently their recommendation not to intervene. These concepts may have distorted their judgment of the coup. During the coup, Thurman did not know what was happening inside PDF headquarters. He did not check the facts on the ground, which contradicted his earlier negative perceptions of the coup and Giroldi. Senior officials in Washington, who depended on him for information and recommendations, consequently also did not know what was really happening.[75]

The U.S. response to the coup also dramatically revealed an enormous gap between Bush's rhetoric and action. In the eyes of the public, Giroldi had created an opportunity to remove Noriega that Bush had failed to seize. Despite his public defense of the inaction, Bush was clearly dissatisfied with the information and policy recommendations given to him during the coup. He reportedly said "amateur hour is over" and instructed his aides to review the handling of the crisis and to prepare better for the next challenge.[76] Indeed, this was an appropriate instruction, for it did not take long for a new challenge to emerge.

AMERICAN MILITARY INTERVENTION

At the end of 1989, the Noriega crisis assumed larger and more critical proportions. The public wanted Bush to fulfill his campaign promise to combat drugs. In his first nationally televised speech from the White House, delivered on 5 September 1989, Bush said: "All of us agree that the gravest domestic threat facing our nation today is drugs" and called the drug problem "the toughest domestic challenge we've faced in decades."[77] The controversial Giroldi coup occurred just a month later.

Despite the failure of the Giroldi coup, Bush continued to encourage this option through a new covert operation. This time, however, he wanted a change in the operational rules. American covert operations against individuals were limited by an executive order banning U.S. government involvement in assassinations.[78] In October 1989, after the failure of the Giroldi coup, Bush determined that planning an assassination would still be prohibited, but U.S. officials would not be prosecuted if a coup accidentally caused the death of the coup target. Bush then authorized Panama 5, a new covert operation to topple Noriega through another PDF coup. The CIA received a budget of $3 million and was granted greater freedom to use force, although it was still prohibited from directly assassinating Noriega.[79] However, Panama 5 was not implemented, because it was

---

[75] Terry Deibel, "Bush's Foreign Policy: Mastery and Inaction," *Foreign Policy* 84 (Fall 1991): 19.

[76] Woodward, *The Commanders*, 128.

[77] George Bush, "National Drug Control Strategy," *Vital Speeches of the Day*, vol. lv, no. 24 (1989): 738–740.

[78] Executive Order 12333 of the U.S. Intelligence Activities, 4 December 1981, *46 Federal Register*, 59941. Also see Mark Sullivan, "Panama: U.S. Policy After the May 1989 Elections," CRS Issue Brief IB89106 (Washington, DC: Congressional Research Service, Library of Congress, 1989), 12.

[79] See Scranton, *The Noriega Years*, 195; Buckley, *Panama: The Whole Story*, 221.

leaked to the media and articles about it were published in the middle of No-vember.[80]

Noriega continued to provoke the United States and particularly to harass the American armed forces in Panama. On 15 December 1989, the Panamanian National assembly appointed Noriega chief of the government and "maximum leader of national liberation." The assembly also declared Panama to be in a state of war with the United States. The departure of Noriega seemed to be delayed indefinitely. After the Giroldi fiasco, a PDF coup was unlikely, and Panamanians were tired and weak.

The United States interpreted the declaration of war as a license to harass Americans. Indeed, in the following days, there were several serious incidents between the PDF and the U.S. forces in Panama.[81] On 15 December, PDF soldiers stopped a U.S. military patrol car and held the police officer at gunpoint. On the next day, they fired at an American vehicle in a checkpoint and killed Marine Corps Lieutenant Robert Paz. A Navy lieutenant and his wife who witnessed the shooting were arrested and beaten. The woman was also sexually assaulted. In a separate incident, other U.S. soldiers were detained at the airport and their weapons were taken. One day later, on the morning of 17 December, a U.S. officer shot a PDF policeman, thinking the Panamanian was reaching for his weapon.

Noriega's continuing rule in Panama and the new provocations created a personal problem for Bush, because they validated his wimp image. He used tough language against Noriega and made him the number one public enemy of the United States. Still it appeared that Bush was doing little to force him out of office. The gap between words and actions became too wide and Bush's own credibility was put on the line. This came at the worst possible time for him. The international system was on the verge of a major structural transformation. The Soviet Union was already disintegrating, and the United States was about to become the sole remaining superpower. If the United States could not handle a low-level dictator in a country where it maintained bases and large forces, how would it be able to deal with far more serious international challenges? The stakes were high for Bush in Panama: the issue was no longer just Noriega, but Bush's ability to conduct the war on drugs, to promote democracy in Latin America, and to lead world affairs.

In a crucial policy meeting held on 17 December 1989, Bush asked his principal advisers if a limited snatching operation would be sufficient.[82] Powell advocated a large scale intervention whose goal would be to destroy the PDF and the entire Noriega regime and not just the capture of Noriega. His rationale was that it could be difficult to find Noriega and arrest him at the beginning of

---

[80] See, for example, the report published in the *Washington Post*, 17 November 1989.

[81] Donnelly, *Operation Just Cause*, 94–97; Scranton, *The Noriega Years*, 198–199.

[82] Woodward, *The Commanders*, 167–171; Donnelly, *Operation Just Cause*, 98–99; Buckley, *Panama: The Whole Story*, 228–233.

the operation, but destroying the PDF would ensure Noriega's capture. Powell also thought that the PDF's destruction would be required to establish democracy in Panama. Bush agreed and approved the plan for large-scale military intervention in Panama.

CONCLUSIONS

Noriega's conflict with the United States escalated from one crisis to another, and each crisis ended with an actual or symbolic victory for him. Each victory strengthened his position inside Panama and motivated him to challenge the United States even further. Following each victory, the United States had to use tougher measures, ending with the most extreme one of military intervention. The United States continually redefined the Noriega problem, which finally became an issue larger than just Noriega and Panama. At stake was Bush's image as a weak president, his ability to take the lead in world affairs and to fulfill his campaign promise to combat drug abuse in the United States. During the first crisis, the Reagan administration considered Noriega's contributions valuable enough to override any liabilities. The policy was to pressure him to modify his behavior through persuasion and warnings. After the indictments in Florida, however, the United States wanted to remove Noriega from his powerful position while keeping his PDF-controlled regime intact. But Bush's decision to use force, which entailed greater political and economic costs, again changed the U.S. objectives in Panama. The new goals were to remove Noriega from power, destroy his regime, and establish democracy in the country.

Initially, the United States cultivated a relationship with an unscrupulous leader in the name of a cause ostensibly larger than his liabilities. The greater cause was helping the contras overthrow the Sandinistas in Nicaragua. But by employing Noriega, the United States compromised the long-term, more fundamental American interests of stability, security, human rights, and democracy in Panama. U.S. officials ignored Noriega's criminal activities and for a long period of time let him believe he would be protected from prosecution and retaliation. Noriega thought that only a few State Department officials wanted him removed from power, and he considered his allies in the intelligence and the national security establishments more influential than the diplomats. It was difficult for both Noriega and his supporters to change their perceptions of each other. Noriega's supporters in Washington were slow to understand his growing threat to U.S. interests, and Noriega failed to notice the transformation of his status from an ally to an enemy.

Bureaucratic infighting and mixed signals reinforced Noriega's misperceptions. This fighting, particularly inside the White House and between the State Department, CIA and DOD, was often leaked to the press and received wide attention. The internal feuds were responsible for many of the confusing signals. Reagan was unable to prevent the competing branches of his administration from supporting different strategies toward Noriega, who assumed the split would prevent the administration from using extreme measures against him, especially the use of force. The split in Congress and congressional disagreements with the White House also reinforced Noriega's misperceptions.

U.S. policies and threats in the Noriega crisis lacked credibility, which was one of the major factors in the escalation that led to the U.S. invasion. The United States preferred a Panamanian solution to the Noriega problem—a PDF coup or a popular uprising. American officials, including Bush, encouraged PDF officers and the people to remove Noriega, implying that the United States would help the Panamanians once they initiated such an action. But when the Giroldi coup took place, the United States did very little to help. Similarly, when Noriega brutally suppressed public demonstrations, the United States did very little to support the people.

On several occasions the United States dispatched forces to Panama and conducted military exercises. The main purpose of these actions was to send Noriega a message. However, in the absence of true intention to use force against Noriega, these actions only reenforced Noriega's belief that the United States was bluffing. The growing gap between the tough rhetoric and the meager action exposed the Bush administration to charges of weakness and impotence, which eventually contributed to Bush's decision to use force.

Noriega negotiated several times with various American and OAS officials. These officials assumed that Noriega was willing to resign if he was offered appropriate incentives. It is also probable that he never intended to step down regardless of the incentives and that he was just using the negotiations to play for time and to further embarrass the United States. Resignation could have meant death for him. Out of power, he could have become a target for drug-lords and other criminals whom he had double-crossed over the years. This may have been why he rejected all the deals offered to him. American policy makers should have examined realistically the potential to achieve an agreement through negotiations and revised their strategy accordingly.

The way in which the United States handled the Noriega affair was not an isolated case in how the United States has managed international crises in recent years. Several critical issues and mistakes made in this confrontation reappeared in subsequent international crises, most noticeably in the 1990–1991 Gulf crisis and war.[83] Like Noriega, Iraq's Saddam Hussein did not believe the United States

---

[83] For sources on the Gulf War, see Laurie Mylroie, "Why Saddam Hussein Invaded Kuwait," *Orbis* (Winter 1993): 123–134; Woodward, *The Commanders*, Part Two; Lawrence Freedman and Efraim Karsh, *The Gulf Conflict, 1990–1991* (London: Faber and Faber, 1993); Joseph Nye, Jr. and Roger Smith, eds., *After the Storm: Lessons from the Gulf War* (Lanham, MD: Madison Books, 1992); U.S. News and World Report, *Triumph Without Victory: The Unreported History of the Persian Gulf War* (New York: Times Books, 1992); Stephen Graubard, *Mr. Bush's War* (New York: Hill and Wang, 1992); Robert Tucker and David Hendrickson, *The Imperial Temptation: The New World Order and America's Purpose* (New York: Council on Foreign Relations Press, 1992); Elaine Sciolino, *The Outlaw State: Saddam Hussein's Quest for Power and the Gulf Crisis* (New York: John Wiley, 1991); David Scheffer, "Use of Force After the Cold War: Panama, Iraq, and the New World Order" in Louis Henkin, et al., *Right versus Might: International Law and the Use of Force* (New York: Council on Foreign Relations Press, 1991), 109–172.

would use force against him. Like Noriega, he received mixed and confusing messages from the United States, which led him to assume that he could take aggressive actions against the Iraqi opposition and neighboring states without risking a major confrontation with the United States. Indeed, as in the Noriega case, Washington considered Saddam a valuable ally serving a larger cause, in this case the battle against Iran's effort to spread Islamic fundamentalism in the Middle East.

Saddam attacked Teheran with Scud missiles in 1988, used chemical weapons against the Kurds, threatened Israel with the same weapons, and then threatened Kuwait before he invaded the country in 1990. The U.S. response was weak and confined to a few critical statements. Before the invasion, some congressional leaders recommended that the Bush administration impose sanctions against Saddam. Bush not only opposed this recommendation but even went on to provide Iraq with substantial loan guarantees and access to advanced technology. This policy might have encouraged Saddam to believe that the United States would issue verbal denunciations of the invasion but would not use force to roll back the Iraqi forces. Following the invasion, the Bush administration used the same means to deal with Saddam that it had employed against Noriega, including dispatching forces, imposing economic and diplomatic sanctions, negotiating with Saddam's representatives, and calling upon the Iraqi army and people to rebel against Saddam. But just as in the Noriega case, all these means failed to resolve the crisis peacefully.

After the damage of bureaucratic infighting and miscommunication was evident in the Panama and the Gulf crises, one would have expected American policy makers to have learned the appropriate lessons. Also, after two decisive and highly publicized demonstrations of American determination to use force against challenging dictators, leaders in conflict areas such as Bosnia and Somalia were expected to take U.S. threats of intervention more seriously. Yet, neither American policy makers nor the dictators were able to draw the proper lessons.

In the case of Bosnia, the White House, the military, and Congress all had different attitudes towards U.S. military intervention.[84] The military opposed any intervention in the Bosnian civil war, because it feared an endless large-scale ground war in a difficult mountainous terrain. Congress was split on this issue, while President Bill Clinton made a strong statement warning the Serbians that if they did not stop the systematic shelling of cities and towns, the United States would intervene to halt the fighting. Serbian leaders Radovan Karadzić and Slobodan Milošević were aware of the contradicting messages coming from Washington, which reenforced their belief that despite its rhetoric, the United States would not use force in Bosnia. The aggressors in Bosnia have felt free to continue

---

[84] On the crisis in Bosnia, see William Pfaff, "Invitation to War," *Foreign Affairs* 72 (Summer 1993): 97–109; Dusko Doder, "Yugoslavia; New War, Old Hatreds," *Foreign Policy* 91 (Summer 1993): 3–23; Sabrina Petra Ramet, "War in the Balkans," *Foreign Affairs* 70 (Fall 1992): 79–98; James Goodby, "Peacekeeping in the New Europe," *Washington Quarterly* 15 (September 1992): 153–171.

their indiscriminate attacks on noncombatants, and military intervention might still be the only way to stop the fighting. As in the Noriega and Saddam crises, internal disagreements and confusing American messages led the Serbian leaders to ignore U.S. warnings.

In the case of Somalia, the United States, as well as the United Nations, sent confusing messages to clan leader Mohammed Aideed, who was fighting other clan leaders over control of Somalia. U.S. troops had originally been sent to Somalia in December 1992 to stop the civil war and protect supply routes to hunger stricken areas.[85] In May 1993 most U.S. troops were withdrawn except for 1,400 soldiers who remained under UN control. After this withdrawal, the United States sent mixed messages to Aideed, who was not sure whether the Clinton administration wanted him as a legitimate participant in Somali peace negotiations or whether it wanted him captured and his forces destroyed. Aideed felt threatened but thought he could attack American and other troops from UN command without triggering a major U.S. response. But like Noriega and Saddam, he miscalculated. In October 1993, Aideed attacked U.S. troops, killing seventeen American soldiers. Clinton then ordered a counterattack and sent thousands of American troops back to Somalia.

The United States tried hard to resolve the post cold war crises through peaceful means. However, persuasion, warnings, negotiations, sanctions, and threats, all failed to convince Noriega to resign or Saddam to withdraw from Kuwait. These same means also failed to persuade Karadzić and Milošević to end the fighting in Bosnia, or Aideed to refrain from attacking U.S. forces in Somalia. Under certain circumstances, lengthy negotiations and moderate means may send the wrong signals to ruthless authoritarian leaders who play foreign policy games by their own rules. If the United States had delivered tougher and clearer messages early enough to Noriega, Saddam, and Aideed, it might have avoided using large-scale force against them, saving both lives and resources.*

[85] On the U.S. mission in Somalia, see Henry Kissinger, "Somalia: Reservations," *Washington Post*, 13 December 1992; Jonathan Stevenson, "Hope Restored in Somalia?" *Foreign Policy* 91 (Summer 1993): 138–154; Michael Elliott, "The Making of a Fiasco," *Newsweek*, 18 October 1993, 8–11; George Church, "Anatomy of a Disaster," *Time*, 18 October 1993, 40–50.

* I would like to thank Louis Goodman and Philip Brenner of the School of International Service, The American University in Washington, DC, Andrea Barron, Liesl Scullen, Michael Leib, and Nate Persily for their assistance in the preparation of this article.

"Disobedient" Generals and the Politics of Redemocratization: The Clinton Administration and Haiti

MORRIS MORLEY
CHRIS McGILLION

U.S. policy toward political transitions in postwar Latin America has centered around the goal of securing regime changes that ensure the continuity of the state. This is true of Republican and Democratic administrations under both conservative and liberal presidents. While issues of democracy and dictatorship have remained secondary, the task of preserving the institutions of the state (civil bureaucracies, judiciaries, military and police, etc.) have taken priority. The level of Washington's concern over challenges to the state has been incomparably greater than over changes in regime because the state, especially its coercive institutions, is perceived as the ultimate arbiter of power and guarantor of basic U.S. interests in these societies.

Consequently, Washington's policy toward the state in Latin America has remained constant; toward the regime it has been variable. Whether we are discussing Eisenhower policy toward Cuba, the Kennedy-Johnson approach toward the Dominican Republic and Brazil, Richard Nixon's hostility toward Allende's Chile, Jimmy Carter's policy toward Nicaragua and El Salvador, or Ronald Reagan's support for redemocratization in Guatemala, the thread that linked them all was a singular determination to preserve key state institutions

MORRIS MORLEY is an associate professor of politics at Macquarie University (Sydney, Australia) and a senior research fellow at the Council on Hemispheric Affairs, Washington, DC. He is the author of *Imperial State and Revolution: The United States and Cuba, 1952–1986* and *Washington, Somoza and the Sandinistas: State and Regime in the U.S. Policy toward Nicaragua, 1969–1981*. CHRIS McGIL-LION is the opinion page editor of the *Sydney Morning Herald* (Australia). He has written extensively on U.S.–Latin American relations and hemispheric politics for newspapers and journals in Australia, England, and the United States.

(not least, the armed forces) in the event of a political transition, together with a flexible approach regarding support for elected regimes or dictatorial rulers.

Moreover, given the willingness of U.S. governments to support such autocratic regimes as Fulgencio Batista in Cuba or Anastasio Somoza in Nicaragua over extended time periods in the absence of challenges to the regime or state, an abrupt policy change cannot be adequately explained by reference to a White House commitment to promoting or imposing democratic values. Rather, U.S. policy makers have interpreted a change from dictatorship to democratic regime, first and foremost, as a mechanism for preserving the state, not as a mode of promoting democratization and the values that accompany it.

Where state structures are threatened by broad-based social and political movements, Washington has sought to hive off those sectors compatible with the state and U.S. interests and promote a political settlement in which electoral processes are incorporated within the "old" state; where such movements achieve power and signal their intention to change state structures, Washington has traditionally moved to apply pressure on these nationalist or populist regimes to modify their policies and appoint moderate/conservative individuals to key decision-making positions.

However, as in the case of Haiti, once a decision is made to dump recalcitrant clients in order to "save" the state, it is never a question of the United States automatically achieving what it wills. One particularly difficult task in brokering a desired political transition has been in those circumstances where the target regime is tightly connected with the state, all the more so where the authoritarian client or ruling generals have built up strong political loyalties in the armed forces that resist pressure from the outside. Such circumstances can and do determine Washington's preferred policy options more than any pressing need to protect human rights or pursue the goal of redemocratization.

Bush Policy toward Haiti

It was almost five years after the toppling of the Duvalier family rule before Haiti tasted democracy for the first time in its history. In December 1990, following an interregnum of military-dominated governments, a populist priest, Jean Bertrand Aristide, was elected president with an overwhelming 67 percent of the total vote. Aristide campaigned on a platform of politically, socially, and economically empowering the country's largely peasant population and reforming key state institutions, including the armed forces. On assuming office, however, he confronted two active centers of resistance: a local economic elite that branded him a "Bolshevik" and "the devil" and a military leadership that opposed his efforts to reform the institution and implement existing constitutional provisions affirming civilian authority over the armed forces. During his short-lived presidency, Aristide not only antagonized the Haitian business community but also U.S. investors with his proposals to double the minimum wage, initiate new public works projects, make the wealthy pay their fair share of taxes, impose export levies on assembly plant operators, and support the growth of trade unions.

Aristide's presidency lasted a mere nine months; in September 1991 it was terminated by a military coup. Initially, Washington joined with other regional governments in denouncing the junta and calling for the reinstatement of the ousted Haitian leader. Secretary of State James Baker said the junta would "be treated as a pariah, without friends, without support, without a future. . . ."[1] Days later, though, the Bush administration began to back away from unqualified support for the deposed president's return with all his former powers intact. Demands that Aristide disavow an imagined mobocracy "and work toward sharing power with the Parliament"[2] indicated a new vision of what administration officials had in mind when they spoke of the restoration of Haitian democracy: it must not antagonize the military or the traditional political class which had largely accommodated itself to the coup.

This policy shift was linked to a concern over Aristide's populist orientation. The White House was ambivalent about supporting an elected leader who was committed to empowering the poor through changes in the economy, the regime, and the state. And as the policy unfolded, it soon became clear that support for Aristide's return was predicated on the latter's willingness to accept specific limitations on his presidential powers, not least because his efforts to democratize the Haitian state were perceived as a potential threat to longer-term U.S. objectives: the restoration of political stability; the survival of an, albeit reformed, military institution with its external linkages to the Pentagon intact; and the promotion of an open economy and a development strategy that accorded foreign investors a central role.

Within the foreign policy bureaucracy, the Central Intelligence Agency (CIA) emerged as the locus of hostility to a U.S. policy approach based on Aristide's return. Soon after his election in 1990, the agency began waging a systematic campaign to discredit the Haitian leader, in the process forging close links with Aristide's domestic opponents. Among them was Emmanuel Constant, the head of the Front for the Advancement and Progress of Haiti (FRAPH), a violent paramilitary organization with close links to the armed forces. After the September 1991 coup, Constant was placed on the agency payroll, in return for which he provided continuing information about the nature and activities of Aristide's local protagonists.[3]

For all its professed aversion to the *golpistas* (ruling generals), the United States dragged its feet on endorsing an Organization of American States (OAS)

---

[1] Quoted in Kim Ives, "The Unmaking of a President," *NACLA Report on the Americas* 27 (January/February 1994): 16.

[2] Clifford Krauss, "In a Policy Shift, U.S. Pressures Haitian On Rights Abuses," *New York Times*, 7 October 1991; also see Thomas L. Friedman, "U.S. Won't Link Aristide Return and Democracy," *New York Times*, 8 October 1991.

[3] See R. Jeffrey Smith, "Haitian Paramilitary Chief Spied for CIA, Sources Say," *Washington Post*, 7 October 1994.

trade embargo, which weakened the regional body's effectiveness in denying the military its oil or the wealthy their smuggled-in luxury goods paid for in hoarded dollars. In early February 1992, the Bush administration dealt another powerful blow to the economic sanctions strategy when it lifted those restrictions affecting American-owned assembly plants, which comprised most U.S. investments in Haiti.[4] This was the clearest indication to date that Washington was reluctant to commit itself to a formula based on substituting Aristide for the Duvalierist armed forces.

Later that same month, the State Department sought to broker an "acceptable" political comprise that included a role for the military. Under intense pressure from his American hosts, Aristide agreed to sign an accord with Haitian parliamentarians appointing an interim prime minister, Conservative party leader Rene Theodore, and establishing a timetable for his return in effect as little more than a figurehead president at some future, unspecified date. But after the parliament, bowing to military opposition, failed to approve the agreement, Washington quickly revealed a disposition to tolerate the existing political arrangements.

Meanwhile the generals' brutal rule had precipitated a refugee problem for the Bush administration, which it attempted to solve in a fashion guaranteed to reaffirm the junta's belief that it had little to fear from Washington. Following the September 1991 coup, temporary restraining orders by U.S. courts prevented the forced repatriation of Haitian boat people. This ban was lifted by the U.S. Supreme Court on 31 January 1992, but Naturalization and Immigration authorities continued to prescreen interdicted Haitians at the U.S. naval facility in Guantanamo Bay, Cuba, allowing just under one third to enter the United States to seek asylum. By the end of May, however, concern over the domestic political consequences of thousands of Haitians fleeing military terror produced a major policy shift. Bush reinstituted a 1981 agreement between Washington and the Duvalier regime permitting the U.S. Coast Guard to intercept refugee boats on the high seas and return all undocumented passengers to Haiti. Washington's line was now based on the assumption that boat people were fleeing economic deprivation, not political repression. In future, Haitians could only apply for refugee status at the American embassy in Port-au-Prince. This decision subsequently affected more then 30,000 refugees.

By mid-1992, while still going through the motions of calling for the restoration of Aristide's government, the United States was simultaneously encouraging the exiled leader to negotiate with the new military-imposed Prime Minister Marc Bazin, a former World Bank official and the favored Bush candidate in the 1990 elections in which he received only 14 percent of the total vote. In the process, State Department officials "dropped the none-too-subtle hint that if he passed up this 'important window of opportunity,' the United States may

---

[4] See Al Kamen and John M. Goshko, "U.S. Eased Haiti Embargo Under Business Pressure," *Washington Post*, 7 February 1992.

drop or ease the embargo."[5] A July CIA memorandum, which lavished praise on Bazin and described General Raoul Cedras "as a conscientious military leader who genuinely wished to minimize his role in politics, professionalize the armed services, and develop a separate and competent civilian police force," mirroring as it did the attitudes of many Defense and State officials, provided more evidence of the conditional nature of administration support for Aristide's return: it had to be acceptable to Haiti's military and economic elite.[6]

CLINTON POLICY: JANUARY 1993 TO APRIL 1994

The transition from George Bush to Bill Clinton did not signal any major policy shift on Haiti. While the newly appointed Secretary of State Warren Christopher acknowledged that Aristide "ha[d] to be part of the solution to this [crisis]," both he and President Clinton balked at setting a firm deadline for the exiled Haitian leader's return. Senior administration officials spoke of his "eventual" return "when conditions permit."[7] During their first meeting, Clinton sought to assuage Aristide's concern about the strength of Washington's commitment to his speedy return, but he stressed that this could only take place "under conditions of national reconciliation and mutual respect for human rights."[8]

The initial uneasiness and ambiguity in Clinton's approach to the "Aristide problem" was partly a function of domestic political factors, specifically the refugee issue. In the course of the 1992 presidential election campaign, Clinton vigorously denounced the Bush policy of forcible repatriation of Haitian refugees as "appalling" and promised to overturn it.[9] Within days of his inauguration, however, Clinton backtracked on this pledge following warnings that the United States might soon be confronted by a new wave of at least 200,000 Haitians fleeing the brutality of military rule. Sensitive to the electoral damage suffered by the Carter administration in the wake of the 1980 Mariel boatlift of over 125,000 Cuban refugees to Florida, Clinton tumbled from the high moral ground of the election campaign and announced that the existing policy would remain in place.

[5] Lee Hockstader and Douglas Farah, "U.S. Presses Haiti's Civilian Leaders to Find Accord," *Washington Post*, 5 July 1992.

[6] Quoted from memorandum dated 21 July 1992, prepared by Brian Latell, the CIA's national intelligence officer for Latin America, in Christopher Marquis, "CIA Memo Discounts 'Oppressive Rule' in Haiti," *Washington Post*, 19 December 1993.

[7] U.S. Congress, Senate, Committee on Foreign Relations, *Nomination of Warren M. Christopher to be Secretary of State*, 103rd Congress, 2nd sess., 13 and 14 January 1993 (Washington, DC: U.S. Government Printing Office [GPO], 1993), 75.

[8] See Gwen Ifill, "Haitian Is Offered Clinton's Support on an End to Exile," *New York Times*, 17 March 1993.

[9] Quoted in Ann Devroy and R. Jeffrey Smith, "Debate Over Risks Split Administration," *Washington Post*, 25 September 1994.

The absence of a sharp break in policy was further reinforced by Clinton's decision to temporarily retain until May the architect of Bush's Haiti strategy, Bernard Aronson, as assistant secretary of state for inter-American affairs, and Clinton's reluctance at the White House meeting with Aristide to take a strong stand on the question of justice for victims of the military terror. To Aristide's demand that the coup leaders must be brought to account for the killing of some 3,000 of his supporters and other human rights abuses since September 1991, Clinton offered little but the vaguest of promises.

Having reversed his position on refugee policy Clinton moved quickly to limit its impact by committing the new administration to "step up dramatically" diplomatic efforts to restore the ousted Haitian leader to office.[10] To facilitate this goal, the former U.S. ambassador to Nicaragua, Lawrence Pezzullo, was appointed a special envoy to secretary of State on Haiti policy.

Over the next fifteen months, the Clinton White House searched for an internal political solution to the Haitian conflict that could accommodate the military, the local economic elite, and Aristide. This attempt to produce an acceptable coalition government that would effectively circumscribe Aristide's power had as one of its by-products a sustained pressure on the exiled leader to capitulate on army demands for immunity from prosecution for its brutal rule since September 1991. U.S. policy was distinguished by its effort to bludgeon Aristide to agree to give amnesty to those who had engaged in a "systematic and ruthless" program of murder, torture, and indiscriminate repression throughout Haitian civil society—targeting not just pro-Aristide slum dwellers but also the political, peasant, trade union, and other leaders of the opposition movement.[11]

To lure and prod the military leaders to relinquish power, Clinton resorted to a carrot and stick strategy. The carrot was the White House offer of a seat at the negotiating table for the ruling troika—Army Chief Lt. General Raoul Cedras, his deputy and Chief of Staff General Philippe Biamby, and the Port-au-Prince Police Chief Michel Francois. The stick consisted largely of a gradual tightening of the global, regional, and bilateral trade embargos. In June, Clinton announced new sanctions, preventing all civilian and military coup supporters from entering the United States and freezing the latter's American assets; later that month, the United Nations imposed a global oil and arms embargo on Haiti. In tandem with the resignation of the military-appointed Prime Minister Marc Bazin, the conditions were deemed propitious for a resumption of talks involving Aristide and the military *golpistas*.

On 3 July 1993, under considerable pressure from United Nations Special Envoy Dante Caputo and the Clinton administration's Lawrence Pezzullo, Aristide and Cedras signed the so-called Governor's Island Agreement, which outlined a redemocratization scenario for Haiti. The steps included Aristide's

---

[10] Quoted in ibid.

[11] Americas Watch, *Silencing a People: The Destruction of Civil Society in Haiti* (New York: Human Rights Watch, February 1993), 1.

nomination of a prime minister to assume office after being confirmed by a re-constituted parliament; the suspension of global economic sanctions; the provision of international aid to facilitate reforms of the civil bureaucracy, the judiciary, the armed forces, and the establishment of a new police force; a political amnesty for the perpetrators of the September 1991 coup; and Army Chief Cedras's retention of his position until Aristide's resumption of the presidency on 30 October 1993. In light of the accord's concessions to the military and its lack of any enforcement mechanisms for ousting the ruling junta from power, it is not surprising that Aristide's signature required much greater effort on the part of the international negotiators than Cedras's.

The Governor's Island Agreement signaled an escalation of the campaign to shrink Aristide's authority while ostensibly working for his return to Haiti. In the course of negotiations, Pezzullo seemed no less preoccupied with the fate of the armed forces and the local economic elite than with Aristide's restoration to office. The accord asked much of the exiled civilian president, little of the military leaders, and relied on a groundless belief in the junta's commitment to "good faith" negotiations.

Although Pezzullo, Caputo, and the other international negotiators had been only too willing to accept Cedras's commitments at face value, the "recalcitrant" Aristide displayed the greater willingness to abide by the terms of the agreement. After his nominee for prime minister, Robert Malval, was approved by the reformed parliament in late August, all regional, global and U.S. sanctions were suspended. Almost immediately, the tempo of military-authored violence accelerated. The army and police unleashed their thuggish paramilitary "attaches," who threatened Malval and a number of his cabinet ministers, and assassinated or attempted to murder prominent Aristide civilian and political supporters. The audacious nature of this offensive, reflecting the military's intransigence and belief that it could and would hold onto power, elicited a relatively muted response from Washington. Ultimately, the accord unravelled: while Aristide exhibited flexibility to excess and honored his commitments, Cedras did not.

Throughout this period, U.S. policy makers seemed less committed to restoring democracy than to creating political stability in Haiti. The State Department's Pezzullo strategy was based on the assumption that the military was a stabilizing factor, and that it should and had to be part of any political solution. Hence, there was relentless pressure on Aristide to negotiate some kind of power-sharing arrangements with the generals, to give priority to national reconciliation at the expense of justice, and to be willing to modify or forego long-held policy positions. But it was becoming increasingly clear that on these issues Aristide was not the problem. He accepted the reversal in Clinton refugee policy, agreed to a political amnesty for the military, and appointed a business figure acceptable to the Haitian elite and Washington to be his prime minister. By contrast, Cedras and his colleagues persistently refused to accommodate U.S. demands. Instead, they revealed themselves to be disobedient clients—

obdurate, intransigent, and implacably opposed to relinquishing their hold on political power.

In early October, the military reaffirmed their opposition to Aristide's return and simultaneously dealt a telling blow to the Pezzullo approach. In preparation for Aristide's return on 30 October and as part of a larger United Nations observer and training force destined for Haiti under the Governor's Island Agreement, the U.S.S. *Harlan County*, with 200 lightly armed U.S. soldiers and twenty-five Canadian military trainers aboard, arrived within sight of Port-au-Prince on 11 October, only to find that the military leadership had reneged on its promise to allow the ship to dock. While Haitian soldiers stood by doing nothing, armed civilian thugs, organized by the FRAPH, whose leader Emmanuel Constant was still on the CIA payroll,[12] bluffed the *Harlan County* into turning around and heading for home. This was the clearest possible sign that the ruling clique would not cede power without a struggle.

The Pentagon, determined to avoid any repetition of the debacle in Somalia less than two weeks earlier, which led to the deaths of eighteen American soldiers, played a leading role in the bureaucratic debate that produced the decision to recall the *Harlan County*. If this humiliating episode triggered the image of "America turns tail"[13] and a loss of "credibility," as well as dealing an almost fatal blow to the accord, the Defense Department was far from displeased. Having constantly opposed sending any American troops to Haiti, it felt vindicated. Deputy Under Secretary for Policy Walter Slocombe expressed the agency's view of Aristide in no uncertain terms: it was opposed to risking soldiers' lives to put "that psychopath" back in power.[14] At the same time, other administration officials, so angered over what had occurred, requested that serious consideration be given to the interventionist option. National Security Council (NSC) Adviser Tony Lake, signaling this possible future course of action, directed his subordinates to construct the first of the Haiti invasion scenarios. For the moment, however, according to another involved official, "cooler heads . . . prevailed."[15]

While support for Aristide's return raised hackles in the Pentagon, the exiled leader was still the target of malicious CIA allegations and leaks that largely questioned his sanity. In October, the agency's national intelligence officer for Latin America, Brian Latell, prepared a psychological profile on Aristide that concluded he was mentally unstable. Such studies provided ammunition for anti-Aristide legislators on Capital Hill and other foreign policy influentials such as former Bush NSC adviser, Brent Scowcroft, who described

---

[12] See Stephen Engleberg, "A Haitian Leader of Paramilitaries Was Paid by C.I.A.," *New York Times*, 8 October 1994.

[13] U.S. official, quoted in Devroy and Smith, "Debate Over Risks Split Administration."

[14] Quoted in Elaine Sciolino et al., "Haiti Standoff: The U.S. Will Try Again," *New York Times*, 29 April 1994.

[15] This unnamed administration official is quoted in Devroy and Smith, "Debate Over Risks Split Administration."

the Haitian leader as "erratic" and concurred with Senator Jesse Helms that he was "probably a certifiable psychopath."[16]

If the *Harlan County* fiasco indicated the military leadership's resolve, further provocative actions testing the outer limits of Washington's tolerance followed. Emboldened by Clinton's shambolic foreign policy performance, and despite White House warnings that the generals were responsible for the safety of the new civilian government, gunmen assassinated the newly appointed Justice Minister Guy Malary on 14 October. Malary was then preparing legislation to bring the police force under civilian control.[17] The United Nations immediately reimposed its oil and arms embargo—this time enforced with the support of six U.S. Navy warships. Washington also reinstituted its bilateral sanctions. Just as significant, though, was Clinton's footdragging on proposals to implement more draconian trade penalties against the military, notably a December 1993 French-Canadian plan to impose a comprehensive ban that only excluded food and medicines. The explanation was not hard to find: the administration still clung to a belief in the possibility of a solution to the conflict based on a power-sharing formula, or what special envoy Lawrence Pezzullo described as "a political coalition in the center."[18] Not even the Haitian military troika's recent provocations were able to completely disabuse the Clinton administration of this illusion.

The refusal to jett the belief that the military could still be part of the solution to the conflict also explained the White House reluctance to exploit the generals' cocaine-generated personal wealth. Ignoring Drug Enforcement Administration evidence implicating the Haitian military commanders in drug trafficking extending back to the early 1980s,[19] Clinton avoided virtually any mention of the subject in his public pronouncements, precisely because to have made an issue of these activities would have rendered the existing power-sharing approach politically untenable.

However, by December the frustration among key administration officials over the behavior of the military leadership was palpable. The junta was increasingly perceived not just as an obstacle to political stability, solving the refugee problem, and getting Haiti off the domestic political agenda; but it was also seen as an impediment to Washington's longer-term third force goal—identifying and promoting a civilian alternative to Aristide. According to a *New York Times* report, an exasperated Warren Christopher told his newly appointed deputy, Strobe Talbott, "that the administration's policy was at a dead

[16] Quoted in Mark Danner, "The Fall of the Prophet," *New York Review of Books*, 2 December 1993, 44.

[17] See Congressional Research Service, Issue Brief, *Haiti: The Struggle for Democracy and Congressional Concerns in 1994*, 22 September 1994, 9.

[18] Quoted in Daniel Williams and Julia Preston, "U.S. Policy on Haiti Includes Search for Moderates," *Washington Post*, 8 December 1993.

[19] See Congressional Research Service Issue Brief, *Haiti: Prospects for Democracy and U.S. Policy Concerns*, 16 October 1992, 10.

end because no viable alternative to Aristide would be found while the nation remained under a military dictatorship."[20]

By the 15 January 1994 deadline, the military had failed to meet any of the conditions set down in the Governor's Island Agreement. Although Washington had previously threatened to request expanded United Nations sanctions if this situation arose, it now declined to do so. Instead, it once again sought to apply pressure on Aristide to be more flexible, which translated into additional concessions to ensure a political solution. This new attempt to lean on the exiled Haitian president, largely orchestrated by Pezzullo, took the form of a plan proposed by a delegation of Haitian parliamentarians during a visit to Washington in late February 1994. Pezzullo's objective was to present the image of a politically balanced proposal drafted by a representative group of centrist legislators that could provide the basis for a negotiated resolution of the conflict.

The so-called Monde Plan, named after one of the delegation, a founding member of the paramilitary FRAPH whom the U.S. special envoy preferred to describe as "a right wing politician,"[21] was basically an American production. The visit was sponsored by a private conservative organization, the AID-funded Center for Democracy, and it was composed of figures vetted by U.S. officials. As Pezzullo conceded during congressional testimony: "Well, we selected people who we thought would be a representative group to come up here."[22] More than half of the delegation belonged to the Alliance, a pro-coup coalition that had consistently sided with the military leadership since September 1991.

The proposed plan represented a visible retreat from the Governor's Island Agreement: only one military leader would be required to step down (the others receiving amnesties); the national police, a major perpetrator of violence against Aristide supporters, would remain in place; the exiled president would appoint a new prime minister responsible for establishing a broad-based government that included allies of the current regime; and no date would be set for the military's transfer of power to Aristide and the latter's return to Haiti. In contrast to the earlier accord, there was no provision for an international mission to train and create a more professionalized armed forces. Aristide was bluntly told that this plan was the quid pro quo for a tightening of economic sanctions against the country's ruling generals.

Not surprisingly, Aristide balked at these demands, accusing its supporters of "acting in 'complicity' with the military regime in delaying his return,"[23] and

[20] Devroy and Smith, "Debate Over Risks Split Administration."

[21] U.S. Congress, Senate, Committee on Foreign Relations, Subcommittee on Western Hemisphere and Peace Corps Affairs, *U.S. Policy Toward Haiti*, 103rd Congress, 2nd sess., 8 March 1994 (Washington, DC: GPO, 1994), 112.

[22] Ibid., 113.

[23] Congressional Research Service, *Haiti: The Struggle for Democracy and Congressional Concerns in 1994*, 5.

insisting that the generals would treat this proposal with the same contempt they had lavished on the Governor's Island Agreement. Irritated State Department officials interpreted Aristide's dismissal of the plan as another instance of his inflexibility and refusal to compromise. That, not the military's intransigence, constituted the main obstacle to a political solution and his return to Haiti.[24]

But the chairman of the Senate Foreign Relations Subcommittee on the Western Hemisphere, Christopher Dodd, provided the most trenchant and damning critique of the plan and its policy implications. Following sustained questioning of special envoy Lawrence Pezzullo, he concluded on the following note:

> Larry, you understand my point here. We handpick a group of people. We finance their trip to Washington. We put together a proposal. You have some people who hardly could be called centrists craft this thing and put it together. Label them as sort of the moderate group, then put the pressure on the fellow who got 70 percent of the vote, and if he does not go along with these conditions, which do not even include the entire structure of the hierarchy of the military, that we are not going to impose the sanctions any longer. Why are we putting so much pressure on him?[25]

The State Department-Pezzullo strategy was premised partly on the notion of a reformed coercive apparatus of the "old" state maintaining its power and prerogatives in any transition from Cedras to Aristide—illustrative of the historic U.S. perception of the Latin American armed forces as the ultimate guarantor of Washington's vital interests within its traditional sphere of influence. This concern was echoed by Pentagon officials. While conceding that "there would have to be a change at the very top," Deputy Under Secretary Walter Slocombe told a congressional subcommittee in early March that "there are significant forces within the Haitian military who would support and participate actively in the program of modernizing it and professionalizing [it]. . . ."[26] The achievement of this goal was also linked to a desire to circumscribe and limit Aristide's power in the event of his return to Haiti. Perceived in exile as a transitional figure by many U.S. officials, the Pezzullo-led pressure on Aristide to negotiate a political solution that embraced the military, the local economic elite, and his civilian political opponents was intended to erode the powers of the presidency, and make it more of a ceremonial position without substantive decision-making authority. This desire to encumber a revived Aristide presidency within a powerful set of constraints explained, for instance, the considerable emphasis Washington attached to the naming of a new prime minister as soon as possible; this would facilitate the undermining strategy through the appointment of Aristide political and military foes to cabinet posts.

---

[24] See Steven Greenhouse, "Which Way Forward on Haiti?," *New York Times*, 9 March 1994.

[25] U.S. Congress, Senate, *U.S. Policy Toward Haiti*, 113–114.

[26] Ibid., 126.

At the end of March, U.S. policy still seemed wedded to the Pezzullo approach. The announcement by President Clinton that Washington would intensify its pressure on the generals, especially Cedras, to relinquish power was essentially motivated by twin concerns: saving the military and implementing the political preconditions for Aristide's return. Only with the junta's commitment to leave could Aristide name a new prime minister, thus establishing the basis for the eventual passage of an amnesty law through the Haitian parliament. The exiled leader's failure to appreciate the significance of this policy shift did not sit well with administration officials, provoking one to declare in a mood of barely controlled anger: "These adjustments are a way of trying to meet some of his concerns and get him to join in the process of finding a practical approach to solving this crisis. . . ."[27]

Ultimately, Aristide's stubborn refusal to accommodate each and every U.S. demand for flexibility, compounded by the military leadership's obduracy and disobedience, forced Washington's hand. In late April, the Clinton administration abandoned its attempts to extract more compromises from Aristide and its military-as-part-of-the-solution approach. The ruling junta's defiance and provocations had finally exhausted White House patience. The policy shift took the form of a request for United Nations Security Council support for imposing a global trade embargo on the country, together with financial sanctions (the freezing of overseas assets) and travel bans against 600 military officers who supported the autocratic regime or participated in the September 1991 coup that toppled Aristide from power.[28] One State Department official described these measures to tighten the economic embargo as incorporating "the basic components of the . . . approach" contained in a bill introduced into the House of Representatives in March by the Congressional Black Caucus, a leading domestic critic of Clinton's Haiti policy.[29]

Another clear indicator that the generals were about to be dumped was the almost simultaneous resignation of special envoy Lawrence Pezzullo, the official most closely identified with the power-sharing strategy, and his replacement by the former head of the Congressional Black Caucus, William Gray. But, despite Clinton's decision to get tough with Haiti's military rulers, the resort to stepped up sanctions was not accompanied by any plan of action in the event the sanctions failed to achieve their strategic objective.

CLINTON POLICY: MAY 1994 TO SEPTEMBER 1994

On 2 May, Clinton signaled a dramatic shift in U.S. policy toward Haiti. Referring to the leaders of Haiti's military junta, the president said that "it was time

---

[27] Quoted in Steven Greenhouse, "Aristide Cool to U.S. Shift in Haiti Policy," *New York Times*, 31 March 1994.

[28] See Julia Preston, "U.S. Shifts on Haiti, Gets Tougher on Army," *Washington Post*, 29 April 1994.

[29] Quoted in Steven A. Holmes, "With Persuasion and Muscle, Black Caucus Reshapes Haiti Policy," *New York Times*, 14 July 1994.

for them to go," and for the first time he refused to rule out the use of U.S. force to get them going.[30] But these statements reflected the level of frustration with the Haitian military in the Clinton administration much more than they did a new resolve in the White House to see the crisis ended quickly. Cedras, Biamby, and Francois had dealt themselves out of any U.S.–brokered negotiated settlement by their obstinacy and, to a lesser extent, their continued brutality (OAS and UN human rights monitors in Haiti reported fifty politically-motivated killings for the month of April alone). Administration policy makers, however, remained deeply divided over how the United States should respond to the deadlock created by the junta's refusal to step down. One faction, led by Anthony Lake and Strobe Talbott, favored the invasion option and were preparing plans for it; another faction, led by William Perry and senior military and intelligence officers, cautioned strongly against the use of force. A consensus approach did emerge for the next four months, and even then it was tenuous enough to allow the final twist in the saga—Jimmy Carter's deal with the junta allowing for U.S. military intervention into Haiti and the phased exit of Cedras and his cohorts from power.

Between April and August, Clinton himself remained aloof from the debate within his own camp. In electoral terms, there was little to be gained by getting the approach right on Haiti; and especially after the debacle in Somalia the previous October, there was much to lose by putting another foot badly wrong. Moreover, the president was preoccupied with domestic policy issues, especially the troubled passage of his health and crime bills through the House of Representatives and the Senate. Those White House officials with day-to-day responsibility for Haiti had to consider limitations on their options. According to opinion polls, Americans disapproved of Clinton's handling of foreign policy generally and strongly opposed his sending U.S. troops into Haiti. Congress was hostile to an invasion and, apart from the Black Caucus which was pushing for tougher measures to hasten Aristide's return, deeply suspicious still of the exiled Haitian president and his democratic credentials. Aristide himself remained opposed to any invasion. Finally, it was clear that if Washington were to get the UN's imprimatur for interventionist action, it would have to disabuse UN Secretary-General Boutros Boutros-Ghali of the notion that Haiti represented a case of sphere-of-influence peacekeeping in which the U.S. military should play only a minor role.

Clinton elaborated on the change of policy tack at an 8 May White House press briefing, when he announced the appointment of William Gray to replace Lawrence Pezzullo as the administration's special adviser on Haiti. After declaring that Gray "will be the point man in our diplomacy and a central figure in our future policy deliberations," Clinton outlined a set of tougher economic sanctions on Haiti in line with the previous day's UN Security Council Resolu-

---

[30] Quoted in Barton Gellman and Ruth Marcus, "U.S. Boosts Pressure on Haitians," *Washington Post*, 4 May 1992.

tion 917. These included a freeze on assets in the United States belonging to the Haitian military leaders and their civilian allies, a ban on nonscheduled flights in and out of Haiti, and a tightening of the economic embargo on everything but humanitarian supplies. As well, the president announced changes in migration policy toward Haiti: the U.S. would continue to interdict all Haitian boat people, but instead of automatic repatriation, it would process applications for political refugee status aboard ship or in other countries. "I am committed," Clinton declared, "to making these new international sanctions work." But once again he refused to rule out other options if these failed to convince Haiti's military leaders to step down.[31]

The following day, Secretary of State Christopher, speaking in Mexico City, sought to drive home the message: "If Haiti's military leaders refuse to resign or leave Haiti," he said, "they will find that the international community has both the will and the means to make them pay the price for their illegitimate actions, and to restore the legitimate elected authorities."[32]

This new White House posture looked and sounded much harsher than it was. The circumstances of Gray's appointment, for instance, suggested that it would be much easier for the junta in Port-au-Prince to ignore him than had been the case with his predecessor. Unlike Pezzullo, Gray's brief was to advise rather than represent the administration; moreover, he insisted on performing these duties while retaining his status as a private citizen, not on the payroll of the U.S. government.

In announcing the sanctions, Clinton said that the United States was "working with" the Dominican Republic to improve enforcement procedures along its border with Haiti. But Washington balked at pressing the corrupt Balaguer regime to seal the border against smuggling with threats to reconsider the Dominican Republic's U.S. sugar quota or other economic benefits the country received under the Caribbean Basin Initiative. As for the new arrangements for processing applications for refugee status by fleeing Haitians, these were no more generous than the Bush administration had allowed during the months immediately following the 1991 coup,[33] despite the accumulated evidence since then of the new regime's brutality. In fact, publicly at least, the White House was doing little more than ratcheting up its sanctions policy in line with UN initiatives and adopting minimum changes in its refugee policy to avoid condemnation from its domestic critics. Privately, the Clinton administration had adopted a two-track policy of forcing the Haitian military junta from power while "preparing" Aristide for his return.

If the ruling generals had become expendable, the fate of the coercive institution was another matter altogether. Paramount importance was attached to

---

[31] "Clinton Takes New Steps to Oust Haitian Military Leaders," *USIA Wireless File*, 9 May 1994.

[32] Quoted in Deputy Secretary of State Strobe Talbott, "Pursuing the Restoration of Democracy in Haiti," U.S. Department of State, *Dispatch*, 23 May 1994, 332.

[33] Congressional Research Service, Report to Congress, *Cuban and Haitian Asylum Seekers: Recent Trends*, 1 September 1994.

the survival of the armed forces in the event of Aristide's return. But in recent weeks the weight of opinion among senior policy makers had shifted away from the idea of major personnel cuts and organizational changes as being too fraught with unintended consequences. The new emerging consensus was based on a hitting from the top strategy (getting rid of Cedras et al.) and working with those elements willing to accommodate Aristide's return. Secretary of Defense William Perry put it succinctly, if rather clumsily: "We would want to use as much of the military and military police as is capable. . . ."[34]

Resistance to an invasion was fuelled by continuing CIA advice that Aristide was unreliable and that dispatching U.S. troops to restore him to power would have little impact on Haiti's corrupt and thuggish political system.[35] Within the Defense Department, there was the added concern that the use of force lacked a clear objective and cut-off point. "The problem is not getting in," said a Pentagon-based general. "It is getting out."[36] Exploring options short of direct U.S. intervention seemed preferable. One scenario involved buying off Haiti's military leaders and sending the bill to the country's economic elite.[37] Amid increasing skepticism about whether or not the sanctions would achieve their intended goal in the time period allotted by the White House, a State Department official commented in late May: "It's by a process of subtraction that we're getting to the military option."[38] However, sending in the marines to enforce a political transition based on a restored Aristide presidency was unlikely as long as the exiled leader remained wedded to a program of radical social and economic reform.

During his 8 May briefing, Clinton emphasized that one of the administration's fundamental policy objectives was to promote a "broad-based, functioning representative government that can relate to the business community as well as to the ordinary citizens of Haiti."[39] Given that Aristide was now perceived as an integral part of Washington's equation, it therefore became imperative to reconfigure his populist socioeconomic outlook. This meant jettisoning his commitment to redistribute wealth, end exploitative labor relations, and pursue a growth strategy based on rural, not export-driven development in favor of a more economically "responsible" capitalist development strategy; and appointing the kind of moderate, technocratic officials who would faithfully oversee the implementation of this program.

As part of their efforts to remake Aristide, officials from the U.S. Agency for International Development (AID), World Bank, and the International

---

[34] Quoted in Elaine Sciolino, "Exile in Style Being Offered to Haitian Chiefs," *New York Times*, 20 June 1994.

[35] Devroy and Smith, "Debate Over Risks Split Administration."

[36] Quoted in Michael R. Gordon, "Weighing Options, U.S. Aides Assess Invasion of Haiti," *New York Times*, 30 May 1994.

[37] See Sciolino, "Exile in Style Being Offered to Haitian Chiefs."

[38] Quoted in Gordon, "Weighing Options, U.S. Aides Assess Invasion of Haiti."

[39] "Transcript of May 8 White House News Conference," *USIA Wireless File*, 9 May 1994.

Monetary Fund (IMF) began examining every aspect of his plans for rebuilding Haiti; in the process they instructed him in the kinds of economic programs and public administration rebuilding they deemed suitable for the country's revival.[40] The United States was not only in a position to pressure Aristide directly but also to control his public profile. Aristide's radio broadcasts to Haiti were monitored, the National Security Agency admitted to bugging his telephone calls, and he was not even consulted about U.S. plans for his return—especially the deal Jimmy Carter stitched together with Haiti's military leaders in September.

Washington's goal of getting Aristide "to see eye to eye" with a "critical mass" of the Haitian elite—to appreciate what William Gray called "the political realities"—proved effective as the exiled leader began to tone down his radical theology and class struggle rhetoric.[41] In mid-July he outlined a ten-point reconstruction plan for Haiti that included a commitment to "promote goals in the private sector."[42] With few, if any, alternatives, his acceptance of IMF-World Bank-AID development blueprints calling for large-scale privatization, major tariff cuts, the elimination of import quotas, and a halving of personnel in the civil bureaucracy had become, in effect, one of the preconditions for his return. U.S. officials also managed to procure from Aristide a written pledge to uphold the Haitian Constitution and to hand over power to a successor when his term expired in February 1996. As AID Administrator J. Brian Atwood later recalled: "When we first met he was running for president, he [had] a real attitude about the United States and the West. But I think he really has grown. He knows all the practical issues now."[43]

As these efforts continued, events in Haiti were reeling out of anyone's control. Clinton's decision to modify the refugee processing arrangements produced a dramatic increase in the number of Haitians fleeing their country by boat. During the whole of 1993, around 2,000 Haitians put to sea in search of asylum in the United States; in June 1994 alone, the number jumped to 5,603; and then the floodgates really opened as close to 6,000 decamped in the first four days of July.[44] Attempting to strike an optimistic note, Defense Secretary William Perry told reporters that an invasion was still not on the cards: "I think we should . . . give some time to see that sanctions work itself out, and I think we may see some very substantial results from that. The conventional wisdom is that sanctions cannot be effective, that they cannot force governments to change their actions. This may be a counter-example." The following day (1

---

[40] See Elaine Sciolino, "Aristide Adopts a New Role: From Robespierre to Gandhi," *New York Times*, 18 September 1994.

[41] U.S. Congress, House, Committee on Foreign Affairs, *U.S. Policy Toward Haiti*, 103rd Congress, 2nd sess., 8 June 1994 (Washington, DC: GPO, 1994), 11.

[42] Quoted in Daniel Williams, "U.S. Looks for Moderation in Aristide's Mixed Signals," *Washington Post*, 18 July 1994.

[43] Quoted in Sciolino, "Aristide Adopts A New Role: From Robespierre to Gandhi."

[44] See Congressional Research Service, *Cuban and Haitian Asylum Seekers: Recent Trends*.

July), Secretary of State Christopher, when asked if the administration favored an invasion to overthrow the Haitian military, replied: "The option we're pursuing now is . . . sanctions."[45]

These comments only served to undercut Washington's efforts to spook the ruling generals into stepping down. Such efforts included an announcement by U.S. officials that a naval task force with 2,000 marines was steaming toward the Haitian coast. Complementing this show of gunboat diplomacy were a Pentagon news leak that more than 1,000 commandos had just returned from Florida after secretly rehearsing a plan to seize Haiti's airfields and ports, and William Gray's warning that any threat to the lives of the 3,000 Americans still in Haiti would trigger immediate and forceful White House action. Frustrated over the seeming inability of any measure to stem the refugee tide, the White House unsuccessfully tried to pressure Aristide into making radio broadcasts to Haiti to discourage people leaving.[46]

The US. response to the continuing exodus of Haitians was complicated by the unwillingness of regional allies to absorb large numbers of the boat people. Panama's President Guillermo Endara abruptly reneged on his country's agreement to temporarily house 10,000 Haitians; other Caribbean countries were slow to offer assistance. Meanwhile, Haiti's military rulers were clearly losing their grip on the situation. On 13 July they expelled all international human rights monitors amid a marked escalation in the junta's reign of terror. Clinton responded by saying the expulsion validated his decision to consider possible military action. But no definitive decision was taken.

By the end of July, the United States had secured UN Security Council approval for military intervention in Haiti. Within the foreign policy bureaucracy, however, disagreements persisted over the efficacy of such action. The Pentagon, unlike the State Department, remained steadfastly opposed to an invasion; nor did it believe that the options for inducing the junta leaders to relinquish power for a comfortable exile had been fully exhausted.[47] At the same time, these interagency conflicts could not mask the fact that Washington's patience and imagination were running out. "We're seized by the refugee surge," one senior administration official explained, "and this has accelerated the discussion of other options."[48] But the quickened drift toward a more activist response was temporarily halted by a simultaneous outflux of boat people from Cuba.

Beginning in August, the number of people seeking to leave Cuba by boat or raft rose precipitously. For the whole of 1993, only 3,656 Cubans were inter-

[45] Quoted in Ann Devroy and Barton Gelman, "Exodus From Haiti Strains U.S. Policy," *Washington Post*, 7 July 1994.

[46] See Pilita Clark, "Haiti Risks Invasion After Expulsions," *Sydney Morning Herald*, 13 July 1994, 10; Elaine Sciolino "Haiti Invasion Imminent, Envoy Says," *New York Times*, 4 July 1994.

[47] See Elaine Sciolino, "Top U.S. Officials Divided in Debate on Invading Haiti," *New York Times*, 4 August 1994.

[48] Quoted in Devroy and Gellman, "Exodus From Haiti Strains U.S. Policy."

cepted by the U.S. Coast Guard en route to Florida; between the beginning of August and early September the number surged to 30,000. The Cuban exodus made a final settlement in Haiti all the more imperative. But it also distracted attention from Haiti. Although UN Ambassador Madeleine Albright informed the Security Council at the end of July that the United States was prepared to lead a multinational force into Haiti, it was not until 26 August, after this latest Cuban refugee problem had been contained, that Clinton authorized "the final version of an invasion plan that the military had been drafting for months."[49]

While Deputy Secretary of State Strobe Talbott quickly headed to a meeting of Caribbean foreign and defense ministers in Jamaica to secure unequivocal regional backing for the move, the White House authorized one last-ditch effort to promote an internal solution to the crisis: a $12 million CIA covert operation to topple the junta leaders by offering funds, communications equipment, and weapons to "friendly elements" in the military. As one involved U.S. official put it: "We are using every means at our disposal to get rid of this regime in the hopes of avoiding the necessity of an invasion. . . . Every means."[50] But the agency's failure to crack the loyalty of the armed forces to Cedras made direct U.S. intervention inevitable; all other options had finally been exhausted. It was now time to prepare the U.S. public for the invasion.

Apart from perfunctory remarks labeling Haiti's coup leaders criminal and brutal rulers, Washington was forced to wage a low-key rhetorical campaign during the three years of Aristide's exile. After all, Bush and Clinton officials could hardly rail against repression in Haiti, identify the junta as the culprits, and still deny asylum to the great majority of Haitians fleeing tyranny. But that consideration no longer applied. On 13 September, the State Department released its third interim report on Haiti's human rights situation, which said, in part: "The present situation reflects a degree of terror comparable to that of the Duvalier regimes. . . . The [Cedras] regime's human rights record demonstrates its intention not only to eliminate its opponents, but to subjugate the general populace and suppress and intimidate any potential opposition as well."[51] Clinton drew on this report in a televised address to the nation in which he recounted a litany of politically motivated killings, torture, and rape in Haiti and declared that "General Cedras and his accomplices alone are responsible for this suffering and terrible human tragedy."[52] This demonization of the Haitian military leadership made all the more puzzling Clinton's decision to dispatch a negotiating team headed by Jimmy Carter to Port-au-Prince.

[49] John H. Cushman, Jr. et al., "On the Brink of War, a Tense Battle of Wills," *New York Times*, 20 September 1994. On the Cuban refugee figures, see Congressional Research Service, *Cuban and Haitian Asylum Seekers: Recent Trends*; Congressional Research Service, Issue Brief, *Cuba: Issues for Congress*, 6 September 1994, 14.

[50] Quoted in Doyle McManus and Robin Wright, "U.S. Tried Covert Action to Rid Haiti of Rulers," *Los Angeles Times*, 16 September 1994.

[51] "Haitian Regime as Bad as Duvalier, U.S. Says," *USIA Wireless File*, 15 September 1994.

[52] "The Crisis in Haiti," reprinted in U.S. Department of State, *Dispatch*, 19 September 1994, 605.

Officially, Carter was to discuss the "modalities" of the departure of Cedras and the others from power. More likely, the mission was meant to prepare the way for an invasion. It's composition suggests as much. Carter, who opposed Clinton policy on Haiti and had been ignored when he offered to lead a similar diplomatic effort earlier in the year, had resurrected something of a public persona as a conflict resolution ambassador-at-large. If the former president could not talk the Haitian junta around to a peaceful exit, nobody could. To address any lingering congressional misgivings about the use of force, the powerful Democratic Chairman of the Senate Armed Services Committee Sam Nunn accompanied Carter to Haiti. So too did Colin Powell, former head of the Joint Chiefs of Staff and hero of the Persian Gulf War, ensuring that any invasion decision would pass the Defense Department's muster.

The deal Carter unexpectedly concluded with Cedras caught the Clinton administration by surprise and forced a rethink of the invasion plans literally in midflight. The agreement stated only that "certain military officers of the Haitian armed forces are willing to consent to an early and honorable retirement," that their successors "will be named according to the Haitian constitution and existing military law," that the Haitian military and police forces "will work in close cooperation with the U.S. Military Mission" then on its way to Haiti, and that "the military activities of the U.S. Military Mission will be coordinated with the Haitian military high command."[53] The agreement allowed the ruling clique to stay in power up to a month before Aristide's return. It granted a general amnesty for all human rights abuses committed by military officials against civilian noncombatants since the 1991 coup (which Aristide had consistently opposed since the Governor's Island Agreement); and left Cedras, Biamby, and Francois in possession of millions of dollars they made breaking the oil embargo through an alliance with military officials in the Dominican Republic.[54]

These arrangements satisfied the Pentagon. The Somali debacle had demonstrated the risk of trying to fill a law-and-order vacuum in a strife-torn country. Moreover, it guaranteed that the coercive institution of the military-dominated Haitian state would survive intact (but refurbished) in the transition back to an Aristide presidency. The diplomatic agreement also appealed to Clinton and those White House officials concerned about whether a military gambit would pay off in the polls. They were enthusiastic about what Strobe Talbott called "a permissive invasion" resulting in virtually no casualties.[55]

For Aristide, of course, the deal was far less attractive. First, it indicated just how marginal he was to the evolving policy debate. While the NSC's An-

[53] "Agreement Sets Conditions for Haitian Leaders to Retire," Text, *USIA Wireless File*, 19 September 1994.

[54] See Douglas Farah, "U.S. Assists Dictators' Luxury Exile," *Washington Post*, 14 October 1994.

[55] U.S. Congress, House, Committee on Foreign Affairs, *U.S. Policy Toward, And Presence in Haiti*, 103rd Congress, 2nd sess., 13, 27, and 28 September 1994 (Washington, DC: GPO, 1994), 25.

thony Lake and special White House adviser William Gray kept Aristide informed about the Carter mission, the exiled leader's aides later complained that he had no input into the decision-making process.[56] During these briefing sessions, U.S. officials seemed more concerned with drilling Aristide on the importance of free market policies and adhering to the Haitian constitution, which mandated wider political powers to the parliament than to the presidency.[57] Second, it turned the generals who had ousted him from office and conducted a three-year reign of terror on his supporters into "honorable men," to use Carter's term, and elevated them into allies of the U.S. forces in their mission to restore "democracy" in Haiti. Lastly, Carter's brokered outcome further constrained Aristide's room for maneuver: it delayed his return to Haiti, guaranteed the survival of an institutionally cohesive armed forces, provided generous amnesty terms for Cedras and the other junta leaders, and gave the military-backed network of thugs and "attaches" both time and opportunity to mount one last assault on Aristide supporters under the very noses of U.S. peace-keeping troops.

CONCLUSION

Both the Bush and Clinton administrations shared the same overriding objective in Haiti, which was to restore political stability and stop the country being seen as a "problem" for Washington. Each worked through the same preferred policy options to secure this end, with Clinton only returning to the tough choices he advocated on the 1992 presidential campaign trail as his options narrowed and the situation in Haiti threatened to get out of control.

From the beginning of his presidency, Clinton pressured and cajoled the ousted, democratically-elected president of Haiti to adopt a more flexible approach toward dealing with the ruling junta. As long as the junta was perceived as "part of the solution," the White House was content to talk tough about the generals but apply its real muscle to extracting concessions from Aristide. Washington's objectives in seeking to broker a power-sharing solution to the Haitian conflict were primarily twofold: to ensure the survival of the coercive apparatus of the old state, albeit restructured and reformed; and to shrink Aristide's political authority in the event of his resumption of the presidency. American officials were particularly insistent that the army "must be preserved as an institution," convinced that it was "an essential part of the 'iconography' of nationhood."[58]

---

[56] Cushman et al., "On the Brink of War, a Tense Battle of Wills."

[57] Norman Kempster and Doyle McManus, "U.S. Cautions Aristide Over Divisive Action," *Los Angeles Times*, 17 September 1994.

[58] Quoted in Anthony Boadle, "U.S. to Keep Haiti Army Intact Despite Black Record," *Reuters Wire*, 10 October 1994; Larry Rohter, "Some Aristide Supporters Seek Abolition of Military," *New York Times*, 22 November 1994.

Ultimately, the obdurate behavior of the junta leadership proved incompatible with the broader U.S. policy approach. The belief increasingly took hold among Clinton and his senior advisers that these disobedient clients had passed their use-by date and had to go, by force if necessary. The challenge was to replace them with a government that could lay some claim to legitimacy, that enjoyed some degree of popular support, and that would thus put an end to the refugee flow and get Haiti off Washington's political agenda. Given the U.S. commitment to "stability" and the correlation of political forces in Haiti, Aristide effectively became the sole realistic option. But the White House only wanted his legitimacy, not his populist policies. Hence, the need for his political and economic reeducation—a precondition for the invasion.

In mid-1995, Deputy Secretary of State Talbott reassured members of a Senate Committee: "even after our exit in February 1996, *we will remain in charge* by means of USAID and the private sector."[59] The Clinton political objective in restoring Aristide to power reflected less a universal commitment to democracy than an effort to create a permeable democracy in which restructured state institutions (especially the military and police) and an economic development model (free markets) would serve long-term U.S. interests in Haiti, as well as those of the country's international creditors, and, to a lesser extent, the privileged local elites. Washington wanted a government of civilians who could lay claim to an electoral mandate but who, more importantly, would know their place and have little power or opportunity to move beyond it.

Not surprisingly, this objective has contributed to instability and uncertainty in Haiti. By overriding Aristide's initial desire to abolish the military, prosecute officers for human rights abuses, and disarm the paramilitaries, the White House left Haitian democracy vulnerable to its old adversaries. Despite a purge of the security forces in September 1996, political assassinations and plots by armed right-wing groups have forced President Rene Preval to request the continued presence of foreign peacekeeping troops. Meanwhile, as fear of indiscriminate violence spreads, it slowly undermines confidence in the democratic process.

Another source of tension between the Preval government and the popular classes has been the economic reconstruction program imposed on Haiti by Washington and the international financial community. Large-scale aid has been conditioned on the sell-off of state-run enterprises and the shedding of thousands of public sector jobs. This strategy to date has failed to attract significant new foreign investment or produced visible signs of economic recovery. Rather, it has contributed to an erosion of the government's political support.

Disenchanted voters, however, are not turning to Haiti's right-wing parties, which is one reason why these elements remain attracted to an authoritarian

---

[59] Quoted in Worth Cooley-Post, "Haiti Shows It's Ready for Democracy," *National Catholic Reporter*, 28 July 1995, 9. (Emphasis added.)

The United States and South Korean Democratization

JAMES FOWLER

During 1979 and 1980, South Korea experienced a failed transition to democracy. The "Seoul Spring," which took place after the assassination of authoritarian leader Park Chung Hee in late 1979, was brought to a brutal halt when martial law was declared and at least 200 demonstrators were killed at Kwangju in May 1980. Not until June 1987 would South Korea's new leader, Chun Doo Hwan, agree to step down and allow direct elections of the president. Many critics of U.S. foreign policy have studied this period, and the current literature follows two basic schools of thought. One school asserts that the United States had little impact on events in Korea, because it was strategically bound to support the South Korean government regardless of its level of commitment to democratization. This school advances several domestic reasons for the delayed transition, including the lack of labor and middle class support for the opposition and the weakness of the interim civilian government in 1979–1980. The other school focuses on the presence of U.S. troops in Korea and the U.S. "approval" of the use of Combined Forces Command (CFC) units in their bloody crackdown of the Kwangju uprising. These writers claim that the United States could have denied such approval and prevented the crackdown, which led to seven years of rule under the authoritarian Chun regime.

Acknowledging that there are probably many factors that determined the timing of democratic transition, this article will focus on an issue that has yet to be given appropriate attention in the literature: the use of U.S. public pressure. The recent declassification of thousands of pages of telegrams between the U.S. State Department and its embassy in Seoul has especially illuminated the choices that decision makers faced during the period. This evidence indicates that contrary to the opinions expressed throughout the literature, U.S. actions did have an impact on events, though the approval of CFC forces was

JAMES FOWLER is a Ph.D. candidate in the Department of Government at Harvard University.

only incidentally important. Instead, the essential policy tool was the use of public criticism. Ironically, this tool was abandoned under a Carter administration oriented towards human rights and then used by a Reagan administration oriented towards security.[1] The counterintuitive result can be explained by the impact of the Iranian crisis on policy makers in 1979–1980 and the effect of Philippine democratization on policy makers in 1986–1987. Thus this article seeks to illuminate the process whereby conflicts in other countries that had no direct bearing on South Korea ultimately affected the outcome of its own domestic political process.

TWO CYCLES OF SOUTH KOREAN LIBERALIZATION

To better analyze the initial failure and subsequent success of South Korea's transition to democracy, it will be useful to discuss two distinct cycles of liberalization. The first cycle began in 1979, when the government responded to opposition demands by relaxing the application of laws against dissent and securing the release of over 1,000 political prisoners.[2] In spite of these actions, opposition to the Park regime grew. Demonstrations increased in frequency, and even members of the government openly criticized the Park administration.[3] Hardliners began to clamp down in August, arresting key officials of the main opposition party (NDP), confiscating NDP newspapers, and raiding NDP headquarters during the Y. H. Trading Company workers' sit-in.

These actions radicalized the opposition. Kim Young Sam, the leader of the NDP, said in a speech on 10 September that he would start a movement to "overthrow the Park regime."[4] Not surprisingly, the government replied that it would return to strict enforcement of restrictions on dissent.[5] On 4 October, Kim Young Sam was expelled from the National Assembly. Radicals responded in kind on 17 October, when 12,000 students took a demonstration to

---

[1] At President Jimmy Carter's first transition meeting with President Ronald Reagan in 1980, Carter noted that Reagan "expressed with some enthusiasm his envy of the authority that Korean President Park Chung Hee had exercised during a time of campus unrest, when he had closed the universities and drafted the demonstrators." Carter, *Keeping Faith: Memoirs of a President* (New York: Bantam Books, 1982), 578.

[2] Telegrams from U.S. Ambassador to South Korea William Gleysteen to Secretary of State Cyrus Vance, "Reaction to Prisoner Release," 19 July 1979, and "Prisoners Released as Expected on ROK Independence Day," 16 August 1979. These and all telegrams cited were released by the Department of State in response to a Freedom of Information Act (FOIA) request originally filed by Tim Shorrock and can be found in the *Kwangju Documents Collection*, Government Documents and Information Center, Mudd Library, Yale University.

[3] Telegram from Gleysteen to Vance, "National Assembly Finishes Fourth Day of Interpellations," 26 July 1979.

[4] Telegram from Gleysteen to Vance, "Kim Young Sam's September 10 Press Conference," 10 September 1979.

[5] Telegram from Gleysteen to Vance, "ROKG Limits Dissent," 14 September 1979.

downtown Pusan where as many as five students were killed and 500 arrested.[6] Though the Park government was very used to dealing with student protests, these demonstrations were much larger in scope and received widespread support from citizens other than students.[7] In response to continuing demonstrations in Pusan and Masan, the Park government declared martial law for the region including and immediately surrounding the two cities.

The Pusan and Masan riots had a substantial impact on the mood of the nation. However, no one was prepared for the events that would follow.[8] On 26 October 1979, the director of the Korean Central Intelligence Agency (KCIA), Kim Chae Kyu, shot and killed Park Chung Hee at a dinner party. Kim had been embroiled in an argument with Cha Chi Chol, the head of the Presidential Protective Force, over how to respond to the riots in Pusan and Masan. Kim believed that the government should pursue a policy of conciliation, while Cha argued that it was time to crack down.[9] Kim apparently feared an impending purge of reformers in the government (including himself), so he readied his men on the night of 26 October. When it was clear that Park would accept Cha's advice instead of his own, Kim shot both Cha and Park.[10] Believing that he had the support of many reformers in the military, Kim tried to convince the moderate Army Chief of Staff and Martial Law Commander General Chung Song-Hwa to execute a coup that evening, but Chung refused in the name of law and order.[11] Kim was promptly arrested.

Hardliners clamped down, declaring martial law for the whole mainland. The month of November was very confusing. Prime Minister Choi Kyu Hah was the de facto head of state, but he gave no clear signals of whether he was a reformer or a hardliner. The opposition demanded democratic reform and cautiously began to organize. Meanwhile, General Chung tried to soothe hardliner fears of disorder by announcing that "if the North were to attack, ten million South Korean lives would be sacrificed and he would prefer to crack down

[6] Telegram from Gleysteen to Vance, "Situation in Pusan Following Declaration of Martial Law," 18 October 1979.

[7] Telegram from Gleysteen to Vance, "More on Pusan Demonstration; Demonstration at EWHA University in Seoul," 17 October 1979.

[8] Ironically, Gleysteen writes: "None of our contacts, including the dissidents, see the current situation in Pusan as an indication that the Park Government faces real problems in staying afloat." Telegram from Gleysteen to Vance, "Update on Martial Law Situation October 22," 22 October 1979.

[9] Kihl Young Whan, *Politics and Policies in Divided Korea: Regimes in Contrast* (Boulder, CO: Westview, 1984), 76. In private conversations with Ambassador Gleysteen, Kim said that he thought EM-9 should be repealed and that he was concerned about "the accumulation of grievances against the Park government and the relatively depressed economic climate in which such grievances can grow." See telegrams from Gleysteen to Vance, "Meeting with Kim," 17 March 1979, and "Charges of U.S. Complicity in President Park's Death," 19 November 1979.

[10] Telegram from Gleysteen to Vance, "ROK Announce Partial Investigative Results on President's Death," 28 October 1979.

[11] Kihl, *Politics and Policies*, 78.

now on a thousand demonstrators who were inviting such an attack."[12] On 6 December, Choi was elected interim president by the electoral college, and the following day he gave hope to the opposition that he was a reformer by lifting the much-hated Emergency Measure 9 (EM-9) and releasing Kim Dae Jung, a key opposition leader, from house arrest.[13]

On 12 December, Major General Chun Doo Hwan, the commander of the Defense Security Command, and "a group of men very close to President Park,"[14] arrested sixteen military generals, including martial law commander General Chung, and initiated a purge of reformers at all levels of the military.[15] Their primary motivations were a fear that social unrest would break out very soon and a concern that the older, more moderate officers were mishandling the prosecution of Kim Chae Kyu.[16] Chun would later consolidate the purge of reformers by maneuvering into the job of acting director of the KCIA while retaining his post as director of the Defense Security Command.[17]

In spite of these movements by hardliners against reformers in the military, the civilian government continued to pursue liberalization. 1,722 political prisoners were released or had their sentences reduced in December 1979, and in February 1980 the government relaxed press censorship and restored political rights to Kim Dae Jung and hundreds of EM-9 violators.[18] The move briefly appeased radicals,[19] but the probably intentional effect on the moderate opposition was to start up an age-old internecine rivalry between Kim Dae Jung and Kim Young Sam that would hamper their ability to focus on their real opponents.[20]

In April 1980, students participated in massive, but peaceful demonstrations on the twentieth anniversary of the student revolution that toppled Syngman Rhee, Korea's first president. But even as student pressure remained contained, labor pressure was on the rise. A miners' strike at Sabuk turned violent,

---

[12] Telegram from Gleysteen to Vance, "Martial Law Administrator General Chong Song-Hwa Briefs the Press," 29 November 1979.

[13] Kihl, *Politics and Policies*, 77; and telegram from Gleysteen to Vance, "ROKG Announces the Lifting of Emergency Measure 9," 7 December 1979.

[14] Telegram from Gleysteen to Vance, "Younger ROK Officers Grab Power Positions," 13 December 1979.

[15] Yang Sung Chul, *The North and South Korean Political Systems* (Boulder, CO: Westview, 1994), 429; and telegram from Christopher to Vance, "Military Power Play in South Korea," 12 December 1979.

[16] Donald Stone MacDonald, *The Koreans: Contemporary Politics and Society* (Boulder, CO: Westview, 1990), 58; and telegram from Gleysteen to Vance, "Younger ROK Officers Grab Power Positions," 13 December 1979.

[17] Kihl, *Politics and Policies*, 78.

[18] Telegrams from Gleysteen to Vance, "Release of Prisoners on Occasion of Inauguration," 21 December 1979, and "Political Rights Restored," 29 February 1980.

[19] Telegram from Gleysteen to Vance, "ROK Universities: Off to a Calm Start," 14 March 1980.

[20] Kihl, *Politics and Policies*, 78.

and a Pusan steel mill riot left one dead and several injured.[21] Moreover, the Federation of Korean Trade Unions (FKTU) threatened to sue the government if it did not eliminate the Special Measures law that denied rights to labor.[22] This rise in radical pressure on the government did not go unnoticed. By 1 May, the Martial Law Command (MLC) was issuing warnings that labor and campus disturbances would no longer be tolerated.[23] Hardliners were in position.

The first student-MLC clashes took place on 2 May, as students at Seoul National University tried to take a demonstration off campus.[24] The result of the clashes was to reorient student demands to a call for the end of martial law by 15 May.[25] Their patience exhausted, moderates agreed to ally with radicals: Kim Dae Jung joined in the demand on 8 May, and Kim Young Sam and the Catholic Church joined on 9 May.[26] The result on 15 and 16 May was 40–50,000 students in the streets of Seoul alone.[27] In an effort to bolster students' demands, Kim Young Sam and Kim Dae Jung displayed unprecedented unity by jointly calling for the lifting of martial law.[28] For hardliners, this final coalition between radicals and unified moderates was the final provocation. On 17 May 1980, the military arrested several student leaders and pressured President Choi and the Cabinet to extend martial law to the whole country, giving the military direct control.[29] Kim Dae Jung and Kim Young Sam were promptly arrested. That morning newspapers printed the official text of the martial law order, citing "current North Korean movements and the certainty of incidents of unrest all across the ROK" as reasons for the return to military rule.[30]

---

[21] Ibid.; and telegram from Gleysteen to SecState, "More Violence on Labor Scene," 1 May 1980. NB: "SecState" was used in the interim period after Secretary Vance resigned and before Edwin Muskie became secretary of State.

[22] Telegram from Gleysteen to Vance, "Organized Labor Calls for Suspension of Special Measures Law," 29 April 1980.

[23] Telegram from Gleysteen to SecState, "Martial Law Command Threatens Action Against Future Disturbances," 1 May 1980.

[24] Telegram from Gleysteen to SecState, "Student-Police Clashes Occur for First Time This Year," 2 May 1980.

[25] Telegram from Gleysteen to SecState, "Student Activism Turns to National Political Issues," 5 May 1980.

[26] Telegram from Gleysteen to SecState, "National Alliance Calls for Resignation of Prime Minister and Acting Chief of KCIA," 8 May 1980; and telegrams from Gleysteen to Secretary of State Edwin Muskie, "Kim Young Sam May 9 Press Conference," 9 May 1980, and "Catholic Church Calls for Lifting of Martial Law," 9 May 1980.

[27] Telegram from Gleysteen to Muskie, "Seoul Sitrep, 2000 May 15: Demonstrations Out in Force but Police Lines Holding," 15 May 1980.

[28] Telegram from Gleysteen to Muskie, "Kim Dae Jung and Kim Young Sam Join in Call for Lifting of Martial Law and Resignation of Prime Minister and Acting KCIA Chief," 16 May 1980.

[29] Telegram from Gleysteen to Muskie, "Crackdown in Seoul," 17 May 1980.

[30] See Kihl, *Politics and Policies*, 79; and telegram from Gleysteen to Muskie, "ROK Sitrep as of 0900 18 May," 18 May 1980.

On 18 May, thousands of students from Chosun University initiated a demonstration in Kwangju that drew massive support.[31] Demonstrators called for
the release of Kim Dae Jung (who was from Kwangju) and an immediate end
to military rule. Army Special Forces were sent to stop the demonstration and
in the ensuing struggle used fixed bayonets on demonstrators, causing several
deaths. By midafternoon a full scale riot had broken out, attracting thousands
of townspeople and ordinary citizens.[32] Rioting continued on 19 May, as crowds
swelled to 100,000.[33] On 20 May, the Korean Army was forced to withdraw.
After seven days of siege, the regular Korean Army entered the city in the early
morning hours and took control in a "relatively bloodless maneuver."[34] By mid-
day the army had arrested 1,740 civilians, 730 of whom, mostly students, were
detained for investigations.[35] The final death toll for the uprising was officially
put at 230, although unofficial estimates ranged from 600 to 2,000.[36] This first
cycle of liberalization ended in bloodshed without democracy. Chun would rule
with a tight grip for the next six years.

The second cycle of liberalization would not begin in earnest until February
1986, when the opposition launched a petition campaign for a constitution with
direct elections. Under the aegis of the new campaign, the opposition successfully united under a new party (NKDP) and pushed hard for liberalization. Reformers in the government party (DJP) relented, initiating a dialogue on constitutional reform. But subsequent demonstrations, especially the Inchon
demonstration on 3 May, indicated the growing radicalization of certain groups
within the opposition.[37] The growing power of these radicals fueled a reformer
faction in the military that feared that if they did not negotiate with the moderate opposition soon, radicals would become too powerful and attempt to violently overthrow the Chun regime.[38]

Hardliners quickly grew impatient with bickering between and within the
DJP and NKDP. On 13 April 1987, Chun suspended debate on constitutional
reform, and on 10 June he nominated retired General Roh Tae Woo to succeed

---

[31] For an excellent account of the Kwangju uprising, see Nam Koon Woo, *South Korean Politics:
The Search for Political Consensus and Stability* (New York: University Press of America, 1989),
221–224.

[32] See MacDonald, *The Koreans*, 58–59; and telegram from Gleysteen to Muskie, "Korea Sitrep—5
M. May 19," 19 May 1980.

[33] Telegram from Gleysteen to Muskie, "Seoul Sitrep, 1430 May 21," 21 May 1980.

[34] MacDonald, *The Koreans*, 58–59.

[35] Nam, *South Korean Politics*, 223.

[36] Yang, *The North and South*, 429–431. For example, the human rights group AsiaWatch maintains
that 2,000 civilians were killed.

[37] James Cotton, "From Authoritarianism to Democracy in South Korea" in James Cotton, ed.,
Korea Under Roh Tae-woo: Democratization, Northern Policy and Inter-Korean Relations (Canberra:
Allen & Unwin, 1993), 33.

[38] Cotton, "From Authoritarianism," 33; Robert E. Bedeski, "State Reform and Democracy in
South Korea" in Cotton, *Korea Under Roh*, 65; and Edward A. Olsen, "The Challenge of Political
Change Overseas," *Washington Quarterly* 10 (Spring 1987): 177.

him under the unchanged constitution. The opposition exploded as thousands of demonstrators took to the streets in Seoul and elsewhere.[39] Over the course of the next two weeks, reformers began to convince hardliners that they had no choice this time, that repression could not succeed. General Roh sensed this shift away from hardliners in the military and began to "pull away from Chun."[40] Finally, on 26 June, General Roh announced that the demands of the opposition would be met, including for the first time direct and open presidential elections. Thus was democracy born in the second cycle of liberalization.

A MODEL OF LIBERALIZATION

In both cycles, initial liberalization by the government engendered increasing demands by the opposition for further liberalization. The spiraling conflict eventually led to a reversal of liberalization that provoked significant demonstrations (Pusan and Masan in 1979, Seoul and Kwangju in 1980, and the June demonstrations in 1987). However, the outcomes of these cycles were very different (crackdown in 1980 and democracy in 1987). What factors could explain the different outcomes?

The transitions to democracy literature describes the liberalization process generally as a two-stage interaction in which the opposition pushes for reform and the government either reforms or cracks down on the opposition. Following a distinction originating with Guillermo O'Donnell, these reforms can either be described as liberalization (prisoner releases, relaxation of restriction on dissent) or democratization (free and fair elections).[41] The distinction is important because, as Samuel Huntington notes, liberalization without democratization is inherently unstable.[42] Instead of reducing pressure on the government, liberalization gives the opposition more leeway and a greater incentive to increase pressure for democratization. Hence, the interaction between the government and the opposition is repeated through successive stages of partial liberalization until the government either democratizes, cracks down on the opposition, or is overthrown. Adam Przeworski concludes: "These indeed are the alternatives: either to incorporate the few groups that can be incorporated and to repress everyone else, returning to authoritarian stasis, or to open the political agenda to the problem of institutions, that is, democracy."[43]

[39] Don Oberdorder, "U.S. Policy in the 1987 Crisis Compared With Other Allies" in Robert A. Scalapino and Lee Hongkoo, eds., *Korea–U.S. Relations: The Politics of Trade and Security* (Berkeley: University of California Press, 1988), 180; and Okonogi Masao, "South Korea's Experiment in Democracy" in Cotton, *Korea Under Roh*, 11.

[40] Author's interview with U.S. Ambassador to South Korea James Lilley, 28 February 1997.

[41] See Guillermo O'Donnell, "Notas para el estudio de procesos de democratización a partir del estado burocrático-autoritario," *Estudios CEDES* (Buenos Aires: Centro de Estudios de Estado y Sociedad, 1979).

[42] Samuel Huntington, *The Third Wave: Democratization in the Late Twentieth Century* (Norman: University of Oklahoma Press, 1991), 136–137.

[43] Adam Przeworski, *Democracy and the Market: Political and Economic Reforms in Eastern Europe and Latin America* (Cambridge, UK: Cambridge University Press, 1991), 60.

While this explanation illuminates the choices facing the government and the opposition in transitions to democracy, treating these groups as unitary actors obscures the competition to influence strategy that takes place within each group. To enrich the model, we can use the typology introduced by O'Donnell and further elaborated by Przeworski, in which the government is divided into two factions—hardliners and reformers—and the opposition is divided into moderates and radicals.[44] Though these writers use the typology to refer to actors with strictly different preferences, it may be more useful to think of them as existing along spectra from radical to moderate and from reformer to hardliner. For example, some hardliners might be more inclined to support reform than others, while some radicals might be more inclined to support moderate opposition strategies.

Each faction exercises power in two ways—by provoking a response or by changing preferences. For example, if moderates participate in large radical demonstrations, this might cause hardliners to crack down. However, it might also cause some hardliners to be more receptive to reform if the demonstration changes their belief about the probability that a crackdown will have hugely negative consequences. Thus the predictive power of this model may be hampered by an inability to assess the relative weight of cross-cutting effects. This should not, however, discourage the use of the typology as an analytical tool to clarify the interests of each faction and to discover whether explanatory hypotheses can be eliminated because they fall too far outside the realm of the possible.

The most important result of the typology is that the reformer faction is critically important to successful transitions to democracy. To maximize their own benefit in a potential transition, reformers must marginalize radicals by making concessions to moderates. Otherwise, opposition strategies will become more extreme as radicals lose patience with the process, increasing the risk of civil disorder. However, the natural tendency of the opposition to demand greater and greater concessions may increase the probability that hardliners will respond by cracking down to avoid a loss of power. Caught in a high-risk balancing act, reformers must be able to face down or change the hardliners if they are to continue making concessions and complete the process of transition.[45] Thus, a weak reformer faction is a recipe for failure, while a strong reformer faction can dramatically improve the probability of democratization.

The importance of the strength of reformers is empirically verified in South Korea. In the first cycle of liberalization, Kim Chae Kyu tried to initiate a coup in the name of democratization, but the coup failed when reformers failed to support him. Moreover, Chun Doo Hwan was able to purge reformers in the military and in the KCIA, meaning that there were no reformers left to oppose

[44] Ibid., 67.

[45] Courtney Jung and Ian Shapiro, "South Africa's Negotiated Transition: Democracy, Opposition, and the New Constitutional Order," *Politics and Society* 23 (September 1995): 278–280.

garrison decree and the crackdown at Kwangju. However, in the second cycle, Roh Tae Woo led a group of reformers that convinced Chun to step down. In both of these cycles, the relative strength of reformers correlated directly to the likelihood of a transition. When reformers were weakest, hundreds died at Kwangju. When reformers were strongest, democracy bloomed. Any explanation of the timing of the transition must thus be tested for its effect on reformers.

AD HOC EXPLANATIONS

Scholars and other observers have advanced many ad hoc explanations that identify one factor or another as being important to the timing of Korean liberalization. Five of the most common arguments will be addressed here. First, there is widespread agreement that nationwide demonstrations held in June 1987, especially those held on the 18th and 19th, were very important in contributing to Chun's decision to allow direct elections.[46] The most common argument in the literature is that these demonstrations were unique because they drew the support of the middle-class or ordinary citizens.[47] More and more Koreans identified themselves as middle class over the period, and Soo Young Auh hypothesizes that middle-class Koreans as "postmaterialists" were better educated, more physically secure, and thus more likely to place a "high priority on self-expression" and participate in demonstrations.[48] This effect primarily increased civilian support for the opposition, but it also increased the strength of reformers in the lower ranks of the military as they too became middle class.[49] Thus authors like Robert E. Bedeski assert that a critical threshold of support from a "broader cross-section of society" was reached in 1987, which finally led to a "popular reaction" against the government.[50]

However, the middle class also participated to a lesser degree in the first cycle. The Pusan demonstration in October 1979 was the first major demonstra-

---

[46] For samples, see Okonogi, "South Korea's Experiment," 11; Bedeski, "State Reform," 65; and Sam Jameson, "U.S. Reportedly Had Little Influence in South Korean Policy Turnabout," *Los Angeles Times*, 3 July 1987.

[47] See Daniel A. Bell, *Towards Illiberal Democracy in Pacific Asia* (New York: St. Martin's, 1995), 87; Bedeski, "State Reform," 65; Jameson, "U.S. Reportedly," 12; Oberdorfer, "U.S. Policy," 180; and Russell Watson, "Crisis in Korea," *Newsweek*, 29 June 1987, 8. This view was also expressed in the author's interviews with Ambassador William Gleysteen, 27 February 1997 and Deputy Assistant Secretary of State Michael Armacost, 28 February 1997.

[48] Soo, "The Impact of Value Change on Democratization in Korea," (http://www.kois.go.kr/Explore/Studies/15.html), 1 January 1997. See also Tat Yan Kong, "From Relative Autonomy to Consensual Development: The Case of South Korea," *Political Studies* 43 (December 1995): 641. For a description of the theory of postmaterialist values, see Ronald Inglehart, *Culture Shift in Advanced Industrial Society* (Princeton: Princeton University Press, 1990).

[49] Author's interview with Gleysteen, 27 February 1997.

[50] Bedeski, "State Reform," 69.

tion that was widely supported by townspeople;[51] and the Kwangju incident in May 1980 brought thousands of ordinary citizens onto the streets. That this behavior was first observed in 1979 is no surprise; a public opinion poll in early 1980 showed that for the first time, Koreans viewed a greater share in political decision making and a larger measure of personal freedom as more important than economic priorities.[52] Even though the middle class did participate somewhat more in 1987, some observers doubt that they played a significant role in the demonstrations.[53] The weakness of the middle class did not pose a barrier to transitions in countries like the Philippines, for example.

Second, labor is another group that has been cited in the literature as critical to the 1987 demonstrations.[54] With productivity rising twice as fast as wages, workers resented the fact that they had not shared in the fruits of the Korean economic miracle. Moreover, though workers' rights of free association and collective bargaining were included in the constitutions under both Park and Chun, in practice these rights were not protected.[55] The result, it is argued, was that labor increased its support for the radical opposition by joining in student demonstrations or organizing protests of their own during the second cycle of liberalization.

However, labor activity was even more pronounced in the first cycle of liberalization because of the dramatic economic problems experienced in 1979 and 1980. The international oil shock and a disastrous rice harvest because of a severe winter fueled inflation and caused the Korean economy to shrink in 1980 for the first time since the 1950s.[56] If anything, the economic crisis should have made a transition to democracy more likely.[57] Responding to the crisis, students tried to stimulate support for demonstrations by including specific economic demands such as punishment for businesses that lay off workers.[58] As a result, workers began striking for better wages and working conditions.[59] The Y. H. Trading Company sit-in at the NDP in August 1979 and labor support for the demonstrations in Pusan and Masan in October 1979 contributed to the

[51] Telegram from Gleysteen to Vance, "More on Pusan Demonstration; Demonstration at EWHA University in Seoul," 17 October 1979.

[52] MacDonald, *The Koreans*, 127.

[53] See, for instance, Chalmers Johnson, "South Korean Democratization: The Role of Economic Development" in Cotton, *Korea Under Roh*, 105.

[54] See, for example, Bedeski, "State Reform," 64.

[55] Robert E. Bedeski, *The Transformation of South Korea: Reform and Reconstitution in the Sixth Republic Under Roe Tae Woo, 1987–1992* (New York: Routledge, 1994), 115.

[56] Sakong Il, *Korea in the World Economy* (Washington, DC: Institute for International Economics, 1993), 54; and MacDonald, *The Koreans*, 57–58.

[57] Though the empirical evidence is inconclusive, Przeworski intuits that "finer analysis may still show that economic factors operate in a uniform way: Liberalization occurs when an economic crisis follows a long period of growth." Przeworski, *Democracy and the Market*, 97.

[58] Telegram from Gleysteen to Vance, "Second Demonstration at Seoul National University," 20 September 1979.

[59] MacDonald, *The Koreans*, 58.

fall of the Park regime.[60] As the first cycle of liberalization unfolded, labor became more and more active as evidenced by the Peace Market strike, the miners' strike in Sabuk, the FKTU's threat to sue the government over the Special Measures Law, the Pusan steel mill riot, the FKTU rally for the right to strike, and strikes at hundreds of other firms throughout the period, especially as wages were being renegotiated in spring 1980.[61] The Kwangju uprising itself was an example of "labor and student unrest."[62] Recognizing the importance of labor, one of the first actions of the Chun government was to coerce the FKTU to make a statement calling for an end to labor strife.[63] This evidence indicates that labor played an even more important role in the events of 1979 and 1980, meaning that it cannot be credited as a critical factor in the timing of democratization.

Third, Samuel Huntington argues that hardliners in South Korea were constrained by the *nunca más* effect, named for a December 1982 event in Argentina in which the death of a protester led to a call for reconciliation and reduced violence in the transition. In the Korean protests of 1986 and 1987, Huntington notes that Korean authorities were "careful to avoid using firearms so as not to replicate the Kwangju massacre."[64] While this might have been a declared reason to avoid another crackdown, it does not explain why huge peace marches in April 1980 commemorating the twentieth anniversary of the Rhee government's massacre of 200 students failed to have the same effect. Students were undoubtedly screaming "never again" shortly before the massacre at Kwangju. Hence, if we are to believe that hardliners were indeed constrained by the *nunca más* effect in 1987, the failure of this constraint in 1980 must be explained.

Fourth, other observers argue that the 1988 Olympics played a critical role in constraining hardliners by drawing world attention to the government's actions.[65] The conventional wisdom asserts that if Chun had used the military to crack down on demonstrations, the International Olympic Committee would have moved the Games.[66] General Roh contributed to this perception when he

[60] Tat, "From Relative Autonomy," 638; and Kihl, *Politics and Policies*, 76–78.

[61] Telegram from Gleysteen to Vance, "Garment Workers Strike," 11 April 1980; Kihl, *Politics and Policies*, 78; telegram from Gleysteen to Vance, "Organized Labor Calls for Suspension of Special Measures Law," 29 April 1980; telegram from Gleysteen to SecState, "More Violence on Labor Scene," 1 May 1980; telegram from Gleysteen to Muskie, "FKTU Holds Rally for Right to Strike," 14 May 1980; Frederica M. Bunge, ed., *South Korea: A Country Study* (Washington, DC.: U.S. Government Printing Office, 1982), 179; and telegram from Gleysteen to Christopher, "The Labor Scene: Disputes, Remedies and Recommendations," 6 May 1980.

[62] MacDonald, *The Koreans*, 131.

[63] Telegram from Gleysteen to Muskie, "Unions Feel Pressure from ROKG," 3 June 1980.

[64] Huntington, *The Third Wave*, 196; Former Director of Korean Affairs Robert G. Rich, Jr. concurred with this assertion in an interview with the author on 27 February 1997.

[65] Okonogi, "South Korea's Experiment," 11; Cotton, "From Authoritarianism," 33; and Jameson, "U.S. Reportedly," 12.

[66] Johnson, "South Korean Democratization," 104.

announced that liberalization would take place in the name of political tranquility, a smooth transition, legitimate government, and a peaceful Olympic Games.[67] However, the importance of the Games is questionable. They did not lead to liberalization in other nations—the Soviet Union not only did not liberalize prior to games in Moscow in 1980, it invaded Afghanistan. Moreover, the threat of moving the Games in the event of a crackdown was probably overstated. The committee had, after all, decided to locate the Games in Seoul despite the hundreds killed in Kwangju. Chun could just as easily have been convinced that the committee's assignment of the Games to Seoul was based on his ability to maintain order by any means necessary.

Finally, many observers argue that the first cycle of liberalization ended in failure because of the weakness of the leader of the interim government, President Choi Kyu Hah.[68] Choi's lack of "political experience and leadership qualities"[69] became apparent almost immediately after he became the acting president. On 10 November 1979, Choi infuriated opposition leaders when he announced a plan for an interim government before consulting them.[70] By December, both the opposition and the government expressed fears that Choi's refusal to announce an explicit timetable for constitutional reform and new elections was increasing the possibility of North Korean intervention.[71] Ambassador William Gleysteen was so pessimistic about Choi's ability to run the government that he began to focus on other men within the government such as Prime Minister Shin.[72] As tensions between radicals and hardliners increased in 1980, Choi's voice was noticeably absent, "adding to the general sense of suspicion rather than setting forth clearly what needs to be done."[73] He actually left the country in May on a diplomatic mission to the Middle East, and though he returned before the 15 May demonstrations, he did nothing to calm radicals or allay pressure from hardliners.[74] In a last ditch effort to get Choi to act, Am-

[67] Bell, *Towards Illiberal Democracy*, 87.

[68] Author's interview with Rich, 27 February 1997; Jameson, "U.S. Reportedly," 12; and Kihl, *Politics and Policies*, 77.

[69] Kihl, *Politics and Policies*, 77.

[70] Telegram from Gleysteen to Vance, "Acting President's Speech and Dissidents," 10 November 1979. It should be noted that after much prodding, Choi did meet with Kim Young Sam and dissident groups two weeks later. See telegrams from Gleysteen to Vance, "Acting President Meets Opposition Leader," 24 November 1979, and "Acting President Meets Religious Leaders," 26 November 1979.

[71] Telegram from Rich to Holbrooke, "Weekly Status Report—Korea," 7 December 1979; and telegrams from Gleysteen to Vance, "Conversation with NDP Assemblymen," 12 December 1979, and "My December 20 Conversation with NDP President Kim Young Sam," 21 December 1979.

[72] See telegrams from Gleysteen to Vance, "Current Political Scene Review with Member of Acting President's Staff," 30 November 1979, "Discussion of Military Grab With President Choi," 13 December 1979, "New Defense Minister," 15 December 1979, and "Korea Focus—My Meeting With Prime Minister December 18," 18 December 1979.

[73] Telegram from Gleysteen to Christopher, "Korea Focus: Building Tensions and Concern Over Student Issue," 8 May 1980.

[74] Telegram from Christopher to Gleysteen, "Korea Focus—Tensions in the ROK," 8 May 1980; and Kihl, *Politics and Policies*, 77.

bassador Gleysteen met with his secretary general on 17 May to emphasize that Choi was the only one who had a chance of heading off the looming confrontation.[75] The meeting obviously failed.

However harshly history might judge Choi's character, he should not be blamed for the failure of the transition. In the wake of Park's assassination, any acting president would have had three choices: ally with the moderate opposition and seek a negotiated transition to democracy, ally with hardliners and support renewed authoritarianism, or make no commitments. That Choi did not ally with hardliners indicates that he must have desired a transition and believed that it was possible. However, any alliance with the opposition so soon after Park was killed in the name of democracy would undoubtedly have alarmed hardliners. Though Park's assassination was "semi-popular,"[76] reformers were naturally constrained by the subversive nature of this attempted political change. Any stronger action by Choi to move toward transition might have encouraged a purge of reformers, perhaps including civilians like Choi himself, even before 12 December. After the purge, Choi was on his own.[77] An indictment of Choi thus misunderstands that he could only be as strong as the reformers who could help him stand down the hardliners.

THE ROLE OF THE UNITED STATES

None of the above ad hoc explanations are satisfactory, because they leave out what must be considered a crucial variable—the role of the United States. The scholarly literature has addressed U.S. influence, but most of these treatments get bogged down by the debate over the use of CFC forces to put down the Kwangju uprising.[78] Some observers blame the United States for approving the brutal use of force in Kwangju.[79] Others side with the State Department, which

[75] Telegram from Gleysteen to Muskie, "My 17 Meeting with Blue House SYG Choi Kwang Soo," 17 May 1980.

[76] Author's interview with Gleysteen, 27 February 1997.

[77] Even though reformers did retain posts in the military (some of whom would be instrumental in 1987), Chun effectively forced them to remain silent by installing loyalists deep within the ranks. Author's interview with Gleysteen, 27 February 1997. By February, a reformer faction in the military was "virtually non-existent," meaning that a negotiated transition to democracy was unlikely. See telegram from Gleysteem to Vance, "Role of the Moderate Opposition in the Transition Away from Authoritarianism," 11 February 1980.

[78] See Kim Hyun K., "Unification Fever and Resentment: A Comparative Analysis of U.S. and Korean Press Reports on Radical Student Movement" in Tae-Hwan Kwak and Lee Seong Hyong, eds., *Forty Years of Korea–U.S. Relations, 1948–1988* (Seoul: Kyung Hee University, 1990), 194. For an especially balanced treatment, see Donald Clark, *Korea Briefing, 1991* (Boulder, CO: Westview, 1991), 156–159.

[79] See Yang, *The North and South*, 431–432; Selig S. Harrison, "Political Alliance in the Two Koreas: The Impact of the American Presence" in Doug Bandow and Ted Galen Carpenter, eds., *The U.S.–South Korean Alliance* (New Brunswick, NJ: Transaction Publishers, 1991) 123; and Tim Shorrock, "U.S. Knew of South Korean Crackdown: Ex-Leaders Go on Trial in Seoul," *Journal of Commerce* 27 (February 1996).

has repeatedly claimed that it was "not involved."[80] Resolving this debate is important, because it will illuminate the choices that U.S. officials faced during the period.

Until 1994, all South Korean troops were technically under the supreme command of an American officer. The CFC structure was originally designed to enable South Korea to quickly deploy its own forces if needed for emergencies other than an invasion by North Korea. While giving the South Koreans more flexibility, the CFC system still kept a considerable amount of authority in the hands of the Americans.[81] In theory, the South Korean government was supposed to obtain U.S. approval before removing forces from the CFC command. However, there was no logistical reason that would prevent the government from removing units first and notifying the United States later.[82] The CFC procedure was used for the first time prior to the Pusan and Masan riots. Ambassador Gleysteen observed that CFC Commander General John A. Wickham had been consulted and the new system worked "in an orderly manner."[83] Six weeks later General Chun demonstrated that the CFC command could be completely ignored when he moved Korean forces away from the border in order to support his takeover of the military.[84]

American officials assert that the special forces sent to put down the original demonstration in Kwangju on 18 May were not under CFC control.[85] Moreover, they imply that the Korean military was not required to and did not consult American authorities before using them.[86] However, there is evidence that on 7 May the United States released from CFC control the 11th and 13th Special Forces Brigades in anticipation of the 15 May demonstrations.[87] The following day Gleysteen wrote: "In none of our discussions will we in any way suggest that the USG opposes ROKG contingency plans to maintain law and order, if absolutely necessary by reinforcing police with the army."[88] Assistant Secretary

---

[80] Moon Ihlwan, "U.S. Still under Fire for 'Role' in 1980 S. Korea Massacre," *Reuters North American Wire*, 30 November 1995. See also Kim Hyun K., "Unification Fever," 195.

[81] For an interesting discussion of the uniqueness of the CFC system, see Harrison, "Political Alliance," 123.

[82] Clark, *Korea Briefing*, 158.

[83] Telegram from Gleysteen to Vance, "Text of Scope Paper RE State Funeral for Korean President Park," 1 November 1979.

[84] Pae Sung Moon, "Korean Perspectives on American Democracy" in Kim Ilpyong J., ed., *Korean Challenges and American Policy* (New York: Paragon House, 1991), 468–469; and Harrison, "Political Alliance," 123.

[85] Michael Armacost in *Hearings before the Subcommittee on Asian and Public Affairs of the Committee on Foreign Affairs House of Representatives*, 96th Congress, 2nd sess., 25 June 1980 and 28 August 1980, 10. See also Harrison, "Political Alliance," 123.

[86] Armacost, *Hearings*, 10; Kim Hyun K., "Unification Fever," 195.

[87] Telegram from Gleysteen to SecState, "ROKG Shifts Special Forces Units," 7 May 1980.

[88] Telegram from Gleysteen to Christopher, "Korea Focus: Building Tensions and Concern Over Student Issue," 8 May 1980. See also telegrams from Gleysteen to Muskie, "Korea Focus: May 9 Conversation with Blue House SYG Kwang Soo Choi," 10 May 1980, and "May 19 Discussion with FonMin on Domestic Politics," 20 May 1980.

of State Warren Christopher wrote back: "We agree that we should not oppose ROK contingency plans to maintain law and order."[89] Although none of this heavily sanitized evidence specifically applies to Kwangju, it does indicate that the United States was aware of a large-scale preparation for a crackdown, which they explicitly did not oppose.

American officials do admit that they approved the release of units used in the final assault on Kwangju.[90] Again, the State Department telegrams emphasize the concern for law and order that motivated officials not to oppose the use of force. On 23 May: "While we will not deny U.S. approval of troop movements and will affirm our belief that the primary task at present is the restoration of law and order, we will not engage in prolonged debate of these actions."[91] On 26 May: "We were not telling the government to refrain from military action since we recognized the dangers of an extended period of lawlessness in Kwangju. . . ."[92]

Many writers have focused on the U.S. role at Kwangju as though it were crucial to the outcome of the first cycle of liberalization. The belief is that if only the Americans had "disapproved" the use of CFC forces, the crackdown would not have occurred and Chun would have been forced to accept a transition to democracy. However, normative arguments about this choice have misunderstood the positive constraints on U.S. actions. Chun did not ask for or receive approval to m   CFC forces on 12 December. By May he would have felt even less pressure to avoid a crackdown, because he had already purged reformers in the Korean military. Thus it is not likely that General Chun would have complied, even if General Wickham had told him no.[93] The American choice was constrained by the lack of actors within the Korean military who could have used an American signal of disapproval to convince Chun not to crack down. Since U.S. decision makers believed that they could not change the outcome, the choice between giving a tacit green light or ruining relations with Chun was obvious. On the other hand, if the United States could have done something earlier to strengthen reformers, the option to disapprove would have been more lucrative, because it would have increased the probability of a successful transition to democracy.

Other observers have argued that the events at Kwangju demonstrate that the influence of the United States was "limited" or "marginal."[94] The fear of

[89] Telegram from Christopher to Gleysteen, "Korea Focus—Tensions in the ROK," 8 May 1980.

[90] Armacost, *Hearings*, 11. General Wickham approved 20th division reinforcements. See Clark, *Korea Briefing*, 158; Pae, "Korean Perspectives," 469; and telegram from Gleysteen to Muskie, "Korea Sitrep, 1800, May 22, 1980," 22 May 1980.

[91] Telegram from Gleysteen to Muskie, "Possible ROK Domestic Reaction to U.S. Position," 23 May 1980.

[92] Telegram from Gleysteen to Muskie, "May 26 Meeting with Blue House SYG Choi," 26 May 1980.

[93] Doug Bandow, *Tripwire: Korea and U.S. Foreign Policy in a Changed World* (Washington, DC: Cato Institute, 1996), 42.

[94] Sohn Hak-Kyu, *Authoritarianism and Opposition in South Korea* (New York: Routledge, 1989), 146; author's interview with Gleysteen, 28 February 1997; Lee Manwoo, Ronald D. McLaurin, and

North Korea and the importance of security in Northeast Asia prevented the United States from seriously considering the use of economic or military sanctions to promote liberalization. But this does not exhaust the means of influence at the U.S. command. In the second cycle of liberalization, the United States would make its presence felt primarily through the use of public pressure.

For its first six years, the Reagan administration had explicitly followed a policy to avoid public criticism of allies like Korea.[95] However, the silence was broken in February 1987 when Assistant Secretary Gaston Sigur gave an "exceptionally outspoken" speech in which he called on the Korean government to permanently "civilianize their politics" and implied that Chun could not count on American support if he resisted popular demand for change.[96] The United States also publicly called for a dialogue between the government and the opposition to avert a breakdown that might lead to a North Korean intervention.[97] By June, the United States had dramatically increased its public efforts to pressure the government to proceed with constitutional revision.[98] To head off a plan by Chun to declare martial law, the State Department issued a sharp statement on 19 June.[99] In the aftermath of the Roh declaration on 26 June, many American officials credited public speeches and statements for being the "major instrument of persuasion and impact at the U.S. Command."[100]

Public pressure was brought to bear in the first cycle as well. In August and September 1979, the Korean government complained to the State Department about its increasingly vocal criticism of the renewed enforcement of EM-9, the arrest of NDP officials, and police brutality in the Y. H. Trading Company sit-in at NDP headquarters.[101] When Kim Young Sam was expelled from the National Assembly, State Department officials expressed "deep regret" and claimed that

---

Moon Chung-in, *Alliance Under Tension: The Evolution of Korean–U.S. Relations* (Boulder, CO: Westview, 1988), 45, 150; and Holbrooke, *Hearings*, 28.

[95] Claude A. Buss, *The United States and Korea: Background for Policy* (Stanford, CA: Hoover Institution, 1982), 164; Harrison, "Political Alliance," 123; and Bandow, *Tripwire*, 42.

[96] William Gleysteen and Alan D. Romberg, "Korea: Asian Paradox," *Foreign Affairs* 65 (Summer 1987): 1052. See also Oberdorfer, "U.S. Policy," 179; Lee, McLaurin, and Moon, *Alliance*, 44; Kim Chonghan, "Korea–U.S. Relations: The Convergence and Divergence of National Interests" in Kwak and Lee, *Forty Years*, 12; and Morton Kondracke, "Seoul Searching: South Korea Isn't a Democracy—Yet," *The New Republic*, 27 July 1987, 24.

[97] Bedeski, "State Reform," 65.

[98] Harrison, "Political Alliance," 123; and Oberdorfer, "U.S. Policy," 180.

[99] Kondracke, "Seoul Searching," 24.

[100] Oberdorfer, "U.S. Policy," 179. Ambassador Lilley concurred in his interview with the author, 28 February 1997.

[101] Telegrams from Gleysteen to Vance, "Embassy Expresses Concern Over Arrest of NDP Newspaper Editor," 2 August 1979, and "U.S. Criticism of EM-9," 9 August 1979; telegrams from Vance to Gleysteen, "U.S. Criticism of EM-9," 9 August 1979, and "Police Assault on NDP Headquarters in Trading Co Sit-In Incident," 14 August 1979; and telegrams from Gleysteen to Vance, "Police Assault on NDP Headquarters," 14 August 1979, and "Situation Report: Y. H. Incident—August 16," 16 August 1979.

the expulsion was "inconsistent with the principles of democratic government."[102] More importantly, for the first time ever, the U.S. ambassador to South Korea was recalled to Washington.[103] President Park "complained bitterly" to Ambassador Gleysteen about the recall[104] and with good reason—days later, anger over Kim's expulsion would lead to riots in Pusan, which would lead to Park's assassination. Gleysteen later reflected that U.S. public pressure may have "unwittingly contributed" to his death.[105]

Immediately following Park's assassination, U.S. public pressure declined dramatically. On the plane to Park's funeral, Director of Korean Affairs Robert Rich, Undersecretary of State Richard Holbrooke, and Secretary of State Cyrus Vance decided that an opportunity existed for democratization, which meant that "we had to shut our mouths a bit" and instead pursue liberalization through increased private diplomatic pressure.[106] As a result, the State Department maintained relative silence in November and in stark contrast to their protest of the 1960 coup, refused to criticize the actions taken by General Chun in December 1979.[107] American officials instead protested the breach of CFC command through private channels.[108] After the Korean government agreed on a vague timetable for reform, Holbrooke promised that the U.S. government "would not publicly contest the ROKG version of recent events." In January, reformers in the Korean government hoped they could strengthen their hand by holding a Carter-Choi summit meeting, but the request for the meeting was denied.[109] U.S. public comment remained muted throughout 1980, even in the aftermath of the May declaration of military rule and the Kwangju uprising.[110] Carter's statement to the Democratic Platform Committee on 12 June claimed: "We have promoted an increasingly frank and friendly dialogue with the Korean Government." Throughout the trial of Kim Dae Jung, the policy of the State Department was to avoid public comment.[111]

Thus, in 1979 and 1987, public statements by the American government contributed to the progress of Korean transitions by catalyzing the radical op-

[102] Telegram from Rich to Holbrooke, "Weekly Status Report—Korea," 4 October 1979.

[103] Sohn, *Authoritarianism*, 163.

[104] Author's interview with Gleysteen, 27 February 1997.

[105] William Gleysteen in David D. Newsom, ed., *The Diplomacy of Human Rights* (Washington, DC: University Press of America, 1986).

[106] Author's interview with Rich, 27 February 1997.

[107] Pae, "Korean Perspectives," 468.

[108] Telegram from Gleysteen to Vance, "Younger ROK Officers Grab Power Positions," 13 December 1979.

[109] Telegram from Gleysteen to Vance, "Trial Balloon RE Visit of President Choi to US," 7 January 1980.

[110] Lee, McLaurin, and Moon, *Alliance*, 38. For a specific example, see the telegram from Christopher to Gleysteen, "Crackdown in Seoul," 18 May 1980, in which the State Department deliberately delays and weakens its response.

[111] See, for example, the telegram from Christopher to Gleysteen, "Korea Focus: Instructions to See General Chun," 7 August 1980.

position and influencing reformers to act against hardliners.[112] Meanwhile, the failure of liberalization in 1980 can be at least partially attributed to the weakness of reformers, especially after they were purged by Chun on 12 December 1979. While there can be no certainty that sustained U.S. public pressure in late 1979 and early 1980 would have strengthened the reformers enough to make a transition to democracy possible, the result is strong enough to raise two important questions. U.S. officials clearly wanted Korea to democratize in 1980, so why did they eliminate an option that could have catalyzed the opposition and strengthened the reformers as happened in 1987? And if there was a good reason to avoid public statements, what caused officials to use public statements in 1987?

Public Pressure in the First Cycle of Liberalization

The word "caution" rings time and again like a mantra throughout declassified telegrams between Ambassador Gleysteen and the State Department. In the first cycle of liberalization, Gleysteen struggled with the State Department's increasing use of public criticism. Before the Carter-Park summit, Gleysteen cautioned the president not to endorse any individual or group engaged in human rights activities.[113] When discussing the Y. H. Trading Company incident with the Korean foreign minister, he explained that he would not have worded the public criticism so strongly.[114] In September 1979, Gleysteen urged that Washington not denounce the expulsion of Kim Young Sam, but instead call for "mutual restraint."[115] Days later, when Kim Young Sam criticized President Carter's visit and the embassy in a *New York Times* article, Gleysteen refused to rebut in order not to exacerbate tensions in the present environment.[116] Richard C. Holbrooke further noted that public statements had been moderated because of Gleysteen's influence.[117] In October, Gleysteen recommended avoiding comment on military law and the demonstrations in Masan and Pusan.[118]

---

[112] This also appears to be true of 1960, when U.S. statements "catalyzed" the movement that sent Syngman Rhee into exile. See MacDonald, *The Koreans*, 53.

[113] Telegram from Gleysteen to Vance, "Summit Background Paper 3: Human Rights," 25 May 1979.

[114] Telegram from Gleysteen to Vance, "Meeting with FonMin on Y. H. Trading Company Incident," 17 August 1979.

[115] Telegram from Gleysteen to Vance, "Meeting with Blue House Official on Political and Human Rights," 15 September 1979.

[116] Telegram from Gleysteen to Vance, "Kim Young Sam Criticizes President Carter's Visit and Embassy," 17 September 1979.

[117] Telegram from Vance to Gleysteen, "Assistant Secretary Holbrooke's Bilateral with ROK Foreign Minister Park R—Korean Political Developments," 27 September 1979.

[118] Telegrams from Gleysteen to Vance, "Situation in Pusan Following Declaration of Martial Law," 18 October 1979, and "Embassy Thoughts on Current Mood Following Declaration of Martial Law in Pusan," 20 October 1979.

After Park's assassination, Gleysteen was much more successful at restraining comments. After Park's assassination he urged the State Department to work toward political liberalization through diplomatic channels.[119] After the 12 December incident, Warren Christopher noted: "On the basis of Ambassador Gleysteen's recommendation, we are being cautious at this juncture in how we publicly characterize the situation and are avoiding any implication of a coup d'etat."[120] A pattern had definitely emerged, which was carried into 1980. During the Kwangju crisis, Gleysteen recommended that Korea–U.S. planning talks set for June not be canceled.[121] And as Congress considered public punitive action in June 1980, he opposed it, preferring that members of Congress write letters instead.[122] In response to the verdict in the trial of Kim Dae Jung, he opposed a strong public statement.[123]

The Carter administration "relied very heavily" on Ambassador Gleysteen.[124] Moreover, Gleysteen has admitted that he "managed to keep public statements repressed" after Park's assassination.[125] However, it is difficult to believe that this entirely explains the dramatic change observed in the first cycle of liberalization. What conditions existed that would give Gleysteen so much more power over public commentary?

The Iranian revolution and the taking of American hostages in 1979 had a twofold impact on U.S. policy towards South Korea. First of all, it diverted the attention of both the State Department and the administration away from Korea.[126] Gleysteen noted that "Iran distracted the Administration while it disciplined them," which enabled him to exert more control over the use of public criticism.[127] Second, though, it motivated analogies that directly influenced U.S. policy. Kim Young Sam drew the analogy in a speech at Yale: "If the U.S. had made the Shah step down ten years ago and had engaged in dialogue with the opposition, there wouldn't exist a situation in which the embassy is being stormed."[128] In September 1979, Kim compared the embassy in Seoul with that in Teheran just before the shah's downfall.[129]

[119] Telegram from Gleysteen to Vance, "Initial Reflections on Post-Park Chung Hee Situation in Korea," 28 October 1979.

[120] Telegram from Christopher to Vance, "Military Power Play in South Korea," 12 December 1979.

[121] Telegram from Gleysteen to Muskie, "Your Memo to the Secretary for the PRC Meeting," 22 May 1980.

[122] Telegram from Gleysteen to Muskie, "Korean Focus: Consultations with Congress," 12 June 1980.

[123] Telegram from Gleysteen to Muskie, "U.S. Comment on Kim Dae Jung Verdict," 5 September 1980.

[124] Author's interview with Armacost, 28 February 1997.

[125] Author's interview with Gleysteen, 27 February 1997.

[126] Lee, McLaurin, and Moon, *Alliance*, 38.

[127] Author's interview with Gleysteen, 27 February 1997.

[128] Telegram from Gleysteen to Vance, 22 February 1979.

[129] Telegram from Gleysteen to Vance, "Kim Young Sam Criticizes President Carter's Visit and Embassy," 17 September 1979.

The State Department had its own opinions. Robert Rich noted that while the Iran analogy existed at the White House and congressional level, at State it was felt that there was "no possibility" of Korea becoming another Iran.[130] Gleysteen echoed this skepticism, pointing out that the analogy that was drawn depended on the orientation of the person making it. Those who believed the United States should take an active role in promoting Korean liberalization argued that a public perception by the Korean population that the United States is too closely tied to the Korean government could produce anti-American outbursts like those in Iran. Others used the Iran example to warn against pressing too hard on the Korean government.[131]

Meanwhile, newspapers in the United States were drawing their own conclusions in editorials that found their way into State Department telegrams to Seoul.[132] Heavily influenced by Congress and the press, the White House feared the destabilizing effect of unbridled demonstrations, because after Iran "another failure would have been disastrous."[133] On 4 December, Richard Holbrooke directed Gleysteen to work to moderate the opposition's actions:

> I have been talking privately with key Senators and Congressmen, including [Sam] Nunn, [John] Glenn, [Lester] Wolff, [Richard] Stone, and a few others about our strategy. We have their full support at this time. Their attitudes, like everyone else's, are dominated by the Iranian crisis and, needless to say, nobody wants another "Iran"—by which they mean American action which would in any way appear to unravel a situation and lead to chaos or instability in a key American ally. . . . What we have in mind is your sending a clear message to Christian dissidents who are now stirring up street demonstrations. . . . Even when these are in fact not demonstrations, but rather just meetings in defiance of martial law, the U.S. Government views them as unhelpful while martial law is still in effect. . . . The purpose of the message to the Christians is to alert them to the fact that they should not automatically count on the same degree of American support now that they might have had a few months ago. . . . The purpose of this approach, quite frankly, is to enhance U.S. credibility with the leadership on the eve of some tough decisions.[134]

Though Gleysteen refused to issue an explicit message to opposition leaders, he wrote back to Holbrooke: "We have been doing something which resembles your reftel proposal."[135] Thus, the Iranian crisis not only gave Gleysteen a freer

---

[130] Author's interview with Rich, 27 February 1997.

[131] Telegram from Gleysteen to Vance, "Anti-Government Demonstration at YWCA Hall and Leaflets Distributed at Seoul National University," 26 November 1979.

[132] Telegram from Gleysteen to Vance, "Hankuk Ilbo Article on Treatment of ROK Reporters," 13 October 1979; and telegram from Vance to Gleysteen, "New York Times Editorial on Korea," 16 December 1979.

[133] Author's interview with Gleysteen, 27 February 1997.

[134] Telegram from Vance to Gleysteen, "Korea Focus—Nudging ROK Political Leaders," 4 December 1979.

[135] Telegram from Gleysteen to Holbrooke, "Korea Focus—Nudging ROK Political Leaders," 7 December 1979.

hand, but helps to explain why the human rights-conscious Carter administration in 1979 changed its policy of asserting overt pressure on the Korean government for liberalization.

Public Pressure in the Second Cycle of Liberalization

In the aftermath of Park's assassination, Gleysteen was keenly aware of the potential for igniting a strong anti-American reaction if the opposition believed the United States was not supporting liberalization.[136] However, he seemed to fear an anti-American reaction within the Korean military even more. As a result, he argued against pushing "too hard and too crassly" for liberalization.[137] The pivotal event, though, that would cause anti-American sentiment to "explode" and become a significant factor in domestic politics was the Kwangju incident.[138] Amid their struggle in May 1980, the citizens of Kwangju believed that America should and would actively intervene to enforce justice and bring about a much-desired end to military rule.[139] But the United States chose not to intervene beyond approving the use of CFC forces to put down the uprising. American authorities were well aware that this action risked fanning anti-American sentiment.[140] The perception of American collusion with the military authorities was further bolstered by the Reagan administration's hasty move to invite General Chun to be the first foreign head of state to visit the White House.[141] An anti-American backlash that Gleysteen had feared would come from the military came instead from the opposition and quickly spread to mainstream Koreans.[142]

Anti-Americanism conditioned the second cycle of liberalization as Koreans became increasingly disillusioned with America's continued military, diplomatic, and economic support for the Chun regime. Many who had in the past looked to the United States as an example of participatory democracy came to

[136] Ibid.

[137] Telegram from Gleysteen to Vance, "Initial Reflections on Post-Park Chung Hee Situation in Korea," 28 October 1979.

[138] There is widespread agreement on this point. See Lee, McLaurin, and Moon, *Alliance*, 10; Nam, *South Korean Politics*, 223; Kwak Tae-Hwan and Wayne Patterson, "Security Relations Between Korea and the United States 1960–1984" in Lee Yur-Bok and Wayne Patterson, eds., *One Hundred Years of Korean-American Relations, 1882–1982* (University: University of Alabama Press, 1986), 120; Hyun Sing-il, "Anti-Americanism in Korean Student Movement" in Kwak and Lee, *Forty Years*, 36; Bandow, *Tripwire*, 42; and Jameson, "U.S. Reportedly," 12.

[139] Bandow, *Tripwire*, 42; and telegram from Gleysteen to Muskie, "Kwangju Riot and Political Stability," 21 May 1980.

[140] Telegram from Gleysteen to Muskie, "May 22 Meeting with FonMin," 22 May 1980.

[141] Lee, McLaurin, and Moon, *Alliance*, 11.

[142] Nam, *South Korean Politics*, 223; Doug Bandow in Bandow and Carpenter, *U.S.-South Korean Alliance*, 80; and telegram from Gleysteen to Muskie, "Kwangju Riot and Political Stability," 21 May 1980.

believe that the United States was actually "part of the problem."[143] As student unrest increased between 1985 and 1987, radicals began to target American citizens and institutions such as the Chamber of Commerce and U.S. Information Agency. In the street demonstrations of 1987, many protesters blamed America "not only for the political intransigence of the Chun government but for its very existence."[144] Even in the aftermath of Roh's 26 June declaration, demonstrators in Seoul pulled down an American flag and burned it on the balcony of a hotel amid "wild applause" and a "roar of approval among the hundreds of thousands of protesters."[145] The effect of this increased anger toward America was the sense that anti-Americanism itself represented "a long-range problem in Korean-American security relations."[146] Thus, the rise in anti-American sentiment was probably an important catalyst that contributed to the decision to use public pressure. However, it is difficult to believe that this entirely explains the dramatic change observed in the second cycle of liberalization. What conditions existed that would have caused the change in 1987?

Just as the failure of Iran made the Carter administration more risk averse, the success in the Philippines caused the Reagan administration to be more aggressive in South Korea. Before the Philippine events, public criticism would have won little favor as a diplomatic tactic directed toward a friendly foreign government.[147] However, the cry of "people power" in the Philippines reached all the way to Washington.[148] Pressure from the Congress came from Representatives like Stephen J. Solarz, who said: "like the Philippines, South Korea is an example of a country where we can more effectively protect our strategic interests by promoting our political values."[149] The press echoed these sentiments in editorials that called on the government to "replicate its success" from the Philippines in Korea by abandoning "quiet diplomacy."[150]

Pressure to draw the analogy was so strong that one State Department document noted: "[Ronald Reagan] has difficulties with comparisons that are sometimes made between Korea and the Philippines" and tried to outline the reasons they were different.[151] Despite this attempt to draw a distinction, the administration's experience in the Philippines was clearly an important factor in leading to the belief that public speeches and statements were their "major instrument of persuasion" in Korea.[152] "The impact of the Aquino accession on

---

[143] Vincent S. R. Brandt in Lee Chong-Sik, ed., *Korea Briefing, 1990* (Boulder, CO: Westview, 1990), 92.

[144] Bandow, *Tripwire*, 28.

[145] Harrison, "Political Alliance," 123–124.

[146] Kwak and Patterson, "Security Relations," 125–126.

[147] Oberdorfer, "U.S. Policy," 179.

[148] Bedeski, "State Reform," 63.

[149] Olsen, "The Challenge," 173.

[150] Raymond Bonner, "It's Time We Start Backing Democracy in South Korea," *New York Times*, 28 June 1987.

[151] Memo, ID#390429SS, FG001, WHORM: Alpha File, Ronald Reagan Library.

[152] Oberdorfer, "U.S. Policy," 179.

South Korea would be difficult to exaggerate. . . . Though [the opposition] knew that the United States did not topple [Ferdinand] Marcos and install [Corazon] Aquino, they understood clearly the United States role as facilitator of the process."[153] Thus, the influence of the Philippines may help to explain why the security-conscious Reagan administration in 1987 changed its policy of avoiding overt pressure on the Korean government for liberalization.

CONCLUSION

As the story of democratization continues to unfold in South Korea, more and more of its citizens will come to appreciate the freedoms they enjoy and will wonder why the transition did not occur during the Seoul Spring in 1979 and 1980. Participation by the middle class and labor in civil protest seems important because the demonstrations in 1987 were somewhat larger and more national in scope than those in 1980. However, we find that both labor and the middle class were also active in demonstrations in 1980. The memory of the Kwangju incident may have constrained hardliners in 1987, but if so we must explain why the memory of the student revolution did not restrain them in 1980. Similarly, world attention drawn by the Olympics may have constrained hardliners in 1987, but it might equally have encouraged them to enforce order more strictly. We might also posit that the weakness of Choi Kyu Hah made a critical difference, but his weakness seemed to be due more to a lack of strength of reformers in the military. None of these explanations is entirely implausible; each probably played a role in determining the outcome. However, they typically do not address the force that drove the transition: the increased strength of reformers within the Korean military meant that they could stand down hardliners in 1987.

The decision by the United States to "approve" the use of CFC forces appeals to many as a reason for a delayed transition, but it is doubtful that opposing the redeployments would have changed the outcome. The lack of reformers who might have been energized by a strong U.S. stand against a crackdown highlights the real role the United States had to play. From Rhee to Roh, public statements issued by the United States had catalyzed the opposition and strengthened the hand of reformers. Yet from November 1979 to January 1987, the United States was conspicuously silent. This silence seems to have been overlooked as a crucial reason that the transition failed.

Contrasting the first cycle of liberalization with the second, we are left with a puzzle. Why was public pressure muted in the first cycle but used in the second? Though Gleysteen always tried to moderate the statements that came out of Washington, public pressure on the Carter administration to avoid "another Iran" ultimately caused it to abandon the use of public pressure. And while rising anti-Americanism in Korea may have increased the Reagan administra-

[153] Olsen, "The Challenge," 173.

tion's interest in pressuring Chun to democratize, public pressure to repeat the success in the Philippines made the government realize that they had abandoned a powerful tool.

This analysis of South Korea's delay in transition yields three important results. First, external public pressure can be very important in determining the interactions of domestic factions, especially insofar as public pressure affects the relative strength of reformers. Even when strategic reasons prevent a country like the United States from using economic or military sanctions to encourage liberalization, the power of verbal sanctions and public signals should not be underestimated. As ephemeral as public statements might be, in Korea they were used successfully to exert influence and were sorely missed when they were not used.

Second, foreign policy can be driven by less-than-perfect analogies, even if the people who implement policy do not believe in them. At no time did officials at the State Department believe that analogies between South Korea and Iran or the Philippines were valid. Yet pressure from the press and Congress (and perhaps by extension, the American people) caused the policy to change anyway. In spite of the best efforts of policy makers to treat each situation as unique, they are constrained by a populace and their elected officials who use analogies to cope with understanding complex political situations.

Finally, though President Carter is widely known for his commitment to human rights and President Reagan is better known for his commitment to security, we should be very wary of such facile generalizations. The Carter administration clearly abandoned an important human rights tool in the name of security long before Reagan took the reins. Moreover, the Reagan administration would ultimately risk security by using this tool to promote the transition. These counterintuitive changes under presidents that seemed ideologically pure indicate that both administrations were reacting to rather than driving international changes.*

* I would like to thank my professors, Marc Trachtenberg and Leonard Wantchekon, for their continuous support and helpful suggestions; Sandy Peterson for her help in acquiring the declassified documents; and the participants at the 3rd Annual Boston Area Graduate History Symposium for an insightful discussion of the implications of this research. Though the article could not have been written without these individuals, I should emphasize that the views expressed are my own.

The Stinger Missile and U.S. Intervention
in Afghanistan

ALAN J. KUPERMAN

Like much cold war history, the landmark 1986 decision by the United States to arm the Afghan Mujahedin[1] with Stinger antiaircraft missiles—purportedly the first time American-made weapons were supplied to kill Soviet troops—has been distorted by opposing political forces. On one side, and winning the public-relations battle, are conservatives who claim the weapon had a decisive military impact, hastening Soviet withdrawal and the eventual collapse of communism, thereby vindicating their longstanding hawkish approach to the cold war. Opposed are liberals who argue not only that the Stinger did not drive the Red Army out of Afghanistan, but that it actually prolonged the occupation by denying the Soviets an earlier face-saving withdrawal, thereby vindicating their more dovish approach.

The dispute continues, in part because the complete story of the Stinger decision and its impact on the Soviet withdrawal never has been told. Large chunks have emerged in press clippings, investigative reports, and scholarly excavations of the Soviet archives, but they often have been mixed with misinformation and never assembled into a coherent whole. Because of the withholding of key documents by the governments of the United States and Russia, a total picture may not come to light for many years. However, it recently has become possible to tell this fascinating and cautionary tale of cold war decision-making by piecing together and cross-checking earlier fragmentary reports, reviewing newly declassified documents, and consulting former government officials finally willing to speak on the record.

---

[1] The many accepted spellings of this term for the Afghan rebels are standardized in this text, including in quotations where alternate spellings appeared in the original, in order to avoid confusion.

ALAN J. KUPERMAN is a candidate for Ph.D. in political science at the Massachusetts Institute of Technology and research fellow at the Brookings Institution during 1998–1999.

Repeated so often, the Stinger myth has entered political folklore.[2] The year is 1986: Soviet and Afghanistan government forces, utilizing their dominance of the skies, for six years have inflicted terrible punishment on the Afghan Mujahedin rebels and their civilian supporters. Relying on "a combination of scorched earth and migratory genocide,"[3] the Soviets have depopulated large portions of the country, creating an estimated 4.5 million refugees, more than one-quarter of the pre-war population.[4] In desperation, the Mujahedin and their supporters in the United States and Pakistan beg the United States to supply the rebels with an effective antiaircraft weapon to help level the playing field. When the Stinger finally arrives in the fall of 1986, it is a "silver bullet."[5] Soviet and Afghan aircraft begin to fall from the skies as never before. Within two months the Soviet Politburo has set a deadline for withdrawal of its troops, and two years later the last Red Army soldier departs. In quick succession, communism is overthrown in Eastern Europe and, by 1991, the Soviet Union itself has dissolved.

While there is nothing factually incorrect in this chronology, it implies a much greater role for the Stinger than it actually played. It also downplays the Reagan administration's major decision-making failures, which delayed delivery of the missiles for more than a year and led to worldwide Stinger proliferation that continues to haunt American security officials. Most importantly, this widely accepted caricature of history deprives U.S. policy makers of the real lessons of the Stinger experience, essential to avoiding similar mistakes in the future.

A Case Study in Covert-Action Decision Making

By its very nature, covert action is somewhat of a mystery. Decisions are made behind closed doors, memoranda and findings are classified "top secret," and even budget levels are nominally classified, though often leaked to the press. An investigation of the Stinger case, however, reveals that covert-action decision making is not very different from more mundane political matters—replete with rival constituencies, fluid coalitions, legislative lobbying, and as-

---

[2] George Crile, producer, "Charlie Did It," *60 Minutes*, CBS News, 30 October 1988. See also, Fred Barnes, "Victory in Afghanistan: The Inside Story," *Readers Digest*, December 1988; David Ottaway, *Washington Post*, 12 February 1989; Steve Coll, *Washington Post*, 19 July and 20 July 1992; Michael Dobbs, *Washington Post*, 16 November 1992; Tim Weiner, *New York Times*, 24 July 1993; Peter Rodman, *More Precious Than Peace: The Cold War and the Struggle for the Third World* (New York: Charles Scribner's Sons, 1994); Marc Levin, series producer, *CIA: America's Secret Warriors*, Blowback Productions, New York, televised on The Discovery Channel, 1997.

[3] Major Joseph J. Collins, U.S. Army, quoted in Charles Mohr, *New York Times*, 13 April 1986.

[4] Richard P. Cronin, "Afghanistan After Five Years: Status of the Conflict, the Afghan Resistance and the U.S. Role," Report No. 85-20 F, Congressional Research Service, Washington, DC, January 1985, CRS-1.

[5] Congressman Charles Wilson (D-TX), quoted in John Walcott and Tim Carrington, *Wall Street Journal*, 16 February 1988.

sorted backbiting. In this regard, the case confirms Graham Allison's more complex models of governmental decision making, in which "large acts result from innumerable and often conflicting smaller actions by individuals at various levels of bureaucratic organizations in the service of a variety of only partially compatible conceptions of national goals, organizational goals, and political objectives."[6]

The saga begins in December 1979, with the Soviet Union's invasion of Afghanistan and the U.S. decision less than two weeks later to begin supplying weapons to the anticommunist rebels.[7] President Jimmy Carter, who during his first three years in office had publicly denied that the Soviets harbored expansionist intentions, despite mounting evidence to the contrary, simply had had enough.[8] He signed a finding drafted by National Security Adviser Zbigniew Brzezinski, authorizing the covert supply of weapons through Pakistan to help the rebels "harass" Soviet forces—the greatest goal then believed attainable by the ragtag rebels.[9]

Over the next few years, the Red Army gradually transformed inappropriate European-theater military tactics into a more successful counter-insurgency approach. While the rebels proved remarkably committed, they suffered a terrible physical beating under a strategy that took advantage of "virtually complete Soviet dominance in the air"[10] to provide fire-power, reconnaissance, convoy security, tactical lift, mining, ambushes, and dismounted operations. Mujahedin air defenses generally were ineffective, limited to heavy machine guns and a small quantity of unreliable, Soviet-designed SA-7 surface-to-air missiles (SAMs), obtained from defecting Afghan army troops or supplied covertly.[11]

As early as 1983, U.S. Ambassador to Pakistan Ronald Spiers says he recognized the vital contribution the Stinger could make to the rebel cause. Knowing that the recently-developed U.S. missile still was in short supply, Spiers recalls, he sent a classified cable to Lawrence Eagleburger, undersecretary of state for political affairs, urging that "serious consideration" be given to supplying the

---

[6] Graham T. Allison, *Essence of Decision: Explaining the Cuban Missile Crisis* (Boston: Little, Brown, 1971), 6.

[7] Charles G. Cogan, "Partners in Time: The CIA and Afghanistan Since 1979," *World Policy Journal* 10 (Summer 1993): 76.

[8] Robert Gates recently has argued that President Carter was not so naive about Soviet intentions. However, for the first two and a half years the Carter administration limited its covert action to minor propaganda campaigns within the Soviet Union itself. Until the Soviet invasion, covert aid to Afghanistan was limited to less than a million dollars of nonlethal support over six weeks in 1979. Robert Gates, *From the Shadows: The Ultimate Insider's Story of Five Presidents and How They Won the Cold War* (New York: Simon & Schuster, 1996), 142–149.

[9] Rodman, *More Precious*, 216–217.

[10] Alexander Alexiev, *Inside the Soviet Army in Afghanistan*, prepared for the U.S. Army (Santa Monica, CA: Rand, May 1988), 33.

[11] Scott R. McMichael, *Stumbling Bear: Soviet Military Performance in Afghanistan* (London: Brassey's, 1991), 84, 89. See also, Rasul Bakhsh Rais, *War Without Winners* (Karachi: Oxford University Press, 1994), 97.

rebels via Pakistan with Stingers, "when they're available." He also recalls discussing the proposal with Eagleburger during a trip back to Washington, before leaving his post in November 1983.[12] But it appears no significant action was taken on the proposal.[13]

Widespread Opposition to the Stinger Proposal

The rebels themselves took up the plea for effective air defense weapons as early as August 1983, during a visit by two sympathetic U.S. Congressmen, Clarence Long (D-MD) and Charlie Wilson (D-TX). When the American legislators raised the matter with Pakistani President Zia Ul-Haq, however, he instead suggested the alternative of an air cannon like the Swiss-made Oerlikon and rejected any U.S.-made weapons. "If it was American-made the Soviets would trace it to Pakistan and he [Zia] didn't want that," recalled Long.[14] As it turned out, neither did the Reagan administration at the time favor the provision of high-tech U.S. weapons, such as the Stinger, to the Mujahedin. There was virtual unanimity within the administration on this point, although individual agencies often had different reasons for opposition, based on their own parochial concerns.

For the Central Intelligence Agency and especially its cautious Deputy Director John McMahon, directly traceable U.S. involvement raised the danger of public exposure and political scandal that could damage the agency, as had earlier CIA covert operations uncovered by the Pike and Church congressional committees in the 1970s. Despite widespread reports dating back to 1980 that the United States was supplying the rebels tens of millions of dollars in annual aid and coordinating an even larger amount from allies such as Saudi Arabia and China,[15] the agency clung to the tenet of "plausible deniability." As Senator Malcolm Wallop (R-WY) later quipped, the aid program was "bizarrely open for something covert."[16] McMahon insisted that CIA involvement be limited exclusively to the supply of foreign-made weapons to its Pakistani counterpart,

---

[12] Ronald Spiers, interview with author, 16 August 1995. Spiers says the cable was a personal, no dissemination (NODIS) telegram.

[13] Michael Pillsbury, who subsequently worked on the issue at the Pentagon, says he saw no record of the Stinger proposal in the Reagan administration's covert action files prior to 1984 (interview with author, 8 August 1995). Eagleburger can shed no light on this apparently abortive push for the Stinger, saying through a spokesperson that "he just doesn't remember." (Letter from Libby Powell, executive assistant to Lawrence Eagleburger, 28 August 1995.)

[14] Bob Woodward and Charles R. Babcock, *Washington Post*, 13 January 1985.

[15] See, for example , Leslie H. Gelb, "U.S. Said to Increase Arms Aid for Afghan Rebels," *New York Times*, 4 May 1983; Russell Watson with David C. Martin, "Is Covert Action Necessary?" *Newsweek*, 8 November 1982; "Sadat Says U.S. Buys Soviet Arms in Egypt for Afghan Rebels," *New York Times*, 23 September 1981; Michael Getler, "U.S. Reportedly Is Supplying Weapons to Afghan Insurgents; Afghan Rebel Forces Reportedly Getting U.S. Arms Assistance," *Washington Post*, 15 February 1980.

[16] Hearing of the Congressional Task Force on Afghanistan, typescript transcript, 30 April 1986, 53. (Obtained from National Security Archives, Washington, DC.)

the Inter-Services Intelligence Directorate (ISI), which would handle all direct interaction with the rebels. Even though the Mujahedin effort was by far the CIA's largest overseas operation, eventually coming to consume the vast majority of its covert action budget, only a handful of U.S. intelligence officers ever were permitted into the field to observe its implementation.[17]

The agency's other main fear, especially for then-Deputy Director for Intelligence Robert Gates, was the risk of Soviet counter-escalation. In a then-classified 1984 memo, Gates warned that "the Soviets would have to consider more seriously more dramatic action," if the U.S. were to increase aid significantly.[18] In addition, some at the CIA claimed the unsophisticated rebels could not handle a weapon like the Stinger, citing the rebels' past failure to shoot down planes with the Soviet SA-7 missile.[19] Despite retrospective claims that CIA Director Bill Casey had actively pushed for the Stinger starting in the spring of 1983, such assertions are not corroborated by his administration colleagues, and the CIA's institutional stance remained resolutely against providing the missile for several more years.[20]

Pentagon officials too had numerous concerns about supplying the Stinger, but in 1983 they worried most about provoking Soviet retaliation against Pakistan. According to Fred Iklé, undersecretary of defense for policy and the civilian in charge of covert programs at the Pentagon, the danger that "one million Soviet troops" might roll into Pakistan in retaliation was still very real in 1983.[21] Even if the Soviets were to respond only by boosting their cross-border raids into Pakistan, experts warned this could undermine vital Pakistani public sup-

[17] Vince Cannistraro, interview with author, 8 August 1995.

[18] "Nomination of Robert M. Gates," Select Committee on Intelligence, U.S. Senate, S. Hrg. 102–799, Volume II, 24 September, 1–2 October 1991, 449–450. In his later memoirs, Gates is less than frank about the stance he and the CIA took on the Stinger. He claims credit, for himself and the CIA, both for supporting the Stinger decision and for warning of the possible danger of proliferation of Stingers to terrorists. The reality is that U.S. officials who warned about such proliferation were *opposed* to the Stinger decision, as was Gates for a long time. See Gates, *From the Shadows*, 350, 561.

[19] It reportedly later was discovered that the SA-7's given to the rebels had been sabotaged in Poland, explaining their poor performance. (Cannistraro, interview with author, 8 August 1995.) See also, Peter Schweizer, *Victory: The Reagan Administration's Secret Strategy That Hastened the Collapse of the Soviet Union* (New York: The Atlantic Monthly Press, 1994), 118. Others say this is insufficient explanation, given the variety of sources from which SA-7's were obtained. (Pillsbury, interview with author).

[20] Apparently, the original source of many erroneous reports about Casey is a single reference in Joseph Persico, *Casey: From the OSS to the CIA* (New York: Viking, 1990), 312. Persico writes that in 1983 Casey learned "the Afghan rebels wanted American SA-7 Stingers [sic]." Here, Persico confuses the Soviet SA-7 with the American Stinger. Persico then writes: "Yes, Zia told Casey, he would allow these Stingers to be delivered through Pakistan—after he received the first one hundred for himself." Here, Persico apparently conflates a 1983 meeting with one in 1985. Unfortunately, such uncorroborated claims have found their way into otherwise excellent secondary accounts, including James M. Scott, *Deciding to Intervene: The Reagan Doctrine and American Foreign Policy* (Durham, NC: Duke University Press, 1996), 60; and Levin, *CIA: America's Secret Warrriors*.

[21] Fred Iklé, interview with author, 19 August 1995.

port for the Mujahedin.[22] An additional concern was prompted by simulated war games, which indicated the Soviets might retaliate symmetrically by supplying antiaircraft missiles to Central American rebels then confronting the U.S.-supported government in El Salvador.[23]

At the State Department, meanwhile, senior diplomats feared that the spectacle of "Made-in-America" weapons being used to kill Soviet soldiers could upset superpower relations in other, higher-priority areas, such as arms control.[24] Even the Near East desk, which had a more exclusively regional focus, was opposed to such military escalation on grounds it could undercut the nascent negotiating track for peace in Afghanistan.

The Reagan administration also gave great weight to Zia's views, because Pakistan was the linchpin of U.S. strategy in Afghanistan. Although Zia too wanted to help the Mujahedin in Afghanistan, he was under constant Soviet pressure—diplomatically and, near the Afghan border, militarily—to cease funneling aid to the rebels. To retain Zia's allegiance and cooperation, U.S. officials became extremely deferential to his preferences (including overlooking his burgeoning nuclear weapons programs for years after it should have triggered sanctions under U.S. nonproliferation law). Even as late as 1986, when most of the administration had come around to supporting the Stinger proposal, mere reports of Zia's opposition were sufficient to block it.

General Mohammed Yousaf, director of Afghan operations for ISI, learned of Zia's opposition the hard way, according to his memoirs, *The Bear Trap*. In early 1984, soon after being transferred to ISI from the Pakistani army, Yousaf entertained a visiting delegation of private American advocates of the Mujahedin cause. Groups such as the Federation for American-Afghan Action, Free the Eagle, Committee for a Free Afghanistan, and the Freedom Research Foundation played a key role in boosting U.S. aid for the rebels by calling media attention to their struggle and advising conservative members of Congress. When the visiting Americans asked Yousaf which weapon he would recommend to counter Soviet air superiority, he replied frankly, "the Stinger." The Americans, having previously heard CIA reports that Pakistan opposed this weapon, proceeded to the U.S. embassy and accused the CIA station chief of blocking the Pakistani request. He replied that, to the contrary, it was Zia who opposed the Stinger, and the station chief in turn lodged a protest with Yousaf's boss, ISI Chief Akhtar Abdul Rahman. An embarrassed Akhtar invited the delegation back to explain that Yousaf had misspoken: Pakistan did not favor the Stinger.[25]

[22] Barnett R. Rubin, Yale University, testimony before Subcommittee on Asian and Pacific Affairs, Committee on Foreign Affairs, U.S. House of Representatives, 1 May 1986.

[23] Ottaway, *Washington Post*, 12 February 1989.

[24] See, for example, George P. Shultz, *Turmoil and Triumph: My Years as Secretary of State* (New York: Charles Scribner's Sons, 1993), 692.

[25] Mohammed Yousaf and Mark Adkin, *The Bear Trap* (London: Leo Cooper, 1992), 180–181.

Zia often illustrated his opposition to the supply of U.S.-made weapons by utilizing a favorite analogy. The key in Afghanistan, he told CIA Director Bill Casey in late 1982 and a visiting congressional official in early 1984, was to "keep the pot boiling."[26] In other words, the Mujahedin should be armed only enough to continue harassing the Soviets. Too much escalation would cause the "pot to boil over," provoking a Soviet retaliation against Pakistan, he cautioned another U.S. delegation the following year.[27] Indeed, the Soviets explicitly had warned Pakistan against permitting introduction of the Stinger.[28] Zia also reportedly feared that a Stinger could fall into his enemies' hands and be used to shoot down his presidential plane, an ironic footnote in light of his ultimate demise in a suspicious plane crash in 1987.[29]

Although Zia maintained the pot-boiling analogy until at least 1986,[30] it appears he reversed his specific opposition to the Stinger as early as November 1984. That month, he requested U.S. supply of the missile from a visiting congressional delegation led by Senator Sam Nunn (D-GA), ranking member of the Senate Armed Services Committee.[31] Strangely, CIA officials in Washington continued to characterize Zia as opposed to the Stinger for an additional sixteen months, with significant ramifications for U.S. policy.

A Stinger Advocate Joins the Administration

In 1984, the only American officials calling for supply of high-tech U.S. weapons to the Mujahedin were in Congress or private advocacy organizations, while the administration remained strongly opposed to any escalation that would affect the "deniable" nature of U.S. assistance. Indeed, when Congress took up a resolution by Senator Paul Tsongas (D-MA) in October 1984, calling for "material assistance" to be supplied to the Afghan rebels, the State Department and CIA lobbied vigorously in opposition, watering it down to a more ambiguous call to "support effectively" the rebels.[32] As the *Washington Post* reported in January 1985, "congressional supporters wanted initially to supply

[26] John B. Ritch III, "Hidden War: The Struggle for Afghanistan," A Staff Report to the Senate Foreign Relations Committee, April 1984, 36. See also Gates, *From the Shadows*, 252.

[27] Pillsbury, interview with author, 15 August 1995.

[28] Riaz M. Khan, *Untying the Afghan Knot* (Durham and London: Duke University Press, 1991), 175. Khan was a Pakistani official involved for many years in negotiations on Afghanistan.

[29] Yousaf and Adkin, *The Bear Trap*, 181. There is, however, no indication Zia's plane was shot down by a Stinger.

[30] "If anybody's thinking that the greater the heat of the insurgency, the easier the solution, he is wrong." Rubin, testimony of 1 May 1986, 83–84, citing *Washington Post*, 23 March 1986.

[31] "Zia first asked for Stingers for the Mujahedin during a visit by Senator Nunn," according to then-U.S. Ambassador to Pakistan Deane R. Hinton (letter to author, 18 January 1996). The date of the visit was November 1984, and the congressional delegation also included Senators John Glenn (D-OH), Bennett Johnston (D-LA), and David Pryor (D-AR). Senator Sam Nunn, personal communication conveyed by his staff, 20 May 1997.

[32] Cronin, "Afghanistan After Five Years"; also Robert Pear, *New York Times*, 18 April 1988.

U.S.-made Redeye or Stinger ground-to-air, heat-seeking missiles, but the CIA blocked that because those missiles could be traced too easily to the United States."[33]

The monolithic administration stance was broken in September 1984, when conservative senators succeeded in having one of their staffers, Michael Pillsbury, assigned to the Pentagon, where he soon began working on covert programs under Iklé.[34] One of the key policy issues in Congress at the time was the adequacy of U.S. support for anticommunist "freedom fighters" around the world. By October 1984, Pillsbury had drafted a memo for Iklé to send to Secretary of Defense Caspar Weinberger, requesting authorization to explore the provision of high-tech U.S. weapons to the four anticommunist insurgencies then supported by the administration.[35]

Pillsbury was not an immediate convert to the Stinger and initially shared the widespread concern about provoking Soviet retaliation against Pakistan. He first explored four less provocative air-defense options, but eventually found each inadequate.[36] The Soviet SA-7 already had proved largely ineffective in the conflict, especially after Soviet and Afghan aircraft were equipped with flares to distract such heat-seeking missiles. The Blowpipe, a British-designed SAM available in many countries, could maintain plausible deniability but was not a "fire-and-forget" weapon, so that rebels would be vulnerable to attack as they stood in the open to guide the missile onto its target with a joystick. The Swiss-made Oerlikon antiaircraft cannon, a pet project of Congressman Wilson who had added $40 million onto the CIA covert budget specifically for the weapon,[37] was too bulky to satisfy mobility requirements. The Redeye, an obsolete U.S. missile that had served as the model for the Soviet SA-7, was sufficiently dispersed around the globe to provide deniability, but generally was ineffective against helicopters and vulnerable to the same counter-measures as the SA-7. Pillsbury gravitated to the Stinger by default.

By early 1985, the administration was compelled to reassess its approach to the Mujahedin for a variety of reasons. First and most importantly, Soviet forces had sharply escalated attacks against the rebels and their weapons pipeline on the Pakistan border, putting at risk the continued viability of the opposition according to a Pentagon intelligence study.[38] Second, the U.S. Congress was stirring up public pressure for increased aid to the rebels. The final version

---

[33] Woodward and Babcock, *Washington Post.*

[34] Lee Roderick, *Leading The Charge: Orrin Hatch and Twenty Years of America* (Carson City, NV: Gold Leaf Press, 1994), 219.

[35] Iklé, interview with author, 3 January 1996. Pillsbury had been working for the Senate Republican Steering Committee. According to press reports, the other three U.S.-supported insurgencies were in Angola, Nicaragua, and Cambodia.

[36] Pillsbury, interview with author, 16 August 1995.

[37] Bob Woodward, *VEIL: The Secret Wars of the CIA* (New York: Simon & Schuster, 1987), 316–318.

[38] Leslie Gelb, *New York Times*, 19 June 1986.

of the Tsongas resolution of October 1984 stated that, "it would be indefensible to provide the freedom fighters with only enough aid to fight and die, but not enough to advance their cause of freedom."[39] Soon after, in January 1985, a Congressional Task Force on Afghanistan was established and began holding hearings to showcase the purportedly desperate plight of the Mujahedin.

A third trigger for the administration's reassessment was that in March 1985, the Soviet Union selected a new secretary general, Mikhail Gorbachev, whose commitment to the Afghanistan occupation was unknown. Fourth and perhaps most important, some U.S. officials perceived the Soviets were "tired of the war," so the Red Army was unlikely to increase its commitment of troops sufficiently to invade Pakistan.[40] Indeed, while the Soviets had escalated tactically several times, they stubbornly stuck to a troop cap of 120,000 men. In March 1985, Soviet military expert Alex Alexiev testified, "I don't believe that the Soviet Union can put in half a million men. . . . [A]ctual physical occupation of the country is almost unthinkable." Barring that, he said, "escalation is not really a meaningful concept. Short of open genocide, it cannot get much worse."[41] Nevertheless, there still were dissenting views within the administration, including one official who warned in January 1985: "Consider what they haven't done to Pakistan. . . . You have to believe the Soviets could, if they chose, march in with sufficient troops to do the job."[42]

The formal policy shift occurred in March 1985, when Ronald Reagan signed National Security Decision Directive (NSDD) 166, still classified secret, authorizing assistance to the rebels "by all means available."[43] Even more significant was an annex, classified top secret and signed by National Security Adviser Robert McFarlane, which outlined specific measures the United States would take to assist the rebels.[44] American aid no longer would be limited to enabling the rebels to "harass" the Soviets, but would aim to compel a Soviet withdrawal. The Mujahedin would receive satellite reconnaissance and other U.S. intelligence to assist their targeting of Afghan and Red Army installations, as well as demolition expertise and secure communications technology.[45] Secretary of State George Shultz later reported that both he and the CIA's Casey

---

[39] Pear, *New York Times*, 18 April 1988. Notably, while Congress repeatedly emphasized the immorality of inadequately arming the rebels, this argument does not appear to have figured prominently in the administration's internal deliberations, which hinged on strategic concerns. See also, Woodward and Babcock, *Washington Post*, 13 January 1985.

[40] Iklé, interview with author, 19 August 1995. The CIA's Cogan concurs, saying it became "clear that our concerns about a Soviet intervention in Pakistan were also exaggerated." (Cogan, "Partners in Time," 80.)

[41] Alex Alexiev, Rand Corporation, testimony before Congressional Task Force on Afghanistan. U.S. Senate, typescript transcript, 11 March 1985, 93, 112–113.

[42] Woodward and Babcock, *Washington Post*.

[43] Gelb, 19 June 1986.

[44] Coll, *Washington Post*, 19 July 1992.

[45] Coll, *Washington Post*, 20 July 1992. See also, Coll, *Washington Post*, 19 July 1992.

fully supported the measure.[46] The dollar value of U.S. aid climbed in successive years from $122 million in fiscal year 1984, to $250 million, $470 million, and $630 million in FY 1987,[47] generally matched by equal contributions from Saudi Arabia.[48] The Stinger missile, however, as well as other high-tech weaponry directly traceable to the United States, were conspicuously absent from the annex.

By all accounts, Pillsbury was unsatisfied by this intermediate escalation of aid, continuing to believe that top-quality U.S. weapons should be sent to the Mujahedin. He says this belief was reinforced in meetings with rebel leaders brought to the United States by private American advocacy groups. Pakistan's ISI had ordered the rebels not to meet with CIA officials, but the Pentagon was immune from the ban. In meetings with leaders including General Rahim Wardak and the brother of Commander Ahmad Shah Massoud, Pillsbury says he got the distinct impression the rebels' needs were not being accurately transmitted to Washington via Pakistani and U.S. intelligence agencies. The initiative for high-tech weapons, he concluded, would have to come from outside the U.S. intelligence community.[49]

A Trip to Pakistan

Pillsbury soon managed to convince his boss, Fred Iklé, of the merits of the Stinger, and in May 1985 the two set off for Pakistan. There, ISI Chief Akhtar informed them the rebels did indeed require Stingers to counter the Soviet escalation. Pillsbury, having been told previously by the CIA that the Pakistanis opposed the Stinger, insisted the agency's station chief report Akhtar's request directly to Casey in a cable.[50] In light of Akhtar's behavior in the previous year's meeting with U.S. advocates, hewing to Zia's then-policy of opposing Stingers, this change is further evidence Zia had come to favor the Stinger by this point.

Around this time, Iklé made his first pitch for the Stinger to Secretary of Defense Caspar Weinberger. The secretary responded by asking his assistant, Colin Powell, to check with the Joint Chiefs of Staff (JCS) and the CIA's Casey. When the word came back negative, however, Iklé told Pillsbury they had no support in the administration.[51]

---

[46] Shultz, *Turmoil and Triumph*, 1087.

[47] Olivier Roy, *The Lessons of the Soviet/Afghan War*, Adelphi Papers 259 (London: Brassey's for the International Institute for Strategic Studies, 1991), 35. See also, David Ottaway, *Washington Post*, 8 February 1987.

[48] Kathy Evans, *The Guardian*, 2 January 1992.

[49] Pillsbury, interview with author, 16 August 1995.

[50] Diego Cordovez and Selig S. Harrison, *Out of Afghanistan: The Inside Story of the Soviet Withdrawal* (New York: Oxford University Press, 1995), 195.

[51] Iklé says that Casey, with whom he regularly spoke and often joined for breakfast with Weinberger, favored the Stinger option "in principle," but felt compelled to defer to the CIA's career staff, who were opposed. Iklé, interview with author, 3 January 1996. Also Pillsbury, interviews with author, 8 August and 1 September 1995.

Pillsbury, rather than being deterred, apparently redoubled his efforts. Such behavior may have sprung from his experience as a staff person in Congress, where proposals commonly fail several times before being adopted, or may simply have reflected Pillsbury's peculiar character. Even on Capitol Hill he had earned a special reputation for going outside official channels in pursuit of his objectives.[52] Pillsbury acknowledges this operating style ruffled a number of feathers in the executive branch, where decision making, especially on national security matters, is expected to be hierarchical rather than entrepreneurial. Several of his administration colleagues, however, are more blunt, criticizing Pillsbury as a "loose cannon."[53] For better or worse, his persistence appears to have helped keep the Stinger issue alive when it had little institutional support within the executive branch.

When Senator Orrin Hatch (R-UT) called to ask his former staffer where he might profitably spend the congressional recess of June 1985, Pillsbury seized the opportunity and suggested Pakistan. Discovering that all military aircraft routinely used for official trips already were reserved, Pillsbury also managed to obtain use of the vice-president's Air Force 2, to permit the trip to go forward. Pillsbury and Hatch, along with a bipartisan congressional delegation that included Senators Chic Hecht (R-NV), David Boren (D-OK), and Bill Bradley (D-NJ) traveled to Pakistan, where they met with both President Zia and rebel leaders.[54]

Hatch asked Zia about air-defense needs, but the Pakistani president refused immediately to take the bait. Rather than seeking Stingers directly for the rebels, Zia requested them only for his own army to defend the border area from Soviet aircraft incursions. Zia also hinted he might be able to divert some Stingers to the rebels if they were supplied to his army under an official foreign military sale, but the U.S. delegation explained to his staff that this would violate American law.[55] Apparently, Zia had backed away from his earlier request to Nunn to provide Stingers explicitly for the Mujahedin, but he still appeared to favor the rebels receiving the missiles. Hatch persuaded Zia to put the army request in writing to President Reagan, and the following month the White House announced it was rushing 100 Stingers to Pakistan, accompanied by Sidewinder air-to-air missiles. The rebels, however, were left out.[56]

Iklé and Pillsbury finally gained an ally within the administration in September 1985, when Morton Abramowitz, the State Department's assistant sec-

[52] Roderick, *Leading The Charge*, 218–219.

[53] Then U.S. Ambassador to Pakistan Deane Hinton criticizes Pillsbury for promoting the Stinger option during his trips to Pakistan despite the "official line" of U.S. opposition, terming him a "loose cannon." He adds, "That was OK for Congressmen and staffers, but once Pillsbury joined the executive branch his behavior was quite objectionable." Letter to author from Ambassador Deane Hinton, 29 August 1995. Weinberger cited in Cordovez and Harrison, *Out of Afghanistan*, 197.

[54] Roderick, *Leading The Charge*, 257–258.

[55] Pillsbury, interview with author, 15 August 1995.

[56] Bernard Gwertzman, *New York Times*, 12 July 1985.

retary for intelligence and research, joined a delegation to Pakistan led by Assistant Secretary of Defense Richard Armitage. Abramowitz says he already had a vague sense the war was not going well for the rebels and wanted to see for himself. The Mujahedin's specific need for enhanced air defense was driven home, he says, in meetings with Akhtar, assorted rebel leaders, and General Mirza Aslam Beg, a Pakistani army commander for the border region. "All professed to want the Stinger," recalls Abramowitz. Even the CIA's station chief told him he could not understand why agency headquarters opposed it.[57]

Upon his return to Washington, Abramowitz went to see Casey to get the director's views on the Stinger. Casey was lukewarm, almost disinterested, says Abramowitz. "He wasn't for it, or strongly against it."[58] Others at the agency, however, clearly were opposed to the Stinger. According to Selig Harrison, Deputy Director John McMahon strenuously pushed the alternative of the British Blowpipe on grounds it would maintain plausible deniability and be just as effective.[59]

JCS Objections

In the fall of 1985, Iklé made his second attempt to win Weinberger's support for the Stinger, managing to put the issue on the agenda of the secretary's weekly "tank meeting" with the JCS. Iklé later reported that a "vigorous quarrel" broke out in the meeting, but JCS opposition prevailed.[60]

The military's objections to the Stinger proposal never before have been documented publicly. However, a recently obtained, declassified 1986 Defense Investigative Service report summarizes an interview with General John Moellering, who attended the tank meeting as assistant to the chairman of the JCS. The report reveals Moellering "was initially opposed to the possible release of the [Stinger] weapons to Third World countries for reasons of technology loss, accountability problems and depletion of a finite and small, strategic stockpile."[61]

---

[57] Abramowitz, interview with author, 30 August 1995. Abramowitz notes that he took the station chief's comment with a grain of salt.

[58] Ibid.

[59] Cordovez and Harrison, *Out of Afghanistan*, 196. McMahon ultimately resigned the same month President Reagan approved the Stinger for the rebels in Afghanistan and Angola. Some claim the Stinger decision was a prime motivating factor for McMahon, who had been the object of an intense letter-writing campaign to the White House by American advocacy groups on behalf of the Stinger, calling for his resignation. David B. Ottaway and Patrick E. Tyler, *Washington Post*, 5 March 1986.

[60] Pillsbury, interview with author, 1 September 1995. The Army chief of staff at the time, General John Wickham, confirms that Iklé attended the tank meeting to discuss the Stinger. Wickham, interview with author, 8 September 1995.

[61] Special Agents Larry J. Dobrosky and Samuel Blevins, "Report of Investigation, Unauthorized Disclosure—Stinger Missiles," Defense Investigative Service, 14 April 1986, based on interview of General John H. Moellering, 3 April 1986.

Pillsbury immediately set to work to address each of these three concerns. Technology loss—the risk that the Soviets would obtain a Stinger and use reverse-engineering to copy it and develop effective counter-measures—initially appeared a legitimate concern. Weinberger especially was sensitive to it and years later acknowledged that "I thought there was a great risk in using that technology. . . . In general I felt we should not let our technology out."[62] The JCS viewed its main responsibility as preparing to fight and win a war against the Soviet Union in Europe and did not want to risk undermining its technological edge merely to help rebels in a peripheral struggle. Pillsbury, however, was able to neutralize this argument by uncovering that the Stinger technology already had been compromised to the Soviets a year earlier, through the leak of design information and parts in Greece.[63] Vince Cannistraro, a CIA official delegated to the National Security Council (NSC), suggests this leak stemmed from a 1983 memorandum of understanding between Greece, West Germany, Turkey, and the United States, to produce U.S.-designed weapons in Europe.[64] The Soviets even published a detailed analysis of the Stinger's performance envelope as early as November 1985.[65]

The second JCS concern, the danger of depleting the strategic stockpile, arose despite the army possessing several thousand Stingers, on grounds that all of these missiles were needed for potential hostilities in Europe.[66] The missile's manufacturer, General Dynamics, was reportedly unable to produce a new batch of first-generation Stingers for the rebels, because it was gearing up to produce a more advanced model known as Stinger-POST for the Pentagon. Pillsbury, however, called General Dynamics directly, receiving assurances the manufacturer could boost production to meet both the army's need for the new model and the rebels' need for the original, without net reduction in the army stockpile.[67]

The Joint Chiefs' third ground for objection, accountability, was well-founded, because under the CIA's arrangement with ISI, after weapons arrived

---

[62] Cordovez and Harrison, *Out of Afghanistan*, 197.

[63] Howard B. Means, *Colin Powell: Soldier/Statesman* (New York: Donald I. Fine, Inc., 1992), 210. See also, David C. Morrison, "Fatal Sting," *National Journal*, 21 November 1987; and Ottaway, *Washington Post*, 12 February 1989. Fred Iklé notes with irony that this Soviet espionage backfired. Had the Soviets not already obtained the Stinger design, the United States would have been less willing to supply the weapon to the Afghan rebels. Iklé, interview with author, 19 August 1995.

[64] *Aviation Week & Space Technology*, 17 October 1988, 35. Cannistraro, interview with author, 8 August 1995.

[65] Yossef Bodansky, "SAMs in Afghanistan: Assessing the Impact," *Jane's Defence Weekly*, 25 July 1987, 153.

[66] Iklé recalls that the JCS's "stockpile concern was huge," but that he felt the Joint Chiefs were being short-sighted by insisting on preserving Stingers to fight a future NATO-Warsaw Pact confrontation. In Iklé's view, supplying the Stingers to the Mujahedin could help force the Soviets out of Afghanistan and thereby "reduce the likelihood of World War III" and any need to use Stingers in Europe. Iklé, interview with author, 3 January 1996.

[67] Pillsbury, interview with author.

in Pakistan they effectively left U.S. control. The CIA could establish rules for distribution, but lacked agents on the ground to ensure that Pakistanis and rebels complied. Moreover, ISI was known to give the best weapons to Gulbuddin Hekmatyar—the most radical rebel leader and certainly not the Americans' first choice. Hekmatyar was not the most effective military leader, but ISI reportedly favored him because he supported the Muslim insurgency in Kashmir and, therefore, furthered Pakistan's own regional agenda.[68] Thus, if the United States sent Stingers, there was a real danger they would be stolen from—or sold by—the Mujahedin, ending up in the hands of terrorists or radical states such as neighboring Iran that could use them to shoot down civilian airliners or U.S. military aircraft.[69] Indeed, the rebels earlier had admitted to the CIA's McMahon that, "We do sell some of your weapons. We are doing it for the day when your country decides to abandon us, just as you abandoned Vietnam and everyone else you deal with."[70] To address this concern, Pillsbury began to explore with the CIA whether U.S. military officials could be sent to Pakistan to exercise more control over weapons distribution.

The military brass was not the only roadblock. At the State Department, though Mort Abramowitz had managed to enlist the support of Michael Armacost, Eagleburger's successor as undersecretary of State, there still was vigorous opposition from the regional officers, especially Arnold Raphel, senior deputy assistant secretary of state for Near East and South Asian Affairs. Raphel felt a military escalation risked undermining the negotiating track in Geneva, then just beginning to make progress. Pillsbury, in turn, opposed Raphel's negotiations, fearing they would lead to a sell-out of the rebels. After considerable sniping, the two staffers agreed to a horse-trade: Pillsbury would stop undercutting the negotiating track in return for Raphel ceasing to oppose the Stingers.[71] While this deal did not hold, it momentarily smoothed the path for both efforts.

In December 1985, Secretary of State Shultz finally endorsed the Stinger proposal, explaining in his memoirs:

> The Afghan people were war weary, and Soviet policy was "buying them off." The Soviets seemed to be winning. . . . There would be a narrow window in the next year or two in which pressure on the Soviets might be effective. . . . [T]he resistance did not have the weapons to deal with [Soviet helicopters] and the helicopters were wreaking havoc. . . . In the State Department some people worried that any American weapons system that could turn the tide would so antagonize the Soviets that it would sour our overall effort to improve relations. I strongly disagreed.[72]

[68] See, for example, Roy, *The Lessons*, 35–40.

[69] Persico, *Casey*, 313, citing a mid-1980s fact-finding trip McMahon took to rebel training camps in Peshawar, Pakistan.

[70] Ibid., 313.

[71] The deal is discussed in Cordovez and Harrison, *Out of Afghanistan*, 197. Pillsbury confirms it in interview with author, 15 August 1995.

[72] Shultz, *Turmoil and Triumph*, 692.

The Turning Point

Despite Shultz's support, the proposal continued to face opposition from Weinberger—based on the JCS concerns—and the CIA, continuing to cite Zia's purported opposition.[73] Pillsbury was equipped to challenge the JCS concerns, but not yet the claims about Zia, so he turned again to Capitol Hill. During the congressional recess of January 1986, Pillsbury and Abramowitz escorted a delegation of Senators Hatch and Hecht, and Congressmen Michael DeWine (R-OH), Robert Lagomarsino (R-CA), and James Courter (R-NJ) to Pakistan. Also aboard were Vince Cannistraro, Charles Dunbar (the State Department's Coordinator for Afghan Affairs), and Norm Gardner (from the CIA's operations directorate).[74]

When the delegation met with Zia, the Pakistani president made an unequivocal request that Stingers be supplied to the rebels. "Zia couldn't have been more clear that this was the one weapon the Mujahedin needed or they would be butchered," says Courter.[75] Much to the CIA's embarrassment, Zia also complained that he had been asking for the Stingers "since last year,"[76] which accords with Senator Nunn's account of his 1984 visit. Apparently, the CIA had been conveying Zia's views inaccurately to Washington officials, though it is uncertain whether this lapse arose in the field or at agency headquarters.[77]

To make sure there was no further miscommunication, upon returning home Senator Hatch called Casey personally to brief him on the meeting. Pillsbury then worked out logistical details with the CIA—such as who would train the Mujahedin, in which country, and subject to which kind of polygraphs—winning approval for the plan from the agency's Deputy Director for Opera-

---

[73] Walcott and Carrington, *Wall Street Journal*, 16 February 1988.

[74] Roderick, *Leading The Charge*, 259–260. Before meeting Zia in Peshawar, the delegation first travelled to Beijing, where it obtained an endorsement of the Stinger plan (and other expanded U.S. assistance) from an official of the Chinese government, a key ally in the Mujahedin aid program. Obtaining China's imprimatur, it was thought, might help resolve lingering concerns among Pakistani and U.S. decision-makers.

[75] Walcott and Carrington, *Wall Street Journal*, 16 February 1988.

[76] Cannistraro, interview with author, 8 August 1995. Cannistraro also recalls Zia saying they needed the Stingers because the Soviet-bloc SA-7's were useless.

[77] It is also possible that Zia wavered in his stance on the Stinger in response to fluctuating estimates of what was needed to "keep the pot boiling" at the right temperature. However, Cannistraro says the agency simply was opposed and "kept devising one excuse after another." (Interview with author, 8 August 1995.) Gates, *From the Shadows*, 349–350, reports that in a December 1985 meeting with Casey, Weinberger and Iklé, McMahon pledged the agency would transfer the weapons to the rebels if only the Pentagon would supply them. However, Angelo Codevilla, who spent the early-1980s on the staff of the Senate Intelligence Committee, says that, "The CIA's protestations of willingness to provide anti-air protection [were] insincere," because they were always accompanied by claims that Zia still opposed it. "By early 1986 it was clear to those inside the government who had been working on the Afghan issue that John McMahon and the CIA bureaucracy had lied." Angelo Codevilla, *Informing Statecraft: Intelligence for a New Century* (New York: The Free Press, 1992), 271–272.

tions Clair George in late January.[78] By the end of the month, Pillsbury had prepared a memo for Weinberger reporting how each of the JCS concerns had been addressed and that the CIA had dropped its opposition. The secretary finally relented, setting the stage for a dramatic White House meeting.

In the Reagan administration, covert programs usually were managed by the interagency Planning Coordination Group (PCG), which met regularly in Room 208 of the Old Executive Office Building, chaired by the NSC's Don Fortier. Regular participants included George from the CIA, Iklé from the Pentagon, Abramowitz from State, and Moellering from the JCS, or their deputies, along with other individuals cleared for individual projects. But the meeting to hash out finally the Stinger proposal was special, attended by several more senior officials and held in the White House situation room. In this highly charged setting, a CIA representative declared that Zia and the agency still were opposed to the Stinger. Apparently, the Near East bureau of the agency, which long had opposed the Stinger proposal, had not been briefed on either the Zia meeting or George's decision. Abramowitz reacted with outrage, and the meeting broke down without consensus.[79]

The CIA soon cleared up its error, and on 25 February 1986, the PCG formally approved the Stinger for the Mujahedin, as well as for anticommunist rebels in Angola.[80] Senate Republicans, however, still were concerned that Secretary of State George Shultz might not support sending the Stingers to the anticommunist rebels if asked by the president. Despite the Pillsbury-Raphel nonaggression pact, the State Department's Near East desk had been lobbying hard to block the plan. Senate Majority Leader Bob Dole (R-KS) responded by inviting the secretary to his Capitol Hill office, whereupon Shultz was surprised by a roomful of conservative senators demanding he renew his support for "effective" weapons for the rebels. The secretary complied.[81]

Finally, in March 1986, President Reagan authorized notification to Congress of his decision to provide Stingers to the Afghan rebels, necessitating a "memorandum of notification" modifying Jimmy Carter's six-year-old finding. With the Made-in-America threshold now crossed, the United States also began to supply an array of other sophisticated weapons for the rebels, including mine clearers, satellite-targetable mortars, "mule-mobile" rocket launchers, helicopter detectors, and even rudimentary cruise missiles.[82]

Remarkably, the bureaucratic battle still was not over. At the end of April, the administration lost its leading advocate for the Stinger, when Pillsbury was

---

[78] Pillsbury, interviews with author, 11 August 1995 and 1 September 1995.

[79] Former government official, name withheld upon request.

[80] David B. Ottaway and Patrick E. Tyler, *Washington Post*, 30 March 1986.

[81] Ibid. See also Cordovez and Harrison, *Out of Afghanistan*, 197; Patrick E. Tyler and David B. Ottaway, *Washington Post*, 6 March 1986, which discusses the meeting from the Angola perspective. Also, interview with Pillsbury, 11 September 1995.

[82] Ottaway, *Washington Post*, 12 February 1989. See also Ottaway and Tyler, *Washington Post*, 30 March 1986.

fired from the Pentagon for allegedly leaking the Stinger decision to the press, a charge from which he subsequently was exonerated.[83] Congressional opponents objected to the deal on grounds of inadequate accountability in Afghanistan, with Senator Dennis DeConcini (D-AZ) warning: "We cannot afford to let these particular missiles, the ultimate terrorist weapon, slip into the wrong hands."[84] Army Chief of Staff John A. Wickham, who had been overruled by Weinberger, nominally toed the new administration line but told the press, "we anguish over decisions" about who should get the weapon. On 7 May DeConcini sponsored a last-minute amendment to bar export of Stingers unless the recipient could guarantee stringent controls, conditions that could not be met in the guerrilla environment of Afghanistan. The vote fell short, 62 to 34.[85]

In June, however, administration officials confirmed the Stingers still had not been sent to Afghanistan.[86] CIA and Army officials, long opposed to exporting the Stinger, now claimed to have identified a new Soviet countermeasure that could inhibit the missile's effectiveness, requiring a new evaluation. Field testing at White Sands Missile Range, however, determined the new Soviet defenses were ineffective.[87] Pakistani instructors were flown to the United States in June for training, and by the end of the summer the first Stingers and a training simulator finally were sent to Pakistan. On 25 September 1986, Mujahedin fighters fired their first five Stinger missiles, knocking three Soviet MI-24 Hind helicopters out of the sky on their first try. The military dynamic had shifted.[88]

GORBACHEV PURSUES WITHDRAWAL INDEPENDENTLY

Unbeknownst in Washington during this long wrangling over how to remove Soviet troops from Afghanistan, Mikhail Gorbachev apparently was seeking the same objective from his seat in the Kremlin. Evidence now indicates that Gorbachev sought withdrawal from the moment he was named general secretary in March 1985 and that the Politburo agreed to pursue this goal well before the Stinger missile reached Afghanistan. Even before coming to power in 1983, he had termed the war a "mistake" in a conversation with a Canadian cabinet official.[89] Likewise, in spring 1984, Gorbachev encouraged Marshal Sergei Akh-

[83] Michael Pillsbury, "Drowning in a Leak," *Washington Post*, Outlook, 10 November 1991.

[84] Dennis DeConcini, *New York Times*, op-ed, 30 April 1986.

[85] David Ottaway, *Washington Post*, 21 June 1986. Wickham says that he cannot recall any personal communication with DeConcini on the Stinger issue. Wickham, interview with author, 8 September 1995.

[86] Leslie H. Gelb, *New York Times*, 18 June 1986.

[87] Walcott and Carrington, *Wall Street Journal*, 16 February 1988. Interestingly, the Stingers for Angola were not similarly held up, indicating either that the Soviet counter-measures were not believed to be in use in Angola or that the CIA did not have the same misgivings about the Angolan rebels as they did the Mujahedin.

[88] Yousaf and Adkin, *The Bear Trap*, 176, 182.

[89] Cordovez and Harrison, *Out of Afghanistan*, 187.

romeev, a leading Soviet general in Afghanistan, to share with the Politboro his frank military judgment that the war could not be won.[90] Gorbachev himself says that upon coming to power, the Politburo almost immediately "began to seek a way out of the situation."[91] UN negotiator Diego Cordovez confirms that the new Soviet leader had a marked impact on then-stalled peace negotiations between Pakistan and the Afghan government. "From the time Gorbachev came in things began to change. . . . It was immediate and very significant."[92]

By all authoritative accounts, the main force driving Gorbachev to resolve the Afghan conflict in 1985 was not the direct costs of the war—in terms of rubles, casualties, or public opinion. In this regard, Afghanistan was not a Soviet "Vietnam," as some have argued.[93] The Soviets' deployment cap of 120,000 troops and their 14,000 total deaths were approximately one-fourth of the U.S. totals in Vietnam, drawn from armed forces about twice as large and spread over an approximately equal duration.[94] Moreover, Soviet censorship prevented the growth of Vietnam-like domestic public opposition until Gorbachev deliberately lifted the press ban.

Gorbachev's chief concern, rather, was that the Afghan intervention represented a persistent obstacle to achievement of his main political objective—*perestroika*, or domestic economic restructuring. He believed that so long as the Red Army remained in Afghanistan, the West would not renew the economic and technological cooperation of the deténte years, which he viewed as essential to revitalizing the Soviet economy. Nor could he commence his desired shift in resources from military expenditures (of which Afghanistan per se was only a small part) to civilian spending until East-West tensions were relaxed. Primarily for these reasons, Gorbachev concluded that Soviet troops had to be withdrawn quickly, one way or another.[95] By so doing, he also stood to

[90] Raymond L. Garthoff, *The Great Transition: American-Soviet Relations and the End of the Cold War* (Washington, DC: The Brookings Institution, 1994), 726.

[91] Ibid., 725–726.

[92] Don Oberdorfer, *The Turn: From the Cold War to a New Era: The United States & the Soviet Union, 1983-1990* (New York: Touchstone, Simon & Schuster, Inc., 1992).

[93] While many have made this analogy, at least one scholar goes even farther, arguing that the Soviet experience in Afghanistan was analogous to Napoleon's in Russia, and Britain's in the Suez Crisis, in the sense that a military defeat led to the collapse of an empire. See Douglas Anthony Borer, *Superpowers Defeated: A Comparison of Vietnam and Afghanistan* (Ph.D. dissertation, Boston University, 1993, 397, forthcoming as book: Portland, OR: Frank Cass, 1999).

[94] Mark Urban, *War in Afghanistan* (London: The MacMillan Press Ltd., 1990), 2nd ed., 298.

[95] See, for example, Sarah Elizabeth Mendelson, *Explaining Change in Foreign Policy: The Soviet Withdrawal from Afghanistan* (Ph.D. dissertation, Columbia University, 1993), 200–203; Mike Bowker, *Russian Foreign Policy and the End of the Cold War* (Brookfield, VT: Dartmouth, 1997), 141–142; Tad Daley, *Gorbachev and Afghanistan, The Soviet Debate Over the Lessons of Afghanistan and Consequent Directions in Russian Foreign Policy* (Ph.D. Dissertation, Rand Graduate School of Policy Studies, March 1995), 88–90, 104, 234–236. According to several Soviet sources cited by Mendelson, *Explaining Change*, 246, this belief of Gorbachev's was further reinforced by his experience at the Reykjavik summit of October 1986. Gorbachev, himself, declared in February 1987: "I frankly say that our international policy is, more than before, determined by domestic policy, by our interests in concentrating on constructive work to improve our country." Mendelson, *Explaining Change*, 249. See

reap secondary benefits, including soothing relations with China and the Arab world, boosting the morale of the Red Army, and setting a potential precedent for resolution of other East-West conflicts in the Third World.[96]

Initially, however, Gorbachev's Politburo embraced neither an immediate withdrawal nor the ultimate goal of a "neutral" Afghanistan. To the contrary, Gorbachev at first presided over a continuing qualitative escalation of the military intervention in Afghanistan. While some have characterized this as a last-ditch Soviet effort to "win" the war,[97] that is an exaggeration. At no time did the Soviets increase quantitatively their troop levels necessary to defeat the rebels outright by cutting off their supply lines and occupying large parts of the countryside. Rather, the Politburo strategy in 1985-1986 apparently was to ratchet up military pressure on the rebels sufficient to compel their acceptance of a negotiated settlement that would leave a Soviet-friendly regime in Kabul following Red Army withdrawal.[98]

It is uncertain whether this initially aggressive policy was Gorbachev's own personal preference or resulted from compromise with Politburo hard-liners. Some commentators cite the 1985 escalation as evidence Gorbachev himself initially was not committed to peaceful withdrawal. General Mikhail Zaitsev, the highly-regarded commander of Red Army troops in East Germany, was brought in, and attacks were escalated, especially in areas of the Pakistan border that served as a sanctuary and arms pipeline for the Mujahedin.[99] The Soviets also deployed one-third of their elite *Spetznaz* troops, additional KGB personnel, and "Omsk vans" for secure battlefield communications.[100] Reportedly, Red Army leaders assured the Politburo these moves would enable victory within two years.[101]

---

also Eduard Shevardnadze, translated by Catherine A. Fitzpatrick, *The Future Belongs to Freedom* (New York: The Free Press, 1991), 81; Michael MccGwire, *Perestroika and Soviet National Security* (Washington, DC: The Brookings Institution, 1991), 267; Ted Hopf, *Peripheral Visions: Deterrence Theory and American Foreign Policy in the Third World, 1965-90* (Ann Arbor: University of Michigan Press, 1994), 96, 110–114, which concludes that Gorbachev's overall foreign-policy moderation was motivated "by the costs to detente that previous Soviet policy in the periphery had incurred." See also, Urban, *War in Afghanistan*, 301; Gates, *From the Shadows*, 331, acknowledges that Gorbachev viewed access to new technology as the key to solving Soviet economic problems.

[96] See, for example, Daley, *Gorbachev and Afghanistan*; and Bowker, *Russian Foreign Policy*.

[97] Borer, *Superpowers Defeated*, 341; Coll, *Washington Post*, 19 July 1992.

[98] Nicolai N. Petro and Alvin Z. Rubinstein, *Russian Foreign Policy: From Empire to Nation-State* (New York: Longman, 1997), 246–247. Mark Galeotti, *Afghanistan: The Soviet Union's Last War* (London: Frank Cass, 1995), 153. Odd Arne Westad, "Concerning the Situation in 'A': New Russian Evidence on the Soviet Intervention in Afghanistan," *Cold War International History Project Bulletin* (Winter 1996/1997), Woodrow Wilson International Center for Scholars, Washington, DC, 132, (hereafter referred to as CWIHPB).

[99] Schweizer, *Victory*, 212; Cordovez and Harrison, *Out of Afghanistan*, 188. Urban, *War in Afghanistan*, 175. The largest Soviet offensive began in May 1985. In July 1985, Zaitsev was brought in.

[100] Coll, *Washington Post*, 19 July 1992.

[101] Cordovez and Harrison, *Out of Afghanistan*, 187.

Morton Abramowitz, however, puts this escalation in perspective, arguing that the plans were not Gorbachev's. "When Gorbachev came in, the plans for escalation were already made. . . . It was like Kennedy and the Bay of Pigs." Confirmation comes from Alexander Yakovlev, Gorbachev's foreign policy adviser: "The military-industrial complex pressed him to try this, try that . . . . but it's not true, as some have said, that he himself wanted to try for a military decision."[102] A slightly more nuanced explanation is offered by Viktor Kremeniuk, who argues Gorbachev initially did not push any personal strategy for how to get Soviet troops out of Afghanistan. Rather, Gorbachev the politician walked a fine line between liberals and hard-liners, and "decided to give the military a chance to prove themselves."[103]

A compelling analysis by Sarah Mendelson concludes that such compromise was characteristic of Gorbachev's first two years in office, during which time he laid the groundwork for more fundamental reform through personnel changes in the Communist party and empowerment of nontraditional expert institutions. The personnel overhaul was massive, but could not be achieved overnight. For example, not until Gorbachev's first anniversary, at the 27th Party Congress of March 1986, could changes be made in the Central Committee. At that event, however, some 40 percent of the Central Committee was newly elected—four times the turnover rate of the previous two congresses. Similarly, Politburo membership was altered dramatically by Gorbachev, with eight new members added and five removed in his first year.[104] Still, Gorbachev faced persistent pressure from his right wing and from the Russian and Afghan militaries, which at first opposed the withdrawal decision and later attempted to sabotage its implementation.[105]

In the face of such pressure, Gorbachev pursued a remarkably steady effort to extract Soviet troops from Afghanistan—albeit while initially trying to ensure a "friendly" regime remained. In June 1985, he restarted regional security talks with the United States after a three year hiatus and jump-started the UN negotiations by authorizing Afghan approval of a key provision under which the superpowers would guarantee an eventual settlement.[106] The following

---

[102] Ibid., 187–188. Yakovlev also has said that, "Right from the start the view of [Gorbachev] was that a peaceful withdrawal should be effected." See Foreign Broadcast Information Service (hereafter FBIS) SOV-91-251, 31 December 1991, 3, transcript of "Political Investigation—Behind the Scenes of War," Moscow Central Television First Program Network, 27 December 1991.

[103] Mendelson, *Explaining Change*, 224.

[104] Ibid., 22, 70, 220, 226–227.

[105] On Soviet and Afghan attempts to sabotage implementation of the withdrawal, see FBIS-SOV-91-251, 31 December 1991, 3, where Yakovlev notes, "the implementation was sabotaged. . . . The evacuation was hampered. The road was blocked, cut in two places. Then they found that a bridge had been blown up somewhere. Then it was said that the air force could not get through to Kabul. There was some kind of conference going on there. . . . It became apparent that they were deliberately holding things up, spinning things out in order to put off the moment when it would be possible to say: That's it, we're getting out."

[106] Garthoff, *The Great Transition*, 726; and Cordovez and Harrison, *Out of Afghanistan*, 189.

month, he instructed Soviet newspaper and television reporters to begin reporting the war openly, including the controversial issue of Soviet casualties.[107] Previously, the Soviet public routinely had been told that "soldiers in Afghanistan were planting trees and building schools and hospitals."[108] In retrospect, this media directive can be seen as an attempt by Gorbachev to outflank Politburo hard-liners, by appealing directly to the sensibilities of the Soviet people.

In October 1985, the Politburo approved Gorbachev's strategy of employing "a combination of military and political measures" to "expedite the withdrawal" of Red Army troops while leaving a "friendly Afghanistan" behind. Essentially, this was a three-track strategy: escalate the war to drive the Afghan opposition to seek compromise; accelerate Afghan government reforms to coopt moderate elements of the opposition; and intensify negotiations to harness the results of the first two tracks.[109] One tactic the Soviet leader used to persuade his Politburo colleagues was to read aloud letters from angry mothers questioning how it could be the Soviet Union's "internationalist duty" to destroy villages and kill civilians[110]—letters no doubt triggered by his earlier lifting of media restrictions.

The following month at the Geneva summit, Gorbachev tried to convey this important shift in policy to Ronald Reagan, but the president "did not pick up at all on Gorbachev's lightly veiled hint about pulling out of Afghanistan," according to Shultz.[111] Reagan, however, later claimed he did understand Gorbachev's message even at the time, that "it was a war he had no responsibility—and little enthusiasm—for."[112] By December 1985, Gorbachev's skepticism about the Afghan effort had leaked into official publications, with *Pravda* acknowledging that "far from all the people in Afghanistan, even amongst the workers, have accepted the Saur Revolution."[113] Gorbachev's Foreign Ministry,

[107] Dobbs, *Washington Post*, 16 November 1992. Interestingly, while the ban on reporting individual casualties was reportedly lifted at this early date, and Soviet TV broadcast a report on the anxiety of soldiers' families on 20 October 1986 (see Khan, *Untying*, 178), high-profile press exposes from Afghanistan (notably Artem Borovik's articles in *Ogonek*) did not start to appear until spring 1987, and aggregate casualty figures were not published until two years later (*Pravda*, 17 August 1989), suggesting either that Gorbachev continued to have to compromise with Politburo hard-liners or that Gorbachev himself did not want to undercut too drastically public support for continued prosecution of the war. For discussion of Gorbachev's use of the press to build support for withdrawal, see Mendelson, *Explaining Change*, 238, 253–255. Apparently, the idea of applying *glasnost* to coverage of the war was originated by Politburo liberals and quickly embraced by Gorbachev. See comments of Yakovlev, FBIS-SOV-91-251, 4.

[108] Vladislav Tamarov, *Afghanistan: Soviet Vietnam* (San Francisco: Mercury House, 1992), 1. Tamarov, a 1984 Red Army draftee, writes that "Only a few knew that more and more cemeteries were being filled with the graves of eighteen- to twenty-year-old boys."

[109] CWIHPB, 180. Dobbs, *Washington Post*, 16 November 1992.

[110] Rodman, *More Precious*, 327.

[111] Shultz, *Turmoil and Triumph*, 601.

[112] Ronald Reagan, *An American Life* (New York: Simon and Schuster, 1990), 639.

[113] Gordon Adam, "Afghanistan—The Superpower Trap" in *Detente in Asia?* (The Macmillan Press Ltd, 1992), 33, quoting *Pravda*, 23 December 1985.

under Edouard Shevardnadze, later confirmed that the "political decision of principle on this matter [was] adopted as far back as December 1985."[114]

In February 1986, Gorbachev went public, telling the 27th Party Congress that Afghanistan was a "bleeding wound" and "we should like, in the nearest future, to withdraw the Soviet troops stationed in Afghanistan. . . . "[115] American conservatives, still skeptical, downplayed the importance of this comment by pointing out that Gorbachev continued to blame the war on "counterrevolution and imperialism" rather than Soviet aggression.[116] Foreign Minister Shevardnadze later acknowledged this admittedly mixed message was the product of a compromise with hard-liners, who nearly succeeded in removing the troop-withdrawal reference entirely.[117]

In the spring of 1986, Gorbachev removed yet another barrier to Soviet withdrawal, Afghanistan's ruler Babrak Karmal. Because Karmal had been unable or unwilling to broaden his political base within Afghanistan, the Kremlin believed an immediate Red Army withdrawal would lead to his quick demise and replacement by a regime unfriendly to the Soviets. Karmal also refused to cooperate with Soviet efforts to set a withdrawal timetable, telling Gorbachev, "If you leave now, you'll have to send in a million soldiers next time."[118] But Gorbachev would not permit the Afghan ruler to block his plans, telling the Politburo in October 1985 that Soviet withdrawal must take place "with or without Karmal." On 4 May 1986, Karmal bitterly accepted his forced resignation and was replaced by his chief of intelligence, Mohammed Najibullah, who savvily had aligned himself with the new Soviet policy of withdrawal.[119] In July, Gorbachev ordered a token troop withdrawal to demonstrate the seriousness of his intentions. Although a public relations disaster in the West, because there was little actual reduction in Soviet combat strength,[120] Pakistani officials among others took it as a sincere indication of Gorbachev's intent to leave Afghanistan entirely.[121]

The watershed change in the Politburo's official policy came in November 1986. While Gorbachev had been laying the groundwork for withdrawal for

[114] USSR Ministry of Foreign Affairs, "The Foreign Policy and Dipomatic Activity of the USSR," *International Affairs* (January 1990): 12. See also, Shevardnadze, *The Future*, 68. Shevardnadze was announced as Andrei Gromyko's replacement on 3 July 1985.

[115] Mikhail S. Gorbachev, "The Political Report of the Central Committee of the CPSU to the Party Congress of the CPSU, Moscow, 25 February 1986" in *Toward a Better World* (New York: Richardson & Steirman, 1987).

[116] Rodman, *More Precious*, 327.

[117] Shevardnadze, *The Future*, 47. See also, Cordovez and Harrison, *Out of Afghanistan*, 202.

[118] Oberdorfer, *The Turn*, 239.

[119] Cordovez and Harrison, *Out of Afghanistan*, 202–205. These authors also cite an additional point of contention between Gorbachev and Karmal: the Afghan leader demanded as a condition of his cooperation that the indirect UN negotiations (in which his government and Pakistan communicated exclusively via the UN mediator due to Pakistan's refusal to recognize the Afghan regime) be converted to direct negotiations.

[120] Rodman, *More Precious*, 329.

[121] Yousaf and Adkin, *The Bear Trap*, 223–224.

more than a year, he always had conditioned that goal on arranging to leave behind a "friendly" regime in Kabul. At the Politburo meeting of 13 November 1986, however, this changed dramatically in two ways.[122] First, the ultimate Soviet objective was changed from a "friendly" to a "neutral" Afghanistan—an outcome the Mujahedin and United States would be much more inclined to accept in a negotiated settlement. Second, the Politburo imposed on itself a deadline for withdrawal—in Gorbachev's words, "one year - at maximum two years"—to be enforced apparently even if the first condition were not met.

As Andrei Gromyko stated at the meeting: "Our strategic goal is to make Afghanistan neutral. . . . But most important—to stop the war. I would agree that it is necessary to limit this to a period of one–two years." Edouard Shevardnadze concurred that Gorbachev had "said it correctly—two years." The Politburo also embraced two further steps to lay the groundwork for a Red Army withdrawal: establishing a separate Afghan-run military command to assume control after the pull-out, and inviting Najibullah to visit Moscow the following month to impress upon him the need to broaden his domestic political base in anticipation of the withdrawal.[123]

General Akhromeev, by this time deputy defense minister, conceded at the Politburo meeting that despite the Soviets' qualitative military escalation, their deployment still lacked sufficient troops either to establish authority on rural territory or to shut down all border supply routes. Soviet-backed forces could continue to win individual military confrontations but, he said, "we have lost the battle for the Afghan people." The Red Army could "maintain the situation on the level that it exists now. But under such conditions the war will continue for a long time." Only KGB Chief Viktor Chebrikov still parroted the hardline position that "not everything was done that could have been done"—but he received no support from the others.[124] Soon after the meeting, Gorbachev went public with at least part of the new policy, telling Indian reporters in late-November 1986 that the Soviet Union now favored a nonaligned, neutral Afghanistan,[125] but Western observers failed to recognize the significance at the time.

Because this momentous decision came just two months after introduction of the Stinger, many previously have argued that the missile's impact triggered the Soviet decision—based on the simplistic logic of *post hoc ergo propter hoc.* Viewed in context, however, the Politburo's establishment of a withdrawal deadline was merely one step in a steady progression of Soviet policy, set in motion more than a year earlier and facilitated by Gorbachev's growing power base in the Kremlin.

Thereafter, Gorbachev adhered resolutely to the Politburo deadline despite substantial hurdles, including a prolonged dispute over the conditions un-

---

[122] CWIHPB, 179–180, contains a full transcript of the meeting.

[123] Cordovez and Harrison, *Out of Afghanistan*, 208.

[124] CWIHPB, 179–180; also Dobbs, *Washington Post*, 16 November 1992.

[125] MccGwire, *Perestroika*, 275.

der which U.S. and Soviet aid to the contending Afghan sides would terminate.[126] In December 1986, he informed Najibullah that Soviet troops would withdraw within one and a half to two years. In July of the next year, during the Afghan leader's visit to Moscow, Najibullah was told he had only twelve months. Also in July 1987, Soviet diplomats were authorized to pass word of the decision to their foreign counterparts,[127] with Shevardnadze personally telling U.S. Secretary of State Shultz in September 1987.[128] In February 1988, the Kremlin publicly announced its plans to withdraw, and on 15 February 1989, the last Soviet troops left Afghanistan, only three months behind the deadline set by the Politburo two years earlier.[129]

THE STINGER'S IMPACT

A number of important questions about the Stinger's use in Afghanistan have never been addressed satisfactorily. Most fundamentally, what was the Stinger's military impact? Second, what was its political impact, if any, on the Soviet decision to withdraw and on the end of the cold war, and did it match U.S. expectations? Third, was the Stinger supply program, once approved, handled responsibly by the CIA? Finally, from a longer-term perspective, what was the net impact of the Stinger decision on global security in light of the hundreds of missiles apparently still unaccounted for?

U.S. Intentions

Before assessing the Stinger's impact, it is necessary to explore precisely what the Reagan administration hoped to achieve by this watershed escalation. Former officials concur on the basic rationale—the Stinger would increase the Soviets' costs in Afghanistan, convince them it was unwinnable, and compel a decision to withdraw. In the words of Peter Rodman, deputy assistant to the president for national security affairs at the NSC, the United States intended to show the Soviets that Afghanistan was "indigestible."[130]

However, Reagan officials differ on several important points. One is the extent to which the Stinger decision was a reaction to Gorbachev's ascension to power. According to former Undersecretary of Defense Fred Iklé, a scholar of war termination and author of the seminal work *Every War Must End*, the decision was not spurred by the presence of a new Soviet leader but rather was part of an older U.S. strategy to escalate the war gradually.[131] Indeed, as early

---

[126] On the contentious debate over "symmetry," see Cordovez and Harrison, *Out of Afghanistan*, 260–266, chapter entitled "The United States Moves the Goalposts."

[127] Oberdorfer, *The Turn*, 240–244.

[128] Shultz, *Turmoil and Triumph*, 1086.

[129] Dobbs, *Washington Post*, 16 November 1992.

[130] Peter Rodman, interview with author, 15 August 1995.

[131] Iklé, interview with author, 19 August 1995.

as 1983, President Reagan had signed NSDD 75, stating: "The U.S. objective is to keep maximum pressure on Moscow for withdrawal and to ensure that the Soviets' political, military, and other costs remain high while the occupation continues."[132] In 1985, NSDD 166 boosted aid for the rebels with the explicit goal of helping them compel a Soviet withdrawal. Thus, the Stinger decision of 1986 can be seen as but one step—albeit a major one—in a steady escalation of U.S. pressure against the Soviet occupation. For Iklé, Gorbachev was "just the beneficiary" of this gradually escalating policy.[133]

According to Mort Abramowitz, however, Gorbachev was the key. The administration's assessment of the new general secretary as a moderate, not personally committed to the war, led it to conclude that escalating the war would compel withdrawal rather than counter-escalation. "If it had been another Stalin, you might have thought about it differently," he explains.[134]

Another bone of contention is whether the Stinger escalation was informed by secret intelligence from high-placed sources in the Kremlin or public reports on Red Army tactics and the deteriorating condition of the Soviet Union. The *Washington Post* reported in 1992 that: "An intelligence coup in 1984 and 1985 triggered the Reagan administration's decision to escalate the covert program in Afghanistan. The United States received highly specific, sensitive information about Kremlin politics and new Soviet war plans in Afghanistan. . . . The Reagan administration moved in response to this intelligence to open up its high-technology arsenal to aid the Afghan rebels."[135]

Similarly, Peter Schweizer's book *Victory* reports that, "In January 1985, the administration received detailed knowledge of Soviet plans to dramatically escalate the war in Afghanistan." According to an account Schweizer attributes to Robert McFarlane, President Reagan responded by telling his national security team: "Do whatever you have to to help the Mujahedin not only survive but win."[136]

Pillsbury likewise was impressed by the "super information about KGB and General Staff decision-making" available to the administration, at least until the CIA's Aldrich Ames began exposing U.S. agents at the end of 1985. Based

---

[132] Christopher Simpson, *National Security Directives of the Reagan and Bush Administrations: The Declassified History of U.S. Political and Military Policy, 1981-1991* (Boulder, CO: Westview Press, 1995), 258.

[133] Iklé, interview with author, 19 August 1995.

[134] Abramowitz, interview with author, 30 August 1995. This concept that political leaders responsible for entry into a war will be less willing to concede in the face of opposing escalation than will incoming leaders with less of a personal political stake in the war is explored formally in George W. Downs and David M. Rocke, Princeton University and UC-Davis, "Intervention, Escalation, and Gambling for Resurrection," unpublished manuscript, 15 April 1992. For a more general discussion of the relationship between domestic politics and surrender in war, see Fred Charles Iklé, *Every War Must End* (New York: Columbia University Press, 1991), rev. ed., chap. 4, "The Struggle Within: Patriots Against 'Traitors.'"

[135] Coll, *Washington Post*, 19 July 1992.

[136] Schweizer, *Victory*, 212–213.

on the reams of unconfirmed intelligence reports that crossed his desk, as well as CIA studies, Pillsbury says he perceived a serious schism in the Kremlin. General Zaitsev, together with the General Staff and KGB, were escalating the war aggressively and distorting their reports to the Kremlin on the war's status and prospects. "I believed the information was going through several filters before reaching Gorbachev and Shevardnadze," says Pillsbury. It was this filtering, he argues, that made it necessary for U.S. officials to find a way to convey directly to Gorbachev that the United States would not permit a Red Army victory. Shooting down Soviet aircraft with American-made missiles, he says, was the perfect solution.[137]

Many other administration officials, however, discount the influence of secret intelligence. Iklé says his support for the Stinger was prompted by the well-publicized 1985 Soviet escalation and by his assessment—based on public reports on the unhealthy state of the Soviet military and economy—that the Red Army would not respond by invading Pakistan.[138] Abramowitz says that while the United States knew "there was a controversy" in the Kremlin about what to do in Afghanistan, he recalls the information coming from open sources rather than raw intelligence. "The highly sensitive intelligence came later," he says.[139] Rodman reports the administration found out only subsequently about the General Staff's secret plan to win the war within two years and that "we just saw they were going for broke." Rather than secret intelligence reports, he says, the Stinger escalation was based more on "objective factors" and "changes in Gorbachev's rhetoric."[140]

The Initial Military Impact

Without question, the Stinger had an immediate military impact. Although initial estimates may have been somewhat overblown—claiming the Stinger downed approximately one aircraft per day during the first three months of its deployment—the missile clearly represented an enormous qualitative improvement in the rebels' air-defense capability. As ISI's Yousaf details in his memoirs, previous antiaircraft technology provided to the rebels paled in comparison. The Oerlikon, for example, required "some twenty mules to transport a section of three guns . . . [making] the weapon more of a liability than an asset." It was especially ill-suited to Afghanistan's mountainous terrain, since "the long, heavy, cumbersome barrel had to be positioned across the animal, making it impossible to go through defiles, where it snagged on every bush." Likewise, the Blowpipe, which arrived in 1986, "was a disaster." During one engagement, thirteen of the missiles were fired at exposed enemy aircraft without a single

---

[137] Pillsbury, interviews with author, 11 August and 15 August 1995.

[138] Iklé, interview with author, 19 August 1995.

[139] Abramowitz, interview with author, 30 August 1995. It should be noted that Abramowitz did not assume his intelligence position at the State Department until spring 1985.

[140] Rodman, interview with author, 15 August 1995.

hit—"a duck shoot in which the ducks won." The weapon was not man-portable "over any distance," says Yousaf, who cannot "recall a single confirmed kill by a Blowpipe" before he left ISI in 1987.[141]

The Stinger was different. While the kill rate and number of targets destroyed are still disputed, the missile unquestionably shot down Soviet and especially Afghan aircraft at an unprecedented rate in its first few months of use.[142] Selig Harrison has attempted to rebut this conclusion relying on Soviet statistics,[143] but even if the reported statistics are accurate, his argument is flawed by several lapses. First, in attempting to prove the Stinger did not trigger an increase in downed aircraft, he counts 1986 as a pre-Stinger year because the missile was used only in its final four months. However, 1986 was the year of the missiles' greatest effectiveness, as opposing pilots had yet to adopt countermeasures. Second, he fails to grasp the significance of his own findings that while the Soviets themselves experienced no significant increase in aircraft losses, there was a sharp jump in the loss of Afghan government aircraft. Rather than indicating any Soviet imperviousness to the Stinger, as he implies, such evidence is consistent with reports the Soviets responded to the missile by abstaining from dangerous missions, shifting them to Afghan pilots. From the Mujahedin perspective, the nationality of pilots was of little consequence so long as enemy aircraft finally were being shot down.

Third, Harrison appears to conflate aircraft losses with aircraft shootdowns, a key distinction underscored in an earlier analysis by Scott McMichael. As McMichael states: "During the first two years of the war, the great majority of Soviet aircraft losses (75-80 percent) must be attributed to non-combat causes, plus losses suffered on the ground due to raids, rocket attacks, and sabotage. . . . There can be no doubt at all that the Stinger turned the ratio on its head."[144] The Stinger's effectiveness was due mainly to six technological advantages: it required little training; it was truly man-portable, weighing just 35 pounds; it was a "fire-and-forget" weapon; it was faster and had greater range than earlier SAMs; it could attack fixed-wing aircraft and helicopters from any angle, unlike the relatively primitive SA-7 and Redeye, which could focus only on a jet engine's exhaust from the rear; and once locked on target, it could not be deflected by flares.[145]

[141] Yousaf and Adkin, *The Bear Trap*, 87–88, 171.

[142] Declassified U.S. intelligence cables (dates withheld but identified as approximately March 1987) reveal the initially enormous perceived impact of the missiles. "The Stinger missile has changed the course of the war because Soviet helicopter gunships and bombers no longer are able to operate as they once did," says one cable. "More tactical and air support changes occurred in the last quarter of 1986 and the first quarter of 1987 than in the previous seven years of the conflict," according to another. (Cables obtained from National Security Archives, Washington, DC.)

[143] Cordovez and Harrison, *Out of Afghanistan*, 199.

[144] McMichael, *Stumbling Bear*, 92.

[145] Ibid., 90, although he appears to attribute one feature to the Stinger, an ultra-violet lock-on, that is found only on the more advanced Stinger-POST, a model not provided to the Mujahedin, at least initially. See also, Yousaf and Adkin, *The Bear Trap*, 175.

Yousaf presents a detailed accounting of the Stinger's first ten months in service until his departure from ISI in August 1987. During this time, he claims, 187 Stingers were fired, of which 75 percent hit their target, for a total of approximately 140 downed aircraft. Such detailed statistics must be based on Mujahedin self-reporting, the reliability of which is unknown. Nevertheless, these figures are more reliable than those in an oft-cited September 1987 U.S. analysis, which estimated "the destruction of about 270 aircraft per year." That study's author, Aaron Karp, acknowledged his projections were pure conjecture based on arbitrary assumptions the Mujahedin would fire all their missiles and achieve a low kill rate of 33 percent.[146] While these two assumptions may have seemed reasonable at the time, evidence suggests both were mistaken. Unfortunately, Karp's study has contributed to popular confusion about the Stinger's performance, as his estimates have been widely reported without indication of their lack of empirical basis.

A more rigorous U.S. Army analysis was conducted in early 1989 by a team sent to "go sit with the Mujahedin" in Pakistan for several weeks. It concludes that by war's end the rebels had scored "approximately 269 kills in about 340 engagements" with the Stinger, for a remarkable 79 percent kill ratio.[147] Selig Harrison rejects such figures, quoting a Russian general who claims the United States "greatly exaggerated" Soviet and Afghan aircraft losses during the war. However, the findings of the U.S. study are not necessarily out of line with the Soviets' own statistics that he cites. From 1986 through 1988, the years that include all Stinger launches, Harrison reports that Soviet and Afghan forces lost a total of 310 aircraft. If one discounts for the number of aircraft shot down in 1986 prior to introduction of the Stinger in September, those lost to attrition, and those shot down with other weapons, it is not implausible that somewhere in the range of 269 were shot down with Stingers.

As for the kill ratio, it is impossible to confirm. A U.S. Army analyst involved in the study claims that "several levels of verification" were used to ensure that rebel descriptions of the engagements were consistent with each other, with the limited amount of available physical evidence, and with known characteristics of the missile system. Among factors reportedly responsible for the rebels' high success rate is that distribution of the weapons was limited to their best educated, most effective warriors, who were trained to hold fire unless a kill was extremely likely.[148] Yousaf also cites the rebels' daring tactics, which included positioning Stinger teams at the ends of Soviet runways. Another tactic was for one team of rebels to stand vulnerably in the open, acting as bait to draw enemy aircraft into range, while a second hidden team waited

---

[146] Aaron Karp, "Blowpipes and Stingers in Afghanistan: One Year Later," *Armed Forces Journal International* (September 1987): 36–40.

[147] Maj. William McManaway, "Stinger in Afghanistan," *Air Defense Artillery* (January-February 1990), 3–8; Maj. William McManaway, "The Dragon is Dead!" *Air Defense Artillery* (July-August 1989); Tony Capaccio, *Defense Week*, 12 June 1989; David Ottaway, *Washington Post*, 5 July 1989.

[148] Former U.S. Army analyst, interview with author, 18 November 1998.

to fire the missiles. By contrast, the Pakistan Army utilized more conservative tactics, necessitated in part by having to stay on its own side of the border, which led to miserable results. Yousaf reports that, to his knowledge, the army "fired twenty-eight Stingers at enemy aircraft without a single kill."[149]

War correspondent Mark Urban, however, claims the Mujahedin Stinger kill ratios reported by the U.S. Army were grossly inflated, venturing his own alternative estimate of only 10 percent.[150] While Urban's skeptical views have been widely cited, it is rarely noted that the primary basis for his conclusions appears to have been the anecdotes of TV journalists, who reported great difficulty in videotaping successful missile hits.[151] In retrospect, there are several plausible reasons why journalists might have observed a lower kill ratio than occurred overall, including: taping Stinger firings on the safer, Pakistani side of the border, where the Pakistani Army reportedly had much lower kill ratios than the Mujahedin; viewing launches of missiles other than Stingers, without knowing the difference; observing Stinger firings during the war's last year or two, after Soviet adoption of counter-measures that significantly reduced the Stingers' effectiveness; and for logistical reasons, being unable to tape Mujahedin employing their most daring and dangerous—and, therefore, most successful—tactics. In sum, a host of selection effects may have distorted the sample of missile firings that TV journalists were able to view, making it unrepresentative of the total universe. In this light, it is possible that the reports of both Urban and the U.S. Army are essentially accurate—the Mujahedin achieved a high Stinger kill ratio overall, but TV journalists witnessed a low kill ratio in the firings they observed.

Soviet Counter-Measures

In response to the Stinger's immediate success, the Red Army initially restricted its pilots to less dangerous missions, shunting the rest onto Afghan flyers. The Afghans, however, soon lost their nerve as well. According to Yousaf, they would pretend to go out on missions, fire off their ammunition, return to

---

[149] See Yousaf and Adkin, *The Bear Trap*, 183–184, although their statistics for the Pakistan Army's success rate should be approached cautiously in light of the memoir's generally negative tone toward that army.

[150] Urban, *War in Afghanistan*, 296. Urban also argues that other weapons and tactics were more important to the Mujahedin's cause than the Stinger, including plastic-cased mines (238, 303), high-tech radios (303), and the rocketing of air fields (223). In addition, he gives evidence that the Soviets still were able to use helicopters effectively after the Stinger's introduction, for example, in the resupply of Khost in late-1987 (303). Finally, Urban even claims that changes in Soviet air tactics in late-1986 were a response not mainly to the Stinger, as generally argued, but to Gorbachev's pre-Stinger decision to scale-down the Soviets' offensive ground posture, which reduced the need for air support (297).

[151] Ibid., 270–271, and fn. 18, 277, which cites "interviews with various journalists . . . between them they witnessed more than 20 launches with only one possible kill."

base, and falsely report success.[152] A former Afghan pilot confirms that he and his fellow "pilots went on strike and refused to fly in areas where Stinger missiles were present."[153]

Fairly quickly, however, Soviet forces adopted a series of technical and tactical countermeasures that mitigated the impact of the Stinger. In the technical area, Soviet aircraft were retrofitted with improved flares, infrared beacons, and baffles on their exhausts to impede the Stingers' ability to lock on target. Aircraft also were equipped with a missile radar warning system to notify pilots of the need for evasive action.[154]

Tactically, the Soviets had numerous responses. Fixed-wing aircraft flew at higher altitudes outside the Stinger's three-mile range, which averted the missile threat but reduced the pilots' effectiveness, earning them the derisive sobriquet "cosmonauts" from Soviet ground troops.[155] Helicopter pilots pursued the opposite strategy, adopting low-altitude, nap-of-the-earth techniques to hide from the Stingers, which function best when hot aircraft are silhouetted against a cool, blue sky. At the lower altitude, however, helicopters became more vulnerable to small-weapons fire. Interestingly, the same tactical countermeasures had been reported as early as the first year of the war and several times thereafter in response to earlier-model SAMs.[156] However, the Stinger's introduction apparently triggered a dramatic renewal and expansion of their use.

The Soviets also reportedly shifted many air operations to cover of darkness, as the rebels initially were not equipped with night-vision equipment.[157] They increasingly relied on human intelligence to discover the location of Stingers, then either destroyed the missiles, purchased them, or avoided the locations entirely.[158] Some daredevil Soviet pilots utilized a tactic that was a mirror-image of the rebels' own: flying in tandem within the Stinger's range but separated by a large distance, the first of two Soviet aircraft would make itself vulnerable in order to flush a Mujahedin Stinger team from its perch, after which the second aircraft would appear and fire on the exposed rebels.[159] For

---

[152] Yousaf and Adkin, *The Bear Trap*, 179.

[153] David Isby, "Soviet Surface-to-Air Missile Countermeasures: Lessons from Afghanistan," *Jane's Intelligence Review*, 1 January 1989.

[154] Ibid., McMichael, *Stumbling Bear*, 89; see also, Bodansky, "SAMs in Afghanistan."

[155] Capaccio, *Defense Week*, quoting Representative Charlie Wilson.

[156] David C. Isby, "Soviet Tactics in the War in Afghanistan," *Jane's Defence Review*, vol. 4, no. 7 (1983), 683–685. See also, Ritch, "Hidden War"; Craig Karp, "Afghanistan: Six Years of Soviet Occupation," U.S. Department of State, Special Report No. 135, December 1985, 1. Prior to the initial introduction of these techniques, the rebels are reported to have downed sixty helicopters with SAMs in 1980, according to Jeffrey T. Richelson, *The U.S. Intelligence Community* (Boulder, CO: Westview Press, 1995), 350.

[157] Gates, *From the Shadows*, 350, says that about five months after the Stinger's original introduction into Afghanistan, the CIA introduced a new sighting system that also worked at night, which forced Soviet and Afghan pilots to fly at higher altitudes both day and night.

[158] Isby, "Soviet Surface-to-Air."

[159] John Gunston, "Stingers Used by Afghan Rebels Stymie Soviet Air Force Tactics," *Aviation Week & Space Technology*, 4 April 1988, 47.

important air support missions that could not be conducted safely in the presence of Stingers, such as facilitating insertion of special operations forces, the Soviets sometimes substituted long-range suppressive artillery fire, which was effective but required more ground forces and sacrificed the element of surprise.[160]

Despite the army's claim that the "Stinger was the war's decisive weapon"[161]—echoed by many others including *60 Minutes*, which declared, "The Stinger is generally credited with having won the war for the Mujahedin"[162]—the net effect of Soviet counter-measures eventually was to offset the Stinger.[163] David Isby, an expert military analyst of the Afghan conflict, concluded in 1990 that, "although none of the Soviets' countermeasures were totally successful, the Stinger . . . did not succeed in forcing Soviet helicopters out of the sky."[164] A leading French expert on Afghanistan, Olivier Roy, confirms from his experience among the rebels in late 1988 that, "by 1989, the Stinger could no longer be considered a decisive anti-aircraft weapon."[165]

Ironically, one of the JCS's original concerns had been vindicated. The combat effectiveness of the Stingers—at least in their original configuration—was indeed compromised. The resulting impact on American security interests, however, was minimal. By war's end, U.S. Stinger technology had already advanced two generations and, more importantly, the cold war was drawing to a close.

Impact on Soviet Withdrawal

A key question is what impact, if any, the Stinger's deployment had on the power struggle between Gorbachev—already seeking withdrawal—and General Staff hardliners claiming Soviet escalation could enable military victory.

---

[160] David C. Isby, "Stinger in Afghanistan: The Soviets Try to Adapt," *Rotor & Wing International*, February 1990, 58.

[161] McManaway, "Stinger in Afghanistan." See also, Capaccio, *Defense Week*.

[162] *60 Minutes*, CBS News, 30 October 1988; see also, Ottaway, *Washington Post*, 12 February 1989, which quotes Congressman Charlie Wilson saying, "Once the Stinger made their helicopters useless, that put the Russians on foot against the Mujahedin and there's nobody on Earth who can fight the Mujahedin on foot."

[163] A few press accounts, dissenting from the common wisdom, voiced this opinion as early as 1987. See, for example, Elaine Parnell, "Stingers in a Tale," *Far Eastern Economic Review*, 5 November 1987, who wrote that the Stinger's impact was "nothing approaching the impression given by some that the Stinger has tilted the balance of the war." See also, Bodansky, "SAMs in Afghanistan," who wrote in July 1987 that, "the primary impact of the Resistance's air-defence capabilities was a modification of Soviet-Democratic Republic of Afghanistan (DRA) tactics. . . . [T]here is no evidence that any Soviet-DRA aerial operation was canceled or aborted because of Resistance air-defence." It should be noted, however, that Bodansky consistently had a hawkish view of Soviet intentions and capabilities, stating in March 1985 that the Red Army was "on its way to attaining total victory." See Congressional Task Force on Afghanistan, 11 March 1985.

[164] Isby, "Stinger in Afghanistan," 58.

[165] Roy, *The Lessons*, 53.

As commonly reported, "the supply of high-tech American weaponry to the Mujahedin played a key factor in the Soviet withdrawal from Afghanistan. . . . [T]here is evidence it helped convince the Kremlin that the war was unwinnable."[166] Likewise, the NSC's Cannistraro says that when the Stingers arrived, the Soviets "started taking losses that were unacceptable."[167] His NSC colleague Rodman attributes the diplomatic breakthrough in part to "the escalation of U.S. military aid to the Mujahedin, especially the furnishing of 'Stinger' antiaircraft missiles."[168]

Former Soviet Foreign Minister Shevardnadze, however, presents a contrary view: "The Stinger definitely prolonged our stay. . . . It made our military men, our hawks, much more determined than ever not to withdraw, not to appear to be giving in under duress." This view is shared by Georgi Arbatov, Andrey Kokoshin, and General Akhromeev,[169] and is the main thesis of Harrison and Cordovez in *Out of Afghanistan.* More generally, George Kennan[170] and Raymond Garthoff argue that the militarized version of U.S. containment strategy, including the Reagan Doctrine, prolonged the cold war as a whole. As Garthoff puts it, "Gorbachev pressed ahead. . . not owing to the Reagan hard line and military buildup, but despite it."[171] According to these authors, reduced U.S. pressure would have enabled an earlier withdrawal by permitting the Soviets to save face while doing so.

Rodman rejects such revisionist assessments of the Stinger as "liberal fantasy."[172] Abramowitz, despite being present when Shevardnadze made his comment, says, "I don't believe that for a minute."[173] Iklé cautions that "too much face-saving might have saved the Soviet regime." He believes the humiliating defeat of the Red Army in Afghanistan was integral to reducing the status and influence of hard-liners in the Kremlin. "Otherwise, we might still have the Cold War."[174] French expert, Olivier Roy, concurs that "by undermining the prestige of both the old Brezhnevian guard and the army, [the failure in Afghanistan] gave Gorbachev more room for manoeuvre."[175]

Implicit in all such assessments of the political impact of the Stinger decision are counter-factual claims—that is, what would have happened in its ab-

---

[166] Dobbs, *Washington Post*, 16 November 1992.

[167] Quoted in Schweizer, *Victory*, 270.

[168] Rodman, *More Precious*, 221. He says that Gorbachev's ascendance was the other key.

[169] Mendelson, *Explaining Change*, 43, 215–216.

[170] See, for example, "Who Won the Cold War? Ask Instead, What Was Lost?" *International Herald Tribune*, 29 October 1992, adapted from "The G.O.P. Won the Cold War? Ridiculous," *New York Times*, 28 October 1992. See also, "The Failure in Our Success," *New York Times*, 14 March 1994.

[171] Garthoff, *The Great Transition*, 775. This argument is also made by MccGwire, *Perestroika*, 386, who states that Gorbachev pressed for reform "despite the assertive policies of the Reagan administration, not because of them."

[172] Rodman, interview with author, 15 August 1995.

[173] Cordovez and Harrison, *Out of Afghanistan*, 198.

[174] Iklé, interview with author, 19 August 1995.

[175] Roy, *The Lessons*, 47.

sence. These must be separated from actual facts and evaluated for plausibility. Two facts are clear. First, when Gorbachev came to power in 1985, he initially escalated the war. Second, had the United States not countered with NSDD 166, followed by the Stinger and other U.S. technology, the Soviets would have gained militarily against the Mujahedin. However, at least three important counter-factual questions remain: How badly damaged would the Mujahedin have been? Would this have reversed the rebels' opposition to the unfavorable negotiated settlement then on the table? How would this military progress have affected Politburo decision making? While counter-factual reasoning never is certain, answers to these questions can be found with relative confidence.

First, despite the claims of some,[176] it is highly unlikely that the Soviet escalation of 1985-1986, if not countered by the United States, would have succeeded in eliminating the Mujahedin. Indeed, the Mujahedin had proved able to survive even in the early 1980s, when they were considerably more outmatched than they would have been in this subsequent scenario.[177] The Soviets' fundamental problem was their unwillingness to increase troop levels, forcing them into a strategy of coercion based mainly on air power.[178] Throughout the twentieth century, such an approach had failed to produce victory against a people on its home territory.[179]

Second, it is extremely unlikely that even substantial Soviet military progress would have compelled the rebels to accept a negotiated settlement that left a pro-Soviet government in Kabul. As demonstrated in subsequent years, the rebels preferred to face death rather than cede power even to each other, let alone to a pro-Soviet regime.

Third, regardless of the situation in Afghanistan, Gorbachev was intent on his two-track strategy of consolidating power, by placing allies in key Communist party positions, and establishing nontraditional sources of expertise. By late 1986, therefore, he likely could have pushed his views through the Politburo despite any military gains in Afghanistan. The ultimate question, therefore, is whether Gorbachev's own preference would have changed had the 1985

---

[176] Gates, *From the Shadows*, 429, for example, claims that, "Thanks to our massive infusion of assistance during 1985-1986, the Mujahedin were able to withstand the Soviet maximum push."

[177] Of course, Soviet tactics had improved by the later time period, but so had those of the rebels. For an insightful contemporaneous view from the rebels' perspective, see Almerigo Grilz, "Afghanistan: The Guerrilla is Changing," *Military Technology*, no. 6 (June 1987), which appends an interview with Abdul Haq. Mujahedin commander in the Kabul area. See also, Ian Kemp, "Abdul Haq: Soviet Mistakes in Afghanistan," *Jane's Defence Weekly*, 5 March 1988, in which the rebel leader contends that some Soviet changes, such as the use of *Spetsnaz* troops, had backfired. Abdul Haq also denies that the Stinger made a decisive difference.

[178] As Galeotti, *Afghanistan*, 17, describes the Soviet escalation that started in 1984: "The aim appears to have been to win by shattering rebel morale and destroying their support infrastructure by, quite simply, encouraging mass emigration from rural areas outside Kabul's control: a policy of 'migratory genocide.'"

[179] Robert A. Pape, *Bombing to Win—Air Power and Coercion in War* (Ithaca, NY: Cornell University Press, 1996).

Soviet escalation gone unopposed and produced military gains in Afghanistan. The key fact here is that Gorbachev's primary objective in Afghanistan was to eliminate a thorn in East-West relations that inhibited Soviet economic revitalization. The West, especially the Reagan administration, would not have dropped its insistence on Soviet withdrawal from Afghanistan as a precondition for renewed détente, regardless of progress in the war. Thus, it is very likely that Gorbachev still would have pushed for the withdrawal deadline in late 1986, even had the Soviets made gains against the Mujahedin.[180] Red Army hard-liners would have protested, as they did in any case, but Gorbachev had sufficient votes in the Politburo to prevail.

Although counter-intuitive and contrary to popular wisdom, it appears the U.S. counter-escalation of 1985-1986 was largely irrelevant to the Soviet withdrawal decision of November 1986.[181] This is clearly the case for the Stinger, which was not utilized in Afghanistan until September 1986, a mere two months before the Politburo's decision to adopt a withdrawal deadline. At the key November 1986 Politburo meeting, no mention was made of the Stinger nor any other U.S. escalation. Rather, Defense Minister Akhromeev blamed Moscow for capping troop levels and Kabul for failing to coopt the opposition. Moreover, the Stinger effectively was neutralized by technical and tactical countermeasures well before the Soviets actually completed their withdrawal. Thus, there is no evidence the Stinger even hastened Soviet withdrawal. Neither is there evidence it delayed the Soviet pullout.

Had Gorbachev not decided autonomously to withdraw, it is unlikely the Stinger could have chased him out of Afghanistan. Prior to his entering office, the Red Army's strategy in Afghanistan had presumed a protracted occupation, relying only on holding key cities and garrisons as bases for attacks on population, infrastructure, and supply lines in rebel-controlled areas.[182] These bases were never seriously threatened by the Mujahedin even after they acquired the Stinger. Previous Soviet conquests had required occupations of far greater duration. Indeed, in the mid-1980s, there was a cottage industry among U.S. Sovietologists trying to figure out which historical model the Soviets would use to absorb Afghanistan: Mongolia,[183] Central Asia,[184] Finland,[185] Eastern Eu-

---

[180] Urban, *War in Afghanistan*, 300, reaches the same conclusion.

[181] This belies the conclusion of Scott in his otherwise excellent account of the Reagan Doctrine: "There is little doubt that the increasing costs of Afghanistan, caused in no small part by the application of the Reagan Doctrine, contributed mightily to the restructuring of Soviet policy." Scott, *Deciding to Intervene*, 78. See also Gates, *From the Shadows*, 350: "There is little question that providing the Stinger was a major turning point in the Afghan war." Mark Urban is closer to the truth in dismissing as "nonsense" the "myth that American supplies, particularly the Stinger missile, won the war in Afghanistan." He concludes: "The West and Pakistan did not win the 20th Century Great Game— Gorbachev simply decided he was not playing any more—not with Soviet soldiers at least." Urban, *War in Afghanistan*, 302–304.

[182] Rais, *War Without Winners*, 102–104.

[183] "A Brief History of Russian and Soviet Expansion Toward the South," Combat Capabilities Analysis Group, United States Central Command, MacDill Air Force Base, 30 June 1985, 71.

[184] Alexander Alexiev, testimony, 11 March 1985, 114.

[185] Rubin, testimony, 1 May 1986.

rope generally,[186] or Poland specifically.[187] In 1982, General Secretary Yuri Andropov reminded Politburo colleagues that it had required almost fifteen years to subdue Uzbekistan, Tajikistan, and Kirgizstan.[188] In June 1985, the United States Central Command, unaware of the changes Gorbachev was bringing to the Kremlin, concluded the Soviets could "be expected to show their historical persistence in Afghanistan, anticipating a slow, gradual domination of the country.... [where] time may be on their side." The study, citing previous Soviet triumphs over indigenous anticommunist movements, concluded that "the Afghans will likely suffer a similar fate."[189] According to a key Pakistani official, Islamabad likewise believed Soviet "costs [in Afghanistan] were not intolerable and appeared to be on the decline."[190]

Unintended Consequences: Stinger Proliferation

As the JCS and Senator DeConcini had warned, Stinger accountability proved grossly inadequate. First, Pakistan skimmed off a percentage of the Stingers for itself—a missile tax—with some reportedly winding up on the black market. Of those that reached the Mujahedin, perhaps half were sold for cash, given to allies such as Iran, lost in ambushes, or hoarded for future conflicts.[191]

According to press reports, Stingers now have proliferated around the globe. While not all of this spread can be confirmed or attributed solely to the Mujahedin supply operation, the missiles originally destined for Afghanistan likely account for much of it. Reportedly, Stingers already have shot down aircraft twice in Bosnia[192] and once in Tajikistan.[193] In 1987, an Iranian boat fired a Stinger that reportedly hit a U.S. helicopter in the Persian Gulf but failed to explode.[194] Tunisian fundamentalists are reported to have used a Stinger in a failed 1991 assassination attempt.[195] Stingers also reportedly have been acquired by Kashmiri militants, Indian Sikhs, the Iranian drug mafia, Iraq,[196] Qa-

[186] Edward Luttwak, testimony before Congressional Task Force on Afghanistan, 30 April 1986, 45.

[187] Thomas Gouttierre, Center of Afghan Studies, University of Nebraska, quoted in Aaron R. Einfrank, *Washington Times*, 17 January 1986.

[188] Dobbs, *Washington Post*, 16 November 1982.

[189] United States Central Command, "A Brief History," 71–72.

[190] Khan, *Untying*, 169.

[191] Parnell, "Stingers in a Tale," 33. According to a report cited in Urban, *War in Afghanistan*, 225, several stolen or diverted Stingers ultimately were sold to the rebels' opponent, Afghan leader Najibullah, for about $25,000 each, although other analysts assume the missiles were captured by the Afghan army in ambushes.

[192] Charles Hanley, AP, *Calgary Herald*, 18 November 1993, reports the 1992 downing of an Italian supply plane. *Washington Post*, 28 July 1995, reports the 1995 downing of a French plane by a Stinger that "almost certainly came from Pakistan."

[193] Anwar Iqbal, *United Press International*, 26 July 1993.

[194] Ottaway, *Washington Post*, 12 February 1989.

[195] Christopher Dobson, *The Herald* (Glasgow), 30 July 1993.

[196] Evans, *The Guardian*, 2 January 1992.

tar,[197] Zambia (most likely from Angola),[198] North Korea, Libya, and militant Palestinian groups.[199] In addition, authorities reportedly have broken up plots to acquire the missiles by the Irish Republican Army, the Medellin Cartel, Croatian rebels, Armenia, Azerbaijan, Chechen secessionists,[200] and Cuban exiles.[201]

Under President George Bush, the CIA attempted to stop this hemorrhaging, motivated especially by the connection of some of the former rebels to radical Islamic terrorists. The agency initially requested $10 million to buy back Stingers, and when that proved inadequate, another $55 million in 1993.[202] Former rebel leader and then-Afghan Prime Minister Gulbuddin Hekmatyar responded that he did "not intend to allow even a round of ammunition to be taken out of Afghanistan."[203] Although a few dozen Stingers apparently were retrieved by the CIA, the main effect of the buy-back program has been to bid up the black-market price of the missile from its original value of $30,000 to as high as $200,000. Intelligence officials worry that those who sell back the Stingers at such exorbitant prices will recycle the profits to buy an even larger quantity of Soviet SA-14 missiles—reportedly based on the Stinger design—potentially exacerbating the overall terrorist threat.[204] Ironically, the $65 million appropriated by the United States to buy back a fraction of the leftover missiles is about twice the original purchase price of all of them.

A still unanswered question is precisely how many Stingers are left over from the Mujahedin supply operation. A variety of sources suggest that 300 Stingers were exported for delivery to the rebels in 1986, growing to a total of between 900 and 1200, together with approximately 250 reusable gripstocks.[205] The U.S. Army reported in 1990 that only about 340 Stingers actually were fired by the rebels prior to the Soviet withdrawal, and the *Washington Post* reported that no missiles were fired subsequently in Afghanistan through 1994.[206] The *Times* of London reported in 1994 that approximately 200 of the missiles were in storage in Pakistan—never delivered to the Mujahedin—and that the CIA had bought back another sixty.[207] If these reports are accurate, some 300 to 600 of the missiles remain unaccounted for. In January 1995, U.S. intelligence

---

[197] Hanley, *Calgary Herald.*

[198] David Ottaway, *Washington Post*, 1 May 1987.

[199] Edward Gorman, *The Times* (London), 14 May 1994.

[200] Hanley, *Calgary Herald.*

[201] Larry Rohter, *New York Times*, 4 June 1994.

[202] Robin Wright and John M. Broder, *Los Angeles Times*, 23 July 1993.

[203] *Los Angeles Times*, from *Associated Press*, 20 August 1993.

[204] Hanley, *Calgary Herald;* Gorman, *The Times;* Brian Duffy and Peter Cary, *U.S. News & World Report*, 30 August 1993.

[205] See, for example, Parnell, "Stingers in a Tale"; Ottaway, *Washington Post*, 12 February 1989; Coll, *Washington Post*, 20 July 1992; Yousaf and Adkin, *The Bear Trap*, 182.

[206] Molly Moore, *Washington Post*, 7 March 1994.

[207] Gorman, *The Times.*

sources were quoted as believing that "over 370 Stingers are still in Afghanistan."[208]

Some commentators have downplayed the terrorist threat posed by these remaining Stingers. Cannistraro has said the battery packs on several Stingers recovered from an Iranian boat in 1988 were found to be run-down, rendering the weapons ineffective.[209] He also recalls being told the weapons had "a shelf life of about a year."[210] However, a partially declassified 1987 analysis by the U.S. Central Command states clearly that, "The BCU, the power source required to activate the Stinger, has a shelf life of at least 10 years with a reliability rate of 98-99%."[211] Pillsbury recalls that a House Armed Services Committee staff person, Tony Battista, originally proposed modifying the Stingers to shorten their shelf life to several weeks prior to delivery to the rebels, but was turned down.[212] Even if some battery units have deteriorated, however, Cannistraro concedes, "it's silly to think" that potential users couldn't buy a battery, or have one engineered, to meet their needs.[213]

A final consideration is whether the Stinger is any more effective than other surface-to-air missiles commonly available in international arms markets. Among the alternatives are the British Javelin, the French Mistral, the Swedish RBS 70, and the Soviet SA-14 and SA-16.[214] Moreover, missiles similar to the Stinger are produced or are under development by China, South Africa, Brazil, and Egypt.[215] As far back as 1986, terrorism expert Robert Kupperman downplayed the significance of potential Stinger proliferation by arguing that the Soviet SA-7B, widely available even then, was sufficient to shoot down a civilian airliner.[216] Nevertheless, the Stinger appears to be in a category of its own, especially as a threat to military aircraft. Former CIA national intelligence officer, David Whipple, says he "would doubt there are missiles as good as the Stinger out there."[217] That would explain why the CIA is willing to spend $65 million to try to get them back.

The CIA's Performance

Confronted in 1993 with the worldwide proliferation of Stingers leaking from Afghanistan, former CIA associate director for covert operations, Edward

---

[208] Behroz Khan, *United Press International*, 14 January 1995.

[209] David Hughes, "FAA Examining Missile Threat," *Aviation Week & Space Technology*, 16 August 1993.

[210] Cannistraro, interview with author, 8 August 1995.

[211] "Stinger: One Year of Combat," Afghanistan Fusion Cell, United States Central Command, 26 October 1987.

[212] Pillsbury, interview with author, 11 August 1995.

[213] Cannistraro, interview with author, 8 August 1995.

[214] James W. Rawles, "Stinger: Requiem for the Combat Helicopter," *Defense Electronics*, November 1988.

[215] Wright and Broder, *Los Angeles Times*.

[216] Robert Kupperman, quoted in Peter Grier, *Christian Science Monitor*, 2 April 1986.

[217] David Whipple, interview with author, 9 August 1995.

Juchniewicz, responded, "Isn't the danger posed by a handful of Stingers worth the dissolution of the Soviet Empire?"[218] Surely it would be, had that been the trade-off. However, in light of the far smaller role actually played by the missiles in ending the Soviet occupation of Afghanistan, let alone the cold war, the security threat they now pose may be the most lasting legacy of the Stinger decision.

The obvious question is whether the CIA could have handled the original distribution of Stingers in a more responsible manner. The CIA's Whipple concedes only that, "in hindsight, that's indisputable."[219] However, even at the time, the CIA should have known better, and could have acted more responsibly. In several key respects the agency's failings were due to poor decision making, not to a lack of concurrent knowledge.

First, the agency relied on the worrisome ISI distribution network for the Stinger in 1986, even though an expert had written as early as November 1984 that "direct supplies to the resistance are increasingly feasible."[220] Such an alternative would have enabled restricting the missile to only the most reliable rebels. By contrast, the agency knew that ISI favored the most radical rebels, many with ties to Iran.

Second, the CIA should have taken into account that the rebels were only a temporary ally of convenience. As later acknowledged by the CIA's former chief of operations for the Near East and South Asia, Charles Cogan, it was obvious at the time that "the long-range aims of a country in which Islamists were at least beginning to have a say would not be, could not be, wholly compatible with the aims of a Western nation."[221] This concern turned out not to be so long-range. As early as 1991, Hekmatyar supported Saddam Hussein in the Gulf War. Two years later, in the wake of the 1993 World Trade Center bombing in New York City, Whipple confirmed that "some of the same people who are actual or potential terrorists in [the United States] are former guerrilla fighters in Afghanistan."[222]

Third, the CIA should have recognized soon after the initial modest deployment of Stingers that it was unnecessary to follow up with additional supplies of such an advanced weapons system. In 1987, the U.S. Central Command reported that due to the initial success of the Stinger and the "extreme difficulty for pilots to differentiate between shoulder-fired SAMs, Soviet pilots appear to treat all launches as Stinger. In numerous instances it has been noted that Soviet aircraft will depart an area as soon as a SAM is fired."[223] Thus, the CIA

[218] Weiner, *New York Times*, 24 July 1993.

[219] Whipple, interview with author, 9 August 1995.

[220] Alexander Alexiev, *The War in Afghanistan: Soviet Strategy and the State of the Resistance* (Santa Monica, CA: Rand, November 1984), 7.

[221] Cogan, "Partners in Time," 74. Nevertheless, as Gates, *From the Shadows*, 349, reveals, the CIA ironically tried to increase the number of Arabs coming to Afghanistan to fight with the Muslim fundamentalists, going so far as to explore establishment of an "international brigade."

[222] Weiner, *New York Times*, 24 July 1993.

[223] "Stinger: One Year of Combat," 11.

could have reduced the danger of Stinger proliferation by substituting lower-technology SAMs in follow-up shipments—without undermining rebel effectiveness.

Fourth, the CIA should have known the rebels would hoard Stingers if supplied a surplus. Even an avid Mujahedin supporter, Congressman Charlie Wilson, had earlier acknowledged that the rebels had a troubling habit of "ratholing" weapons for future use.[224] For all these reasons, the CIA should have kept the rebels on a much shorter tether—at least denying them more Stingers until the original ones were exhausted.

Instead, in its most profound error, the CIA supplied additional Stingers in 1987, just as the rebels were reducing their use of the weapon in response to Soviet counter-measures. Given that the rebels were reported to be downing about one aircraft per day and to be enjoying a 75-80 percent kill ratio, the initial batch of 300 missiles should have lasted at least half a year. At that point, the CIA could have assessed the need for more missiles and found, as *Aviation Week* later reported, that "the number of launch opportunities has declined due to changes in Soviet operating techniques."[225] The agency then could have suspended or sharply reduced supply of Stingers in 1987. Instead, the CIA reportedly shipped another 600 or more missiles in 1987, distribution of which continued to the rebels until mid-1988.[226] Making matters worse, the CIA reportedly loosened restrictions on missile distribution in 1987, rescinding the requirement that an expended tube be presented in exchange for each new missile and permitting individual rebels to receive more than one at a time.[227] The *Washington Post* reported in April 1987 that "so many Stingers are arriving in Pakistan that there is a problem of storing the weapons safely." A U.S. intelligence official later confirmed, "we were handing them out like lollipops."[228]

So far, the United States and its allies have avoided paying a heavy price for this sloppy CIA performance, as no civil airliners outside of Afghanistan are confirmed to have been shot down by Stingers.[229] U.S. intelligence officials, however, do not assume this luck will last and in 1992 established a Federal Aviation Administration study group to assess the terrorist missile threat. *Aviation Week* reports that less sophisticated SAMs were used in at least twenty-two attacks on civil airliners from 1986 to 1993, generally in countries experiencing civil insurgencies. According to a Rand analyst, as airports and airlines

[224] Congressional Task Force on Afghanistan, 30 April 1986, 29.

[225] Gunston, "Stingers Used," 46. Recall that the U.S. Army later reported only about 340 Stingers were launched during the entire war.

[226] Barnes, "Victory in Afghanistan," 93.

[227] David Ottaway, *Washington Post*, 5 April 1987; Yousaf and Adkin, *The Bear Trap*, 175.

[228] Moore, *Washington Post*, 7 March 1994.

[229] The Soviet press reported several times that Stingers had been used to shoot down civil airliners in Afghanistan. See, for example, *Tass*, 14 August 1987, reporting the downing of two AN-26 aircraft, killing thirty-six passengers in February 1987 and fifty-three passengers in June 1987.

boost security to inhibit hijackings and bombings, terrorists are increasingly likely to turn to missiles.[230]

THE STINGER DECISION IN RETROSPECT

The case of the Stinger provides several cautionary lessons about U.S. foreign policy generally and covert action specifically. First, it raises the question of who actually makes U.S. foreign policy and suggests procedures to help ensure its soundness. Second, it highlights shortcomings in the CIA's performance of a top-priority covert action, raising questions about the utility of such action as a tool of foreign policy. Third, it provides insight into perennial questions about the strengths and weaknesses of democracies in the conduct of foreign policy. Finally, it underscores the necessity for scholars to engage in painstaking "process tracing" to draw the proper lessons from history.

Without question, the Reagan administration's notorious lack of centralized policy coordination significantly retarded the Stinger decision and contributed to a nearly eighteen-month delay from initial proposal to final implementation, which effectively changed a good idea into a bad one.[231] When first seriously proposed in early spring 1985, in the wake of a Soviet escalation in Afghanistan, the Stinger plan fit an overall U.S. strategy to prevent Soviet absorption of Afghanistan by increasing the costs of the occupation. Despite misgivings of the CIA, the JCS, and the State Department, the potential benefits outweighed the risks in light of the intensified Soviet air campaign, a new Soviet leader not personally committed to the war, and the low assessed risk of retaliatory escalation. As events transpired, the missiles apparently were unnecessary to ensure the rebels' survival or to compel Gorbachev's withdrawal. However, U. S. officials had no way of knowing that in the spring of 1985, so it does not detract from the merits of the Stinger proposal when originally presented.

By the time the plan eventually was implemented in late summer 1986, however, it made considerably less sense, given that the Soviets already had signaled their intention to withdraw. At this point, the risks outweighed the potential benefits. Though delivery of Stingers at this later date probably did not prolong the war, it was unnecessary and led to two consequences feared by the JCS: missile proliferation and the development of Soviet counter-measures that effectively neutralized first-generation Stinger technology.

The Reagan administration's lack of a strong, hands-on leader in the Oval Office or at the NSC permitted individual agencies to pursue their own agendas even to the point of withholding relevant information. The JCS claimed the

---

[230] Hughes, "FAA Examining."

[231] This is directly contrary to the claims of Scott, *Deciding to Intervene*, 234–235, 250–252, that the White House spearheaded the 1985-86 escalation of assistance to the Mujahedin and generally "dominated policy-making" when issues "involved crisis characteristics." He is closer to the truth in subsequently acknowledging that President Reagan's decisions "were taken only after other actors pushed, prodded, and even manipulated the process," 252.

Stinger plan could lead to loss of this U.S. technology without disclosing that it already had been compromised in Greece. The JCS claimed as well that the plan would negatively impact the U. S. Army's missile stockpile, without disclosing that its supplier could increase production to offset any losses. The CIA continued as late as 1986 to report that Pakistani President Zia opposed introduction of the Stinger, even though he had been telling visiting U.S. officials otherwise since 1984.

As bureaucracies inevitably promote their own interests,[232] it is no surprise the army guarded its stockpile of missiles and the CIA attempted to avoid a covert project that could lead to its embarrassment. However, it is the job of the president, the national security adviser, and their staffs to ensure that such parochial pursuits are subordinated to the national interest. Policy disputes should be brought to a head on a timely basis, debated openly and with full information, decided authoritatively, and implemented with the full cooperation of all agencies. Lack of such decisive leadership was a signal failing of the Reagan administration in the Stinger case. As Rodman observes, President Richard Nixon and his national security adviser, Henry Kissinger, "never would have stood for this."[233]

Some scholars have identified two factors as primarily responsible for this Reagan administration shortcoming—bureaucratic structure and presidential personality. In one of its first directives, NSDD 2, the administration intentionally downgraded the structural authority and coordinating role of the national security adviser to reduce risk of his vying for control with the secretary of State, as occurred in the Carter administration.[234] Reagan's management style, meanwhile, was to avoid making decisions until his subordinates attained consensus.[235] The result was a power vacuum in which "each department was free to pursue its own interpretation of the president's decisions—or to ignore the president altogether."[236] As President Reagan's former chief of staff, James Baker, confirms, the foreign policy apparatus "was often a witches' brew of intrigue, elbows, egos, and separate agendas"—a dangerous model of inefficiency.[237]

---

[232] See Allison, *Essence of Decision*, especially his Model II. Also, Morton H. Halperin, *Bureaucratic Politics and Foreign Policy* (Washington, DC: The Brookings Institution, 1974).

[233] Rodman, interview with author, 15 August 1995.

[234] Christopher C. Shoemaker, *The NSC Staff: Counseling the Council* (Boulder, CO: Westview Press, 1991), 59–60.

[235] Cecil Van Meter Crabb, *American National Security: A Presidential Perspective* (Belmont, CA: Brooks/Cole Publishing Company, 1991), 182. See also, Karl F. Inderfurth, Loch K. Johnson, eds., *Decisions of the Highest Order: Perspectives on the National Security Council* (Pacific Grove, CA: Brooks/Cole Publishing Company, 1988); John Prados, *Keepers of the Keys: A History of the National Security Council from Truman to Bush* (New York: Morrow, 1991); Constantine C. Menges, *Inside The National Security Council: The True Story of The Making and Unmaking of Reagan's Foreign Policy* (New York: Simon and Schuster, 1988).

[236] Shoemaker, *The NSC Staff*, 67.

[237] James A. Baker III with Thomas M. DeFrank, *The Politics of Diplomacy* (New York: G.P. Putnam's Sons, 1995), excerpted in *Newsweek*, 2 October 1995, 53.

The CIA's performance in the Stinger case raises questions about the agency's resources and capabilities for covert action, the quality of its decision making in such secret activities, and the reliability of its intelligence reporting, which together reinforce doubts about the overall worth of covert action and government secrecy as tools of foreign policy. The CIA's error in relying on Pakistan's ISI for Stinger distribution—long after plausible deniability was lost and the agency had established its own connections to the rebels—is often justified on grounds the agency lacked sufficient numbers of trained covert-action personnel.[238] However, the inexcusable error of boosting the supply of Stingers just as their use was waning, which contributed to a gross oversupply of the missiles and worldwide proliferation, can be attributed only to a combination of shoddy intelligence, poor decision making, and bureaucratic inertia. Ironically, the CIA's program to supply the Afghan rebels, its single largest operation during the Reagan administration, is often cited as a rare example of a covert action success.[239] If the above shortcomings are what can be expected from a top-priority "success," however, the overall worth of covert action should be reassessed.[240] Assuming U. S. leaders wish to retain this prerogative, despite its potentially inherent shortcomings, the CIA at a minimum must beef up its in-house capabilities to reduce the risk of again falling prey to the whims of another nation's intelligence service.

The Stinger case also contributes to the long debate on foreign policy and democracy,[241] suggesting that effective foreign policy is fostered by a moderate level of democracy, but can be hurt by too much or too little. The Reagan administration appears generally to have suffered from too much democracy in its making of foreign policy. Disparate interests represented within the executive branch were able to lobby each other, leak information beneficial to their viewpoint, form coalitions with members of Congress, and continue to fight even after their proposals had been rejected formally. Even lone advocates could

[238] Roy Godson, "Covert Action: Neither Exceptional Tool Nor Magic Bullet" in Roy Godson, Ernest R. May, and Gary Schmitt, eds., *U.S. Intelligence At the Crossroads: Agendas for Reform* (London: Brassey's, 1995), 168.

[239] Robert Gates takes issue with the conventional wisdom that the CIA has had few operational successes. However, even he claims that "the greatest of them all was the war in Afghanistan." See Gates, *From the Shadows*, 360.

[240] For a view supporting Gates, that covert action has been and can continue to be a useful tool of American foreign policy, see Roy Godson, *Dirty Tricks or Trump Cards: U.S. Covert Action and Counterintelligence* (London: Brassey's 1995). For an opposing view, see the work of Greg Treverton including in *In From the Cold* (New York: The Twentieth Century Fund Press, 1996), 23; see also Ernest May in Godson et al., *U.S. Intelligence at the Crossroads*, 173–177; and Codevilla, *Informing Statecraft*, 270.

[241] A classic statement is Theodore Lowi, "Making Democracy Safe for the World: On Fighting the Next War" in G. John Ikenberry, ed., *American Foreign Policy: Theoretical Essays* (New York: Harper Collins, 1989). See also, Kurt Taylor Gaubatz, "Political Competition and Foreign Policy Power Sharing" (paper presented at the 1996 American Political Science Association meeting, 29 August–1 September 1996).

affect U. S. foreign policy substantially by applying these tactics with sufficient enthusiasm and disregard for protocol.[242]

By contrast, the CIA's problems in the Stinger case were exacerbated by too little democracy. Government secrecy artificially restricted the circle of informed decision makers, contributing to poor decisions.[243] Had there not been insistence on maintaining plausible deniability, the U. S. government might have debated openly which of the rebel groups were most worthy of assistance, rather than quietly delegating this crucial decision to a foreign intelligence agency with an ulterior agenda. More generally, had the program not been covert, Congress, the executive branch, and the press could have scrutinized its implementation—for example, questioning the wisdom of shipping additional Stingers to Muslim fundamentalists just as the missiles' use was dropping off.[244] Reduced government secrecy also might have prevented the CIA from inaccurately reporting Pakistani President Zia's views on the Stinger for more than a year, which interfered with sound decision making.

According to Abramowitz, the government's interagency process "worked" in that officials eventually were turned around "based on argumentation."[245] However, the combined effects of too much and too little democracy stretched that process out over eighteen months, which had deleterious consequences. The Stinger proposal was rejected when it might have made sense, approved when it no longer did, and implemented in a manner that unnecessarily raised risks to U. S. national security.

An important question is whether the degree of democracy in the making of U.S. foreign policy is subject to strategic manipulation or is the product of inexorable social, technological, and historical forces. Those cited above attribute the free-for-all nature of the Reagan administration's foreign-policy process to specific management style and organizational choices. Others claim, however, that it represented just one step in a historical progression toward the ever-increasing domestic relevance of foreign affairs, which is becoming subject to the intense level of democracy traditionally reserved for domestic affairs.[246] It can be argued that technological advances such as the Internet, CNN, satellite

[242] Scott, *Deciding to Intervene*, 241–245, argues this pattern is inherent in modern American democracy.

[243] Sometimes the circle of decision makers is overly restricted *within* the CIA as well, as certain offices "have been notorious for using security compartmentation to protect themselves from legitimate inquiries that might expose operational failures or uncover financial overruns or schedule slips." See Duane R. ("Dewey") Clarridge, with Digby Diehl, *A Spy for all Seasons* (New York: Scribner, 1997), 405.

[244] The progressively decreasing concern about Stinger distribution in the field is reflected in the comments of Milt Beardon, CIA station chief in Pakistan during implementation of the program: "My philosophy, and one that I think prevailed, was: get the weapons into the hands of the shooters and really let God sort it out." (Quoted in Levin, *CIA: America's Secret Warriors*.)

[245] Abramowitz, interview with author, 30 August 1995.

[246] Scott, *Deciding to Intervene*, 248–250. He also argues that this trend has been exacerbated by the end of the cold war.

communication, faxes, and copy machines have exacerbated this trend by making global information instantly available to ever widening circles and encroaching on the government preserve of classified information.[247] If such an historical trend does exist, the Stinger case suggests it will be beneficial as it broadens decision making from artificially small circles, but deleterious to the extent it undermines the government's ability to expedite, centrally coordinate, and implement its decisions.

Another lesson of the Stinger case is that in order to draw the proper lessons from history, political scientists and foreign-affairs analysts must trace the internal decision making processes of both U.S. and foreign governments, rather than treating them as "black boxes." Such process tracing of the U.S. Stinger decision reveals a surprising lack of consensus about the means and ends of the so-called Reagan Doctrine.[248] On the Soviet side, such close analysis is essential to understanding that the withdrawal decision was driven not mainly by the direct human, financial, or political costs of the war, but by Gorbachev's desire to have Western sanctions lifted. Earlier black-box analyses concluded erroneously that Gorbachev was responding to the U.S. escalation.[249]

Ironically, the two elements of U.S. policy that appear most to have influenced the Soviet decision to withdraw were initiated not by the Reagan administration, but by President Carter immediately after the Soviet invasion of 1979. Carter suspended détente, cutting off access to trade and technology, which the Soviets came to see over time as a significant drag on their economic growth. He also initiated aid to the Mujahedin when they were weakest, establishing a weapons pipeline that helped avert their early defeat by the Red Army. The Reagan administration, spurred by Congress, steadily increased aid to the Mujahedin, no doubt improving the rebels' military prospects. However, the major U.S. escalation of aid in 1985-1986 appears not to have been crucial to the rebels' continued survival, nor to have had significant impact on Soviet decision making. Gorbachev eventually obtained domestic support for withdrawal as the result of his own actions, not due to U.S. escalation. He changed personnel, empowered nontraditional experts, and permitted press coverage of the war. Thus, the Reagan administration's most consequential action to effect Soviet withdrawal may have been holding the Carter line, refusing to normalize economic relations so long as Soviet troops remained in Afghanistan. The Reagan Doctrine, at least in the case of Afghanistan, has been credited with an achievement that had other causes—apparently due to little more than a coincidence of timing.

---

[247] Doug MacEachin, "The Uncertain Future of Intelligence Analysis: Confronting the Faultline" (Oral presentation at Center for Science and International Affairs, Harvard University, 14 February 1997). MacEachin is a retired CIA official.

[248] Interestingly, the policy's name was coined not by the administration, but by columnist Charles Krauthammer. However, Scott in *Deciding to Intervene* adduces evidence that the administration had in place a formal policy of assistance to anticommunist rebels well before this appellation was applied.

[249] See Daley, *Gorbachev and Afghanistan*.

The pervasiveness of the myth that the Stinger slew the Red Army and by implication the Soviet empire and communism demonstrates how the distortive effects of the cold war have survived its passing. For almost half a century, Americans were confronted with apparitions such as the missile gap and the evil empire. Those responsible for erecting such exaggerated images of the Soviet adversary are now, perhaps predictably, exaggerating the credit they deserve for destroying it. Despite mounting contradictory evidence, these cold warriors continue to give the Stinger much of the credit for ending the cold war and to promote the simple lesson that the hawks had it right all along. In reality, the Stinger's impact was far smaller, and the lessons are far more complex.*

* Preparation of this article was assisted with financial support from the Paul Nitze fellowship of the School of Advanced International Studies of Johns Hopkins University, the John M. Olin Foundation, and the Lucian Pye fellowship of the Massachusetts Institute of Technology. The author would like to thank all those who commented on earlier drafts, including Steven Aftergood, Raymond Garthoff, Deane Hinton, Fred Iklé, Barry Lowenkron, Michael Mazarr, Michael Pillsbury, and Steve Van Evera.

Mission Impossible: Creating
a Grand Strategy

ROBERT JERVIS

On 1 May 1919, the acting secretary of the navy, Franklin D. Roosevelt, wrote the secretary of state:

> It is a fundamental principle that the foreign policy of our government is in the hands of the State Department. . . . As it is upon our foreign policy that naval estimates must be based, it will be recognized that the Navy Department has a vital interest in this question. It is probable that certain policies are of such importance to our national interests that they must be defended at all costs. On the other hand certain policies are not, by the expense they would entail, justified if they lead to war. Hence . . . it is necessary for the Navy Department to know what policies it may be called upon to uphold by force, in order to formulate plans and building programs.

In May 1940, the United States chief of Operations wrote the commander of the Pacific Fleet:

> Suppose the Japs do go into the East [without simultaneously attacking United States territory]? What are we going to do about it? My answer is, I don't know and I think that there is nobody on God's green earth that can tell you.[1]

GRAND STRATEGY WITHOUT AN ENEMY?

Leaders of the armed forces always ask Roosevelt's question, but as Roosevelt learned when he was president, if not before, it is rarely easy to answer. Under the current circumstances, it is impossible. To make the point more broadly, it is not possible for the United States to develop and follow a coherent grand strategy over the next decade or so. Fortunately, it is not necessary for the United States to have one, although its absence will annoy scholars, confuse other countries, and make military planning extremely difficult.

[1] Quoted in Robert Butow, *Tojo and the Coming of the War* (Princeton: Princeton University Press, 1961), 190.

The reason that the United States will not develop a grand strategy is the same reason that one is not required: the current world, like the one before the invention of heavy bombers, presents no pressing threats. But it is unlike the earlier eras in that the United States now has less-than-vital interests throughout the world, sufficient power to act on more than a few of them, and an activist ideology—a conscience, as some would put it, or, as others would say, the belief that the United States has the right and indeed the obligation to try to improve the world.

This is then truly a new world, one that is unusual for leaders and scholars alike. For many of them, especially if they are Realists,[2] the external world that states inhabit is a very dangerous one. States need to defend their security interests, and these are always potentially if not actually at risk—a situation that Arnold Wolfers analogizes to a house that is on fire.[3] Under such circumstances, all states must obey the imperatives of the international system. This means that domestic politics is not considered, that all states will behave in the same way under the same circumstances regardless of their internal features (for example, democracies will react in the same way that dictatorships do), that democratic control of foreign policy has little meaning, and that morality can play no role because there is little room for choice. Whether or not this is ever an accurate description has been heatedly debated, but it is irrelevant here because no one would claim that this describes the world the United States now inhabits and shapes. The central implication here is that the United States now has unusual freedom of action, which is, of course, what statesmen often dream about. However, we should not forget the old saying "Be careful what you dream for, because you may get it."

The most vital interest of any country is security from invasion or attack. The second most vital interest, often linked to the first, is the ability to protect the state's closest allies, who either contribute to the state's security or are valued in their own right. A third interest is economic prosperity, which both contributes to security and is valued as a goal in itself. Almost all analysts agree that these three core values are now available to the United States for free—that is, they do not require strenuous efforts to reach them, partly because of nuclear weapons.[4] Indeed, not only are there no plausible direct threats to American security, but Western Europe similarly lacks such threats. Such countries constitute what Karl Deutsch called a "security community,"[5] which means that they do not menace one another and there is little reason to fear extreme eco-

---

[2] For the purposes of this article, I will not distinguish between classical Realism (Thucydides, E. H. Carr, Hans Morgenthau) and Neorealism (Kenneth Waltz).

[3] Arnold Wolfers, *Discord and Collaboration* (Baltimore: Johns Hopkins University Press, 1962), 12–17.

[4] The influence of nuclear weapons on world politics has been hotly debated; my own views can be found in *The Meaning of the Nuclear Revolution* (Ithaca, NY: Cornell University Press, 1989).

[5] Karl Deutsch et al., *Political Community and the North Atlantic Area* (Princeton: Princeton University Press, 1957), chap. 2.

nomic conflict between these countries and the United States. This now appears to be true for Japan as well, contrary to the alarmist claims that were common a few years ago. It is as certain as anything can be in international politics that the United States will not fight a war with the states of Western Europe or Japan. This is a truly revolutionary change in world politics, for there has never been an era in which the major powers have not periodically fought each other. We simply do not know what a world will be like in which this threat has been lifted.[6]

We can conjure up all sorts of threats, such as a resurgent Russia, a belligerent China that continues to grow at 10 percent a year, or terrorism. Because it would take an extremely lengthy analysis to rebut each of these claims, I will be content to assert that they largely represent the political and psychological need to find dangers[7] and say that although one can argue that many goals are worthy of foreign policy effort, security threats are largely absent.[8]

MULTIPLE, BUT SECONDARY, GOALS

The fact that the United States has no pressing security threats does not mean that it has no foreign policy goals. Many secondary threats are worth worrying about and worth pursuing, and doing so is feasible because of America's great power. But the very fact that many goals can be pursued while none are primary is what has generated the current debate. During the cold war, to be sure, arguments about strategy were fierce, but they largely involved perceptions of the Soviet Union. In contrast, some of today's arguments turn partially on assessments of the international environment, but most relate to what the United States values, the prices and risks it should be willing to pay to reach alternative goals, and the priorities of domestic and international objectives.[9] In this environment of greatly reduced threat, people focus on dangers that are less extreme or less plausible. By definition, policy makers and military planners concentrate on threats according to some combination of the likelihood that they will materialize and the menace that they will constitute if they do so. But it is

[6] I have discussed the causes and implications of this in "The Future of World Politics: Will It Resemble the Past?" *International Security* 16 (Winter 1991–92): 39–73; and "International Primacy: Is the Game Worth the Candle?" *International Security* 17 (Spring 1993): 52–67. Also see John Mueller, *Retreat from Doomsday: The Obsolescence of Major War* (New York: Basic Books, 1989); Max Singer and Aaron Wildavsky, *The Real World Order* (Chatham, NJ: Chatham House, 1993); Samuel Huntington, *The Clash of Civilizations and the Remaking of World Order* (New York: Simon & Schuster, 1996).

[7] Frederick Hartmann, *The Conservation of Enemies* (Westport, CT: Greenwood Press, 1982); John Mueller, "The Catastrophe Quota: Trouble After the Cold War," *Journal of Conflict Resolution* 38 (September 1994): 355–75.

[8] For an excellent discussion, see Eric Nordlinger, *Isolationism Reconfigured* (Princeton: Princeton University Press, 1995).

[9] The literature on alternative grand strategies is voluminous. An excellent comprehensive survey is that by Barry Posen and Andrew Ross, "Competing Visions for U.S. Grand Strategy," *International Security* 21 (Winter 1996–97): 5–53.

harder than ever to see how one unlikely threat (rogue states) compares with another (China) on these dimensions. Indeed, perhaps threats of a very different kind deserve the greatest attention, as environmentalists, for example, claim. This plethora of remote but equally plausible menaces would not, of course, be a problem if the grand strategy designed to best deal with one of them suited the others as well. But only those who believe in a deity would expect such a happy coincidence.

Life is both more pleasant and more complicated without threats that are both dangerous and likely. I believe that this is clearly the case today. For example, look at what one typical commission has designated as American vital interests:

> Vital national interests are conditions that are strictly necessary to safeguard and enhance the well-being of Americans in a free and secure nation:
>
> 1. Prevent, deter, and reduce the threat of nuclear, biological, and chemical weapons attack on the United States.
> 2. Prevent the emergence of a hostile hegemon in Europe or Asia.
> 3. Prevent the emergence of a hostile major power on U.S. borders or in control of the seas.
> 4. Prevent the catastrophic collapse of major global systems: trade, financial markets, supplies of energy, and the environment.
> 5. Ensure the survival of U.S. allies.[10]

Not only are all these threats vague or unlikely to materialize, but it is hard to see how we would estimate, even roughly, how probable each is. Yet in order to know how many resources we should devote to preventing or coping with such threats, we would need to do this. Bernard Brodie, justifiably known as the dean of American strategists, noted: "All sorts of notions and propositions are churned out, and often presented for consideration with the prefatory words: 'It is conceivable that . . .' Such words establish their own truth, for the fact that someone has conceived of whatever proposition follows is enough to establish that it is conceivable. Whether it is worth a second thought, however, is another matter."[11]

In previous eras, decision makers were often willing to say that certain eventualities that would be deeply disturbing if they arose were unlikely enough to be dismissed out of hand. Thus in 1924, Winston Churchill opposed the Admiralty's argument that more ships had to be built to meet the menace from Japan by arguing: "A war with Japan! But why should there be a war with Japan? I do not believe there is the slightest chance of it in our lifetime."[12] Of

---

[10] The Commission on America's National Interests, *America's National Interests* (Cambridge, MA: Center for Science and International Affairs, Kennedy School of Government, Harvard University, July 1966), 5.

[11] Bernard Brodie, "The Development of Nuclear Strategy," *International Security* 2 (Spring 1978): 83.

[12] Quoted in Martin Gilbert, *Winston S. Churchill, 1922–1939* (London: Heinemann, 1978), vol. 5, 76.

course, these judgments can be wrong, as was the case here. However, they are both necessary and difficult to make in an era when no threat is salient and pressing. We may be able to make rough judgments of dangers and events as being "very probable," "probable," or "improbable." But it is extremely difficult to distinguish among threats that are "improbable," those that are "very improbable," and those that are "very, very improbable."

It is at least as troublesome and difficult to develop intelligent policy prescriptions for distant and unlikely threats, because we are dealing with so many unknowns. Take the first vital interest on the list given above. How do we go about establishing a grand strategy for "preventing, deterring and reducing the threat of nuclear, biological, and chemical weapons attacks on the United States" unless we know something about the countries that might menace us and the circumstances under which the danger might arise? In the past, while it was not easy to see how to diminish and protect against possible threats, as the debates before the two world wars and during the cold war remind us, at least there was a fairly small set of well-defined issues that needed to be analyzed in order to provide guidance. Difficult as it was to analyze Soviet intentions, this question is easy and well structured compared with estimating whether the People's Republic of China (PRC) is likely to be a major threat ten or twenty years from now. Unless one believes in deterministic theories of history (for example, countries with rapidly increasing economies will expand until they meet a superior power; the Chinese, because of their history and culture, see themselves as the Middle Kingdom and so seek to dominate the barbarians; the center of world power has shifted from Europe to Asia), one needs to examine a large number of pathways by which China might become dangerous and, for each one, to estimate the likelihood that a proposed policy would be effective, ineffective, or misguided. Unfortunately, the world is sufficiently complex and perverse that a policy that would discourage and deter China under one set of circumstances could exacerbate the danger under another, thus ruling out any simple prescription.

This more relaxed environment creates greater room not only for differences of opinion about what policy to pursue but also for the splintering of opinion into unstable segments. In the absence of a clear danger, let alone a clear and present danger, our external environment does not require that we be guided by one set of values rather than another. There is always agreement that the protection of the country comes first, but after that, the consensus breaks down, which is hardly surprising. Individuals and groups vary widely in the priority they assign to self-interest, as opposed to altruism (or, to put it slightly differently, on how narrowly or broadly they construe self-interest), as well as on how they see their own interests and what values they seek for themselves and others. Thus some people give economic interests pride of place; others believe that the United States should give priority to enhancing human rights around the world; and still others believe that a crucial part of the national interest is aiding the countries to which they have ethnic or ideological ties. Still others focus on threats, but not on the same ones: some fear Russia; others worry about China; and still others believe that the most pressing danger is proliferation in general or of specific countries obtaining nuclear weapons. It is not news that the national interest is not entirely objective or that it can be composed of conflicting parts. But in the current era, the lack of a plausible candidate for a single unifying value or a motive that should animate American foreign policy greatly magnifies the difficulties of creating a coherent grand strategy.

PLURALISM WITH A VENGEANCE

What we are likely to see is quite familiar to students of American domestic policy. Because neither any one interest nor the state itself is strong enough to impose coherent and consistent guidance, courses of action are shaped less by a grand design than by the pulling and hauling of varied interests, ideas, and political calculations. This is the model of pluralism, which although often criticized normatively or descriptively[13] is believed by most scholars to capture a great deal of American politics. Furthermore, it is commonly argued that pluralism not only preserves individual liberties and ensures that each group gains at least some of the values about which it cares most, but it also is likely to produce a better overall policy than could be arrived at by a central authority seeking a synthesis of the public interest.[14]

Most scholars feel that this model is neither descriptive nor normative for American foreign policy, however. During the cold war, Realists argued that the national interest abroad—unlike the public interest at home—was not chimerical, because the external environment was sufficiently compelling to override many domestic differences and enable even a relatively weak state to follow a policy of some coherence.[15] The argument that the United States can now adopt a grand strategy rests on the similar notion that it needs and has sufficient unity of interest, purpose, and government structures so that the national interest model still holds. Whatever the virtues of this in normative terms—and I might debate but certainly would not dismiss them—I see no reason to expect this to describe the future. Instead, I think the pluralist model offers much better predictions.

[13] For the former, see Theodore Lowi, *The End of Liberalism* (New York: Norton, 2d ed., 1979); for the latter, see, for example, C. Wright Mills, *The Power Elite* (New York: Oxford University Press, 1956); and Grant McConnell, *The Decline of Agrarian Democracy* (Berkeley and Los Angeles: University of California Press, 1953). On pluralism in general, see Andrew McFarland, *Power and Leadership in Pluralist Systems* (Stanford, CA: Stanford University Press, 1969).

[14] The classic statement is that by Charles Edward Lindblom, *The Intelligence of Democracy* (New York: Free Press, 1965).

[15] This claim was most commonly made by students of security but was affirmed by some of those analyzing foreign economic policy as well: see Stephen Krasner, *Defending the National Interest* (Princeton: Princeton University Press, 1978); and Robert Gilpin, "No One Loves a Political Realist," *Security Studies* 5 (Spring 1996): 3–26.

Henry Kissinger argues that "a conceptual framework . . . is an essential tool [of foreign policy. Its] absence . . . produces exactly the opposite of freedom of action; policy makers are forced to respond to parochial interests, buffeted by pressures without a fixed compass."[16] But for any individual to have such a framework is not sufficient to protect against the danger that Kissinger foresees; rather, there must be widespread agreement on it. Indeed, it was the inability of domestic leaders to maintain such an agreement in the wake of Vietnam and Watergate that Kissinger claims destroyed his policy. That the argument is self-serving does not mean it is entirely incorrect; in any event, the history of the 1970s does remind us of both the importance and the difficulty of gaining domestic support.[17]

"All politics is local," former Speaker of the U.S. House Tip O'Neill famously remarked. Students of foreign policy are offended by this notion—the nation's security and other vital interests are too important to be at the mercy of conflicting values, parochial interests, and partisan politics. When I wrote the first draft of this article, newspapers were reporting that the Senate had voted overwhelmingly to delay the next two rounds of military base closings until it received a study of the economic effects of past and future shut-downs. By voting as it did, the Senate ignored the wishes of President Clinton and military leaders who have argued that the closings of bases still to be determined were central to their efforts to pare the Defense Department budget and allow military officials to shift money from military operations to weapons systems.[18] The location of military bases is the aspect of security policy that has always been most influenced by local and partisan politics for the obvious reason that the ratio between domestic impact and foreign policy importance is so skewed toward the former. Yet in the post-cold war world, this characterizes most foreign policy issues.

In April 1997, the *New York Times* carried a story that may have been equally revealing, if inadvertently so. Indeed, it was only a photograph of the new F-22 fighter plane being rolled out of the Lockheed-Martin plant in Marietta, Georgia. In addition to a stylized American flag, the airplane carried the painted slogan "Spirit of America."[19] Because the military rationale for the expensive advanced aircraft is unpersuasive, the "Spirit of America" is better translated not as the historic American commitment to defend itself, let alone to drop bombs on small countries, but by another slogan: "The business of America is business." Military procurement policy has always been strongly af-

---

[16] Henry Kissinger, *White House Years* (Boston: Little, Brown, 1979), 130.

[17] This need is neglected in most scholarly analyses: even the brief mention of domestic support in Posen and Ross's canvas of candidate grand strategies is more than most treatments offer. See their "Competing Visions," 16, 22, 31. It is usually assumed that the intellectual job of determining the best policy is the hardest part of the task, if not the only part.

[18] Jerry Gray, "Senate, in a Rebuff to Clinton, Votes to Delay Base Closings," *New York Times*, 10 July 1997.

[19] *New York Times*, 10 April 1997.

fected by the domestic political economy,[20] but with the declining persuasiveness of the foreign policy arguments for particular weapons, the influence of local economic pressures is certain to increase.

The broader argument for the rise of American economic diplomacy hardly needs to be repeated here. Although with Commerce Secretary Ron Brown's death American economic salesmanship abroad is not so flamboyant, the basic point remains that when the most important foreign policy objective of security has been reached or is indeterminate, economic goals will come to the fore. To take the most obvious example, it is not surprising that American policy toward the PRC, right or wrong, is driven much more by economic concerns than by the belief that imposing trade sanctions would encourage Chinese aggressiveness or increase human rights violations.

Even if economic objectives were both more important and dominant, it would not be easy to develop a coherent grand strategy, as economic interests would not be united. For example, the interests of importers often are different from those of exporters; the economic stakes of one state or congressional district conflict with those of others; and the interests of different sectors in the economy—and perhaps different classes—diverge. A strong executive branch[21] or a corporatist political structure might be able to weld these interests together, but the United States lacks both. Similarly, a small country whose prosperity depends on trade may behave coherently, especially if it elects its officials by proportional representation.[22] Again, the description does not fit the United States. Our system of a separation of powers, an unruly executive branch, and the dependence of political parties on corporate and union money means that private interests have extraordinary access. Furthermore, the fragmentation creates multiple arenas for political struggles, and so one group, interest, or ideology can prevail on one issue or in one instance but not in others. No more than it can adopt a coherent "industrial policy" is the United States likely to follow the sort of coherent economic foreign policy that could both support and require a grand strategy.

This is not to imply that economic considerations—conflicting or not—will or should dominate American foreign policy. Indeed, I think that conventional wisdom has tended to oversell the extent to which economics will dominate the post-cold war era. Although it is easy to cite some very large figures for the

[20] See, for example, James Kurth, "Why We Buy the Weapons We Do," *Foreign Policy* 11 (Summer 1973): 33–56; and Nick Kotz, *Wild Blue Yonder: Money, Politics, and the B-1 Bomber* (New York: Pantheon, 1988).

[21] In what other country could a trade crisis be sparked by the actions of an obscure federal agency, the Federal Maritime Commission, which took everyone else in the executive branch by surprise? See David Sanger, "U.S. Maritime Agency Moves to Bar Most Japanese Cargo Ships from American Ports," *New York Times*, 17 October 1997; Steven Lee Myers, "Little Panel That Could, Did, Posing Threat of Trade War," *New York Times*, 18 October 1997.

[22] Peter Katzenstein, *Small States in World Markets* (Ithaca, NY: Cornell University Press, 1985); Ronald Rogowski, "Trade and the Variety of Democratic Institutions," *International Organization* 41 (Spring 1987): 203–224.

amount of trade, investment, or financial exchanges the United States engages in, it is far from clear how much these will be affected by foreign policy decisions. A major war involving one of our main trading partners would deeply affect the American economy, but many of the main international factors that structure our economic well-being seem to be firmly established. Our ability to lower trade barriers with specific countries, especially in Asia, can be affected by the policies we choose, and these can reciprocally affect whether these countries buy items such as airplanes and advanced telecommunications systems from us or the Europeans. But in the context of a multitrillion dollar economy, the impact of these cases is not great. Now that the vogue for strategic trade theory[23] has passed, it is easier to see that the main determinants of the American economy's health are internal. Nevertheless, the decline in military threats automatically elevates the relative standing of economic goals.

Although economic considerations play a large role, especially when the economic stakes are high, they do not have the field to themselves. To say that security interests are not pressing does not mean they are completely absent. Likewise, to argue, as I did earlier, that potential threats like proliferation do not readily lend themselves to a judgment of their magnitude or of the policies that would best combat them does not mean that people will not or should not argue for dealing with them. In addition, humanitarian or altruistic values are strongly held in American society. I doubt whether the policy of containment would have had as much public support as it did if people had believed that keeping other countries noncommunist not only increased American security but also was good for the world. Similarly, the current policy of supporting emerging democracies is fed by the argument that this will improve the lives of the people in those countries in addition to making others, including the United States, safer and more prosperous. In other cases, humanitarian motives are the main ones at work, as in Kosovo and what support there was for U.S. intervention in Somalia. Realists may decry such motives and argue that they will entangle the United States in unnecessary quarrels without always helping others, but it is hard to understand American foreign policy in the past or predict it in the future without taking account of them. What is crucial here, however, is not that these impulses cannot be ignored but that they are too weak and

---

[23] See, for example, Paul Krugman, ed., *Strategic Trade Policy and the New International Economics* (Cambridge, MA: MIT Press, 1986); Paul Krugman, *Rethinking International Trade* (Cambridge, MA: MIT Press, 1991); Paul Krugman, *Peddling Prosperity: Economic Sense and Nonsense in the Age of Diminished Expectations* (New York: Norton, 1994); Klaus Stegemann, "Policy Rivalry Among Industrial States: What Can We Learn from Models of Strategic Trade Policy?" *International Organization* 43 (Winter 1989): 73–100; Helen Milner and David Yoffie, "Between Free Trade and Protectionism: Strategic Trade Policy and the Theory of Corporate Trade Demand," *International Organization* 43 (Spring 1989): 239–272; J. David Richardson, "'New' Trade Theory and Policy a Decade Old: Assessment in a Pacific Context" in Richard Higgott, Richard Leaver, and John Ravenhill, eds., *Pacific Economic Relations in the 1990s* (Boston: Allen & Unwin, 1993), 83–105; Marc Busch, *Trade Warriors: States, Firms, and Strategic Policy in High Technology Competition* (Cambridge, UK: Cambridge University Press, 1999).

unfocused to direct policy over a significant period of time and over wide geographic areas. They will wax and wane according to circumstances and the public mood and will be intensified and brought to bear by particularly visible and outrageous atrocities. They are strong enough to contest with other values without being able to dominate them.

Finally, American foreign policy will be influenced by those who favor their coethnics abroad. Again, this is not a new phenomenon: the role of the Irish Americans and German Americans in earlier periods comes to mind. More recently, the American "tilt" toward Greece in its disputes with Turkey cannot be understood apart from the fact that Americans of Greek and Armenian descent vastly outnumber those who came from Turkey. Realists again are horrified by these influences; the textbooks are so embarrassed that they do not even acknowledge them. Nevertheless, I see no reason to reject these ties as a valid part of the national interest of a multi-ethnic country. Furthermore, while observers like Samuel Huntington see internal developments in the United States as dangerously approximating the external "clash of civilizations,"[24] it may well be that only a multi-ethnic country can operate effectively in a diverse world. Various ethnic groups in the United States can form bridges to their coethnics abroad.[25] The main point here is that legitimate or illegitimate, dangerous or helpful, ethnic considerations will play a role in American foreign policy.

Only the cold war held pluralism in check. A longer historical perspective reminds us of states' difficulties in constructing a coherent and stable foreign policy when their interests have been powerful and conflicting. Now it is all the rage to argue that democracies not only do not fight one another but also are especially able to commit themselves to courses of action.[26] In the nineteenth century, however, the conventional wisdom was the opposite, holding that because democracies were under the sway of unstable public opinion, they could not be counted on to carry out threats or promises. Before World War I, it was not entirely disingenuous of British statesmen to tell both France and Germany that they could not make firm commitments about the conditions under which their country would fight a war on the Continent, because the decision would have to be made through democratic processes, which, being responsive to public attitudes, would be influenced by the details of the situation that actually arose rather than being determined by more general and hypothetical questions. This kind of constraint was more the rule than the exception in earlier eras and, I believe, is likely to become familiar again.

[24] Huntington, *Clash of Civilizations*, 304–308.

[25] Yossi Shain, "Ethnic Diasporas and U.S. Foreign Policy," *Political Science Quarterly* 109 (Winter 1994–1995): 811–841.

[26] See, for example, James Fearon, "Domestic Political Audiences and the Escalation of International Disputes," *American Political Science Review* 88 (September 1994): 577–592; the discrepancy between current and past beliefs is commented on by Kurt Gaubatz, "Democratic States and Commitment in International Relations," *International Organization* 50 (Winter 1996): 109–140.

In summary, the United States has a fragmented political system in an external environment in which no single interest, threat, or value predominates. This is a recipe for pluralism with a vengeance but not for a grand strategy, however intelligent it may look on paper. The United States will "muddle through," to use Charles Lindblom's term,[27] rather than follow a coherent plan. A sidelight is that if this analysis is correct, decisions will be hard to explain after the fact, because so many relatively small factors either did or could have influenced them. We are accustomed to trying to account for big and important cases, in which we believe that with so much at stake, only major forces and considerations could have been responsible. Yet when we look at cases like the American intervention in Somalia or even the intervention in Bosnia, this assumption does not hold, because the costs and risks were much lower. For future decisions as well, many values and considerations could be at work because even relatively small perceived gains will be sufficient to set the policy in motion.

MILITARY PLANNING IN AN UNCERTAIN WORLD

None of this means that American foreign policy will be entirely without patterns. I doubt that we will undertake serious economic sanctions to improve human rights in a major trading partner like the PRC. Neither are we likely to deploy massive force for humanitarian goals, to secure secondary economic interests, or to uphold abstract principles of world order. At the other end of the continuum, inertia if not enlightened self-interest will maintain our security commitments to the Organization for Economic Cooperation and Development (OECD) allies, and we are unlikely to permit the military conquest of Taiwan. Furthermore, diplomatic instruments backed by demonstrations of force will be important in certain areas of the world, such as East Asia and East Central Europe, where American interests are important but not compelling. Support is likely to be provided for democracies, countries with large ethnic groups in the United States, and humanitarian values when the cost is predicted to be low. But these boundaries leave a great deal in between. Whether the United States intervenes in cases like Somalia and Kosovo, how it will act if the PRC puts military pressure on its neighbors, whether it would threaten to use force in a conflict between South American countries, whether it would provide guarantees or use force to inhibit proliferation will be determined less, I fear, by any grand strategy than by the balance of domestic interests and the play of domestic politics.

It has often been said that the current American enemy is uncertainty and instability. Whether or not this is true for the country at large, it is true for the American military. The domestic environment that will determine the missions

[27] Charles Edward Lindblom, "The Science of Muddling Through," *Public Administration Review* 19 (Spring 1959): 74–88.

it is asked or told to carry out is an uncertain and unstable one. Security policies will differ from one issue area to another and from one period of time to another as circumstances and domestic opinion vary. As the epigraph opening this essay indicates, leaders of military organizations often ask their political superiors for general foreign policy guidelines so that they can develop an efficient force. In a well-ordered polity, such a request is not only reasonable but mandatory. As Bernard Brodie constantly stressed, we must not lose sight of Carl von Clausewitz's wisdom that politics must direct military policy.[28] But the politics that will guide American foreign and security policy will be pluralism, and its results cannot be codified ahead of time.

Unless and until the United States faces a major and pressing threat, foreign policy will begin at home. No American policy can be sustained without adequate domestic support. One might think that this could be arranged with adequate public education: if the experts develop any sort of consensus about at least the outlines of a necessary grand strategy, the public can be brought around to support it. Indeed, for all the current partisan sniping and for all the annoying behavior of Senator Jesse Helms, the two political parties are not deeply divided on basic issues of foreign and security policy. But multiple fracture lines remain, and the best efforts of Madeleine Albright show that even a secretary of state who places a priority on building domestic support faces severe constraints on her ability to do so.[29]

In the late 1940s, when partisan divisions were greater, those who favored a policy of containment were able to work with opinion leaders throughout society to develop a strong foundation for the policy. I do not think this is possible now, however: our trust in government and many other organizations is very low, and we do not have the sort of civic leaders that were powerful earlier. Only the most extreme conspiracy theorists see the Council on Foreign Relations as anything but a social and status group. "Captains of industry" are gone, with the possible exception of a handful of leaders in the communications and information sectors who lack the breadth of experience that earlier elites had. Union leaders have disappeared even faster than unions. University presidents, who earlier were national figures, now are itinerant money-raisers. Those newspapers that have survived are much less relied on than was true earlier, and television anchors lack the expertise and reputation that would allow them to be influential, even if professioinal ethics and the large corporations that own the networks permitted them to try. Known to the public now are "celebrities," largely from sports and the entertainment industry. I would not expect them to undertake the public educational campaigns we saw in the past.

---

[28] See especially Bernard Brodie, *War and Politics* (New York: Macmillan, 1973), chap. 1.

[29] Steven Lee Myers, "Secretary of State Sells Foreign Policy at Home," *New York Times*, 8 February 1997. For a discussion of decision makers' attitudes toward whether public support is desirable or necessary for an effective foreign policy, see Douglas Foyle, "Public Opinion and Foreign Policy: Elite Beliefs as a Mediating Variable," *International Studies Quarterly* 41 (March 1997): 141–170.

What we are likely to see is that different groups, interests, and values will predominate in different areas and at different times. To take an extreme case, American policy toward Cuba has been "captured" by the émigrés in Florida in a way that is very familiar to students of American regulatory policy. When such a feat is impossible, we will see other patterns familiar in domestic policy making, such as shifting coalitions and logrolling. In return for reciprocation, one group will agree to support another's foreign policy in an area of great concern to the latter but not the former. A recent newspaper carried a plea by the Coalition for International Justice calling for the United States to arrest war criminals in the former Yugoslavia. From one perspective, this diverse coalition is heartening: the Muslim Public Affairs Council, the YWCA, B'nai B'rith, the Arab American Institute, the Anti-Defamation League, the Maryknoll Fathers and Brothers, and several labor unions, as well as individuals as different from one another as Patricia Derian (assistant secretary of state for human rights under Jimmy Carter), Bianca Jagger, and former "hard-liners" such as Max Kampelman, Paul Nitze, and Robert Dole.[30] This is not the sort of coalition, however, that can support a general foreign policy, as it would not be activated by other issues. While it would be an exaggeration to say that every new issue will produce a different alignment, there is little reason to expect the coalitions that form on questions like the United States's policy toward the Congo, maintaining Most Favored Nation status with China, enlarging NATO, or expanding NAFTA to bear much resemblance to one another.

Not only change but also instability over time is likely as the results of each major encounter influence later beliefs and preferences. This phenomenon was not absent in the past: the American experience in Vietnam shaped policy for the succeeding decade. But with less to anchor American policy, smaller events will exert greater influence. Thus I suspect that how the intervention in Kosovo ends will significantly influence the likelihood that the United States will undertake further missions of this kind, just as the deaths of a handful of soldiers in Somalia both forced the United States to withdraw and reduced the American appetite for similar tasks.

Military planning, let alone rational procurement, will be very difficult in such a world. It is easy for a civilian theorist to say that the military should simply plan on being flexible and must be prepared to deal with the unknown. But any military officer knows that the extent to which this is possible is severely limited. In reaction to such instruction and in order to rule out at least the wilder political vagaries, an obvious military strategy is to develop a force that can be used only in certain kinds of circumstances or only in certain ways.

But even with some degree of self-protection, the military is likely to be called on in unpredictable ways and places. The lack of major threats to vital American interests is an incredible boon to America and our allies, but it places unusual burdens on the military.

[30] "Mr. President: Order the Arrest of War Criminals in Bosnia Now!" *New York Times*, 15 July 1997.

This environment will also be a difficult one for civil-military relations, already under significant strain.[31] To employ military instruments for national goals that are secondary at best brings up a whole host of difficulties for the armed services, especially because many of the missions require frequent overseas deployments and retraining. Our military cannot be an overarmed police force that specializes in assisting local "civic action" programs, let alone ambitious nation-building. Yet these are almost certain to be prominent among the missions assigned to it. In this difficult and turbulent atmosphere, close working relations among civil and military officials at all levels are greatly to be desired. But this is extremely unlikely, as the two cultures have grown further apart over the past decade. Fewer civilians have served in the military or had extensive experience in military affairs, and fewer military leaders seem to have a deep understanding of proper civil-military relations.

The result is not so much that one or the other group has grown excessively strong but that both have mishandled their responsibilities and relations vis-à-vis the other. Civilians seem to have great difficulty understanding why many activities pose serious problems for the military and fail to consult adequately on issues with a strong military component, such as the expansion of NATO. Military officials too often use their expertise to inappropriately influence political decisions, if not to actually make them, as the American military commander in Bosnia apparently did when he made clear that NATO troops would not arrest indicted war criminals. Uncertainty about the United States's grand strategy will only exacerbate these problems. Dealing with them calls for excellent working relations and understanding on both sides of the civilian-military divide, but this divide has become deeper. Few seem to be willing or able to begin the efforts necessary to bridge it.

---

[31] See, for example, Richard Kohn, "Out of Control: The Crisis in Civil-Military Relations," *National Interest* 35 (Spring 1995): 3–17; the symposium in the following issue; and A. J. Bacevich, "Tradition Abandoned: America's Military in a New Era," *National Interest* 48 (Summer 1997): 16–25. The difficulties are exacerbated but not caused by Bill Clinton's unique characteristics.